THE BEGINNER'S GUIDE TO HAND BUILDING

Quarto.com

First Published in 2022 by Quarry Books, an imprint of The Quarto Group,
100 Cummings Center, Suite 265-D, Beverly, MA 01915, USA.
T (978) 282-9590 F (978) 283-2742

EEA Representation, WTS Tax d.o.o.,
Žanova ulica 3, 4000 Kranj, Slovenia.
www.wts-tax.si

Quarry Books titles are also available at discount for retail, wholesale, promotional, and bulk purchase.
For details, contact the Special Sales Manager by email at specialsales@quarto.com or by mail at
The Quarto Group, Attn: Special Sales Manager, 100 Cummings Center, Suite 265-D, Beverly, MA 01915, USA.

10 9 8 7 6

ISBN: 978-0-7603-7476-4

Digital edition published in 2022
eISBN: 978-0-7603-7477-1

Library of Congress Cataloging-in-Publication Data

Names: Cobb, Sunshine, author.
Title: The beginner's guide to hand building : functional and sculptural projects for the home potter / Sunshine Cobb.
Description: Beverly, MA : Quarry Books, an imprint of The Quarto Group, 2022. | Series: Essential ceramics skills | Includes index. | Summary: "The Beginner's Guide to Hand Building is a friendly, contemporary take on the classic hand-building book - perfect for new and returning ceramic artists"-- Provided by publisher.
Identifiers: LCCN 2022000406 | ISBN 9780760374764 (print) | ISBN 9780760374771 (ebook)
Subjects: LCSH: Pottery craft.
Classification: LCC TT920 .C6259 2022 | DDC 738.1/2--dc23/eng/20220223
LC record available at https://lccn.loc.gov/2022000406

Design and Page Layout: Allison Meierding
Cover Image: Athena Photography
Photography: Athena Photography; gallery photos courtesy of the artists
Illustration Templates: Sunshine Cobb

Printed in Pontian, Johor, Malaysia, PC032026

THE BEGINNER'S GUIDE TO HAND BUILDING

Functional and Sculptural Projects for the Home Potter

SUNSHINE COBB

QUARRY

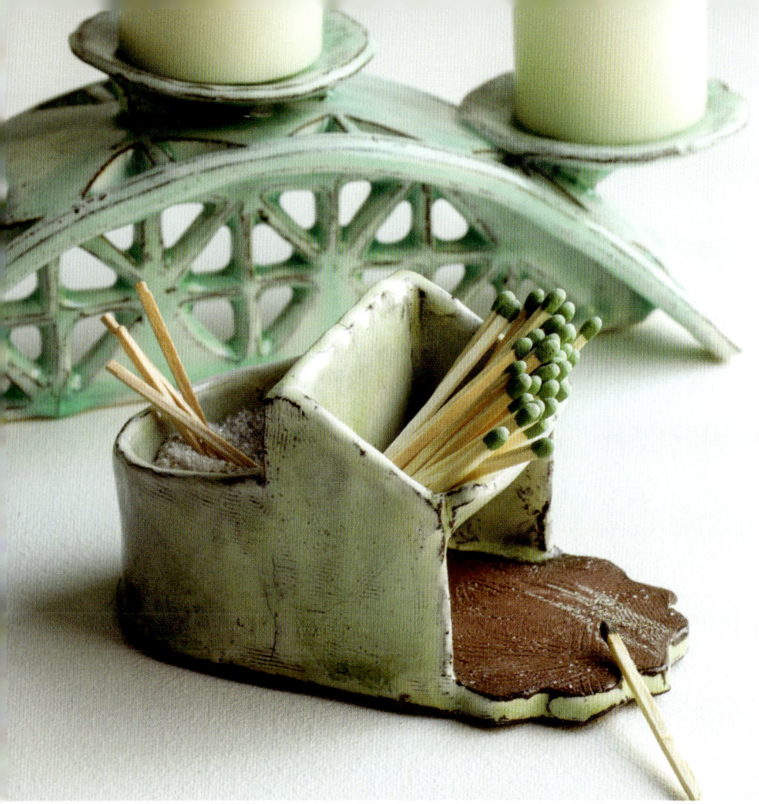
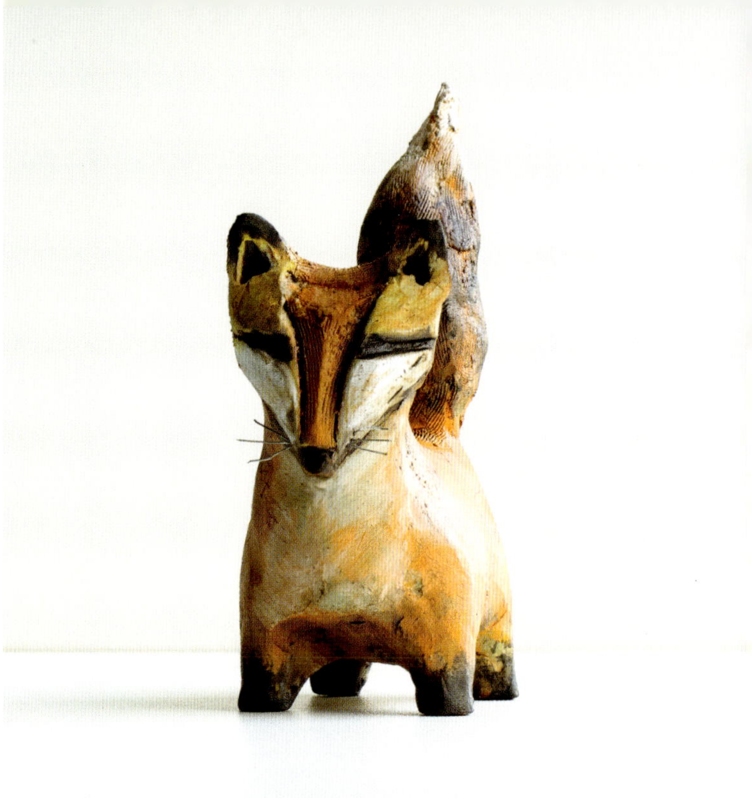
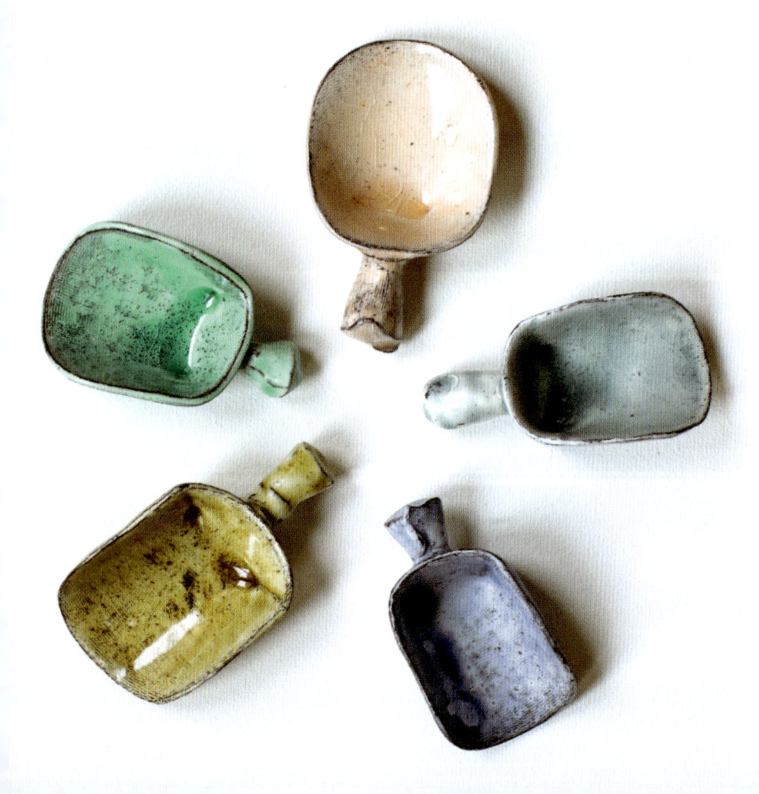
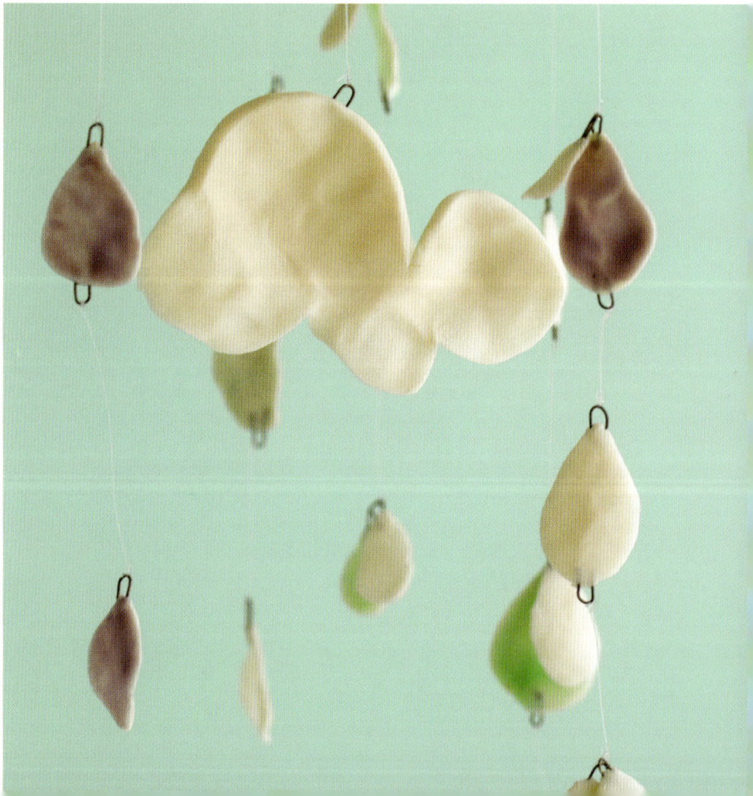

CONTENTS

FOREWORD

I first met Sunshine in person when we presented together on a panel at the National Council on Education for the Ceramic Arts (NCECA). I must admit I was a bit intimidated at first: sure, we were "friends" online, but I had never met this talented, well-known potter in real life. I wasn't sure what to expect. It turns out, I needn't have worried. Sunshine's delightful, down-to-earth way of discussing ceramics, ready smile, and easy-going personality put me at ease. I knew she was the "real deal" and someone I would love to work with again.

Soon after Sunshine published her first book, *Mastering Hand Building*, I had that chance when I invited her to teach a hand building workshop for ClayShare. Her teaching style, philosophy, and gentle yet direct approach was perfectly in line with my own and I knew our students would love learning from her. Her workshop was one of the best attended we have offered and continues to be very popular with our members.

If you haven't heard of it, ClayShare was born in 2017 when I noticed there was a huge boom in potters live broadcasting from their studios. People loved seeing how pottery was made and wanted to be "edutained." I soon realized that there was not only a desire but a need for online ceramic education for those that wanted more than just entertainment. I wanted instructors to be able to share something more structured than social media videos but not as formal as a university class—something that was accessible to everyone, that could be watched over and over, and taught in a caring, compassionate manner.

ClayShare has always drawn multigenerational students from all backgrounds and skill levels, including grandparents sharing their love of pottery with their grandchildren, daughters teaching their mothers, and husbands and wives making pottery together. Girls' night out has turned into girls' night in, thanks to pottery. Combining live broadcasts and workshops with our curriculum of prerecorded classes allow our members to connect and interact with each other live, creating a strong clay community that supports and encourages each other in their pottery journey. From this, something magical has happened: we have seen these connections transcend the studio and evolve into true, real-life friendships.

Of course, we were helped by the monumental shift in pottery, from the traditional institutions of making pottery at a university or community ceramic studio to making pottery at home. Be it at your kitchen table, garage, shed, or other room (my first at-home studio was in the guest bathroom!), any space can become a studio. This change is partly due to living through a global pandemic with lockdowns, isolation, and social distancing. It created a diverse group of new potters. Some have always wanted to try pottery but believed that they were not talented enough or that they are too old (you are never ever too old to learn!)...or that it is too costly, or that requires a lot of equipment. Some are young parents with children to care for (as I was when I was first learning pottery) or adults caring for their aging parents. Others stumble into pottery looking for a side gig, a way to relive stress, or just want to make something with their hands. Whatever starts them on their clay journey, there has never been a better time with more educational resources available on how to make pottery than now.

I for one am energized by this change and am excited to see what will come of it and the fabulous creations being made by these "home potters". People are discovering that they love to make pottery and not only that, that they can do it at home, and that they are also quite good at it.

With *A Beginner's Guide to Hand Building*, Sunshine has created a book that is totally friendly to those who want to make pottery at home. She guides you though each project step by step, giving ideas and options for endless creative possibilities.

Sunshine's wholistic approach to teaching ceramics incudes some very practical and often overlooked practices for the potter's health and well-being. From simple exercises to self-care advice for mind and body to keep you working happier and healthier in and out of the studio. She also includes plenty of information on common materials and tools used in pottery from different type of clays and their stages of workability, firing ranges, health concerns and suggestions for keeping a studio clean (doubly important when that studio is at home!).

I have read a lot of books on hand building ceramics and sculpture, and I must say that Sunshine's approach is refreshing and innovative. In no time, even those who think that they are not sculptors will be making 3D leaves, cacti, clouds, mobiles, wall hangings, and cute little critters that will quickly become an addiction. I know that I for one cannot wait to try these darling projects!

For those who want something functional, Sunshine includes wonderful tutorials on making practical pottery as well. Soon you will be making soap dishes, scoops, citrus reamers, butter boxes, tapas plates, baskets, and more. Before long, your home will be filled with handmade pottery.

In short, the book that home potters have been waiting for is here! Congratulations and thank you, Sunshine, for sharing your brilliant ideas and for writing the book I wish had existed when I began my pottery journey decades ago.

JESSICA PUTNAM-PHILLIPS, M.F.A., *is the founder of ClayShare, an educator, a USAF Veteran, and has been making pottery for over 20 years. Visit her and ClayShare at www.clayshare.com*

INTRODUCTION

Welcome to the mysterious and magical world of clay. Yes, I think clay is its own world! It has its own language and its own paths to navigate, and along the way you'll learn that skills must be developed and practiced to succeed. You will have amazing discoveries and learn a few hard lessons along the way. I am here as your guide as you venture into this new world. However, I am but a guide: you are the adventurer who will lead this journey. (This is a pick-your-own-adventure kind of book. Are you ready?!)

This is a project book, sure, but I've tried to keep everything open-ended. You'll make choices and solve puzzles that are unique to your version of each project. By following the basic scope of each tutorial, you will learn new skills and continue to build a foundation of ceramic knowledge. I hope you'll also find some sparks that fire up your creative brain to continue the journey well beyond this book. I see opening this book and jumping into the projects as the first step in your journey—one that, if you choose, can continue throughout your life.

Before we begin, let me just say it: I am happy you have found clay! I welcome you to the ceramics community, with all its flaws. I have been lucky over the course of my career to visit hundreds of studio spaces. From grade schools, high schools, and colleges to large craft institutions and local community center clay rooms, each is unique. (Although they have similar setups and smells and kiln rooms.) I have only ever been a visitor in most of those spaces, there for a day, a week, or a few months, teaching workshops, demonstrating, or being a sabbatical replacement instructor. I have never worked in a community or school studio for more than about three years.

Believe it or not, it took me more than fifteen years as a professional to invest in equipment of my own because I moved around so much. I followed opportunities and made do with what ceramics spaces I could piece together; sometimes that meant making in one space, firing in another, and finishing the work in a third space. I feel like the label of nomadic potter was invented for me. But really so many people piece meal their studio spaces together from a random assortment of availablity and access. When the pandemic hit, so many folks lost access to their creative spaces. This forced me to think about what was truly essential to my making practice, and what I could do at the kitchen table. Although ceramics requires access to some equipment, hand building is extremely adaptable to almost any place you can set up a table. The clay and tools used for most projects can fit in a small box. Never let the lack of a classic studio space hold you back!

Even if you are working on these projects in a solitary nature at home, keep in mind there is a community of makers out there, and we can connect online, if not in person, anytime. So many folks reached out after my first book was published to let me know I was the only

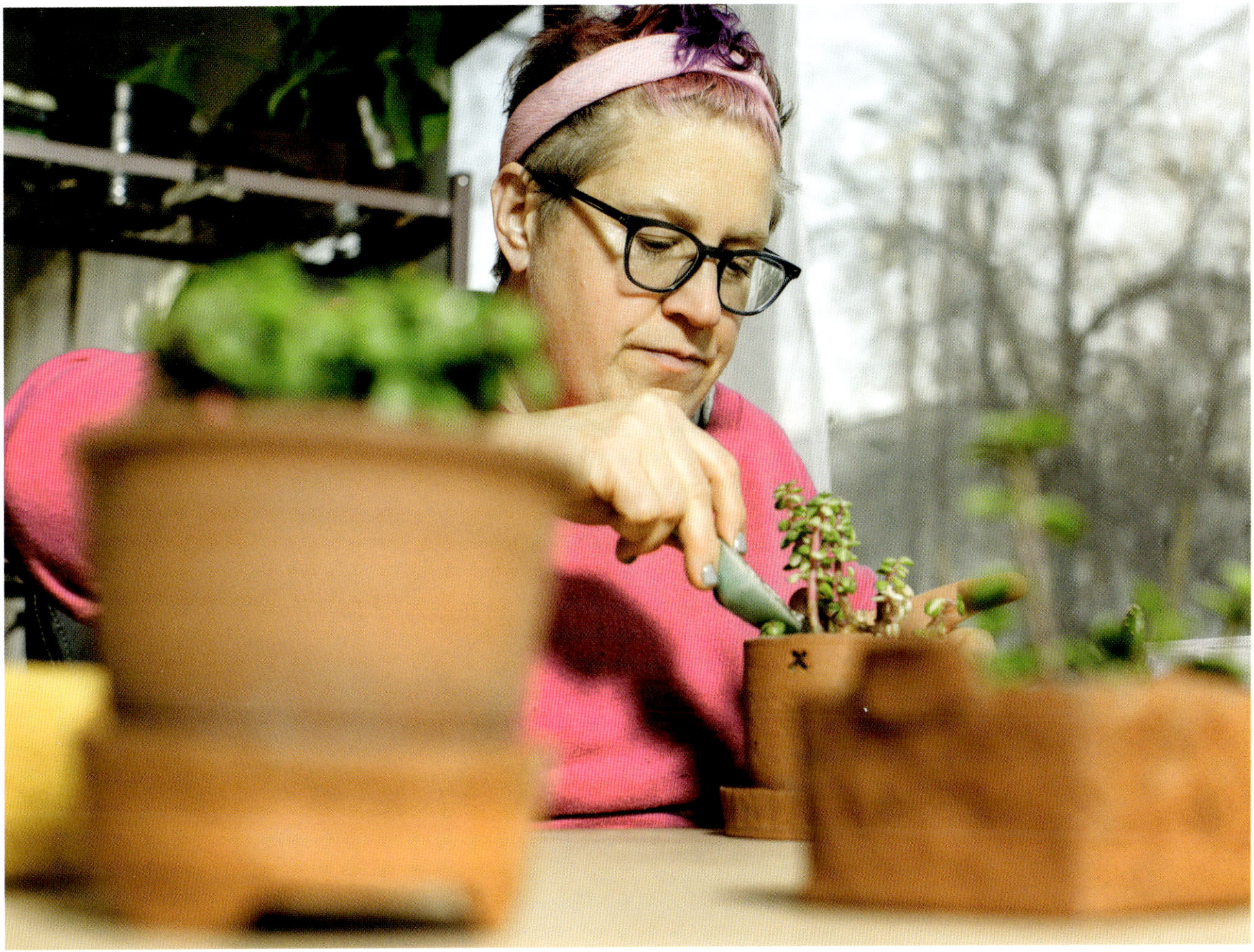

teacher they had access to. They sat at their tables, hand building, with my words on the pages in front of them for company. What I have learned from my twenty years of studio practice—and what lockdown confirmed—is that we are not alone on this creative journey. There is someone somewhere pinching clay at the same time you are. Even if we are sitting at our tables working slowly and steadily, I believe our paths will cross someday. We can share our love of this amazing material and what we have learned about ourselves along the way. In this way, too, clay creates its own world.

Okay, let's get going!

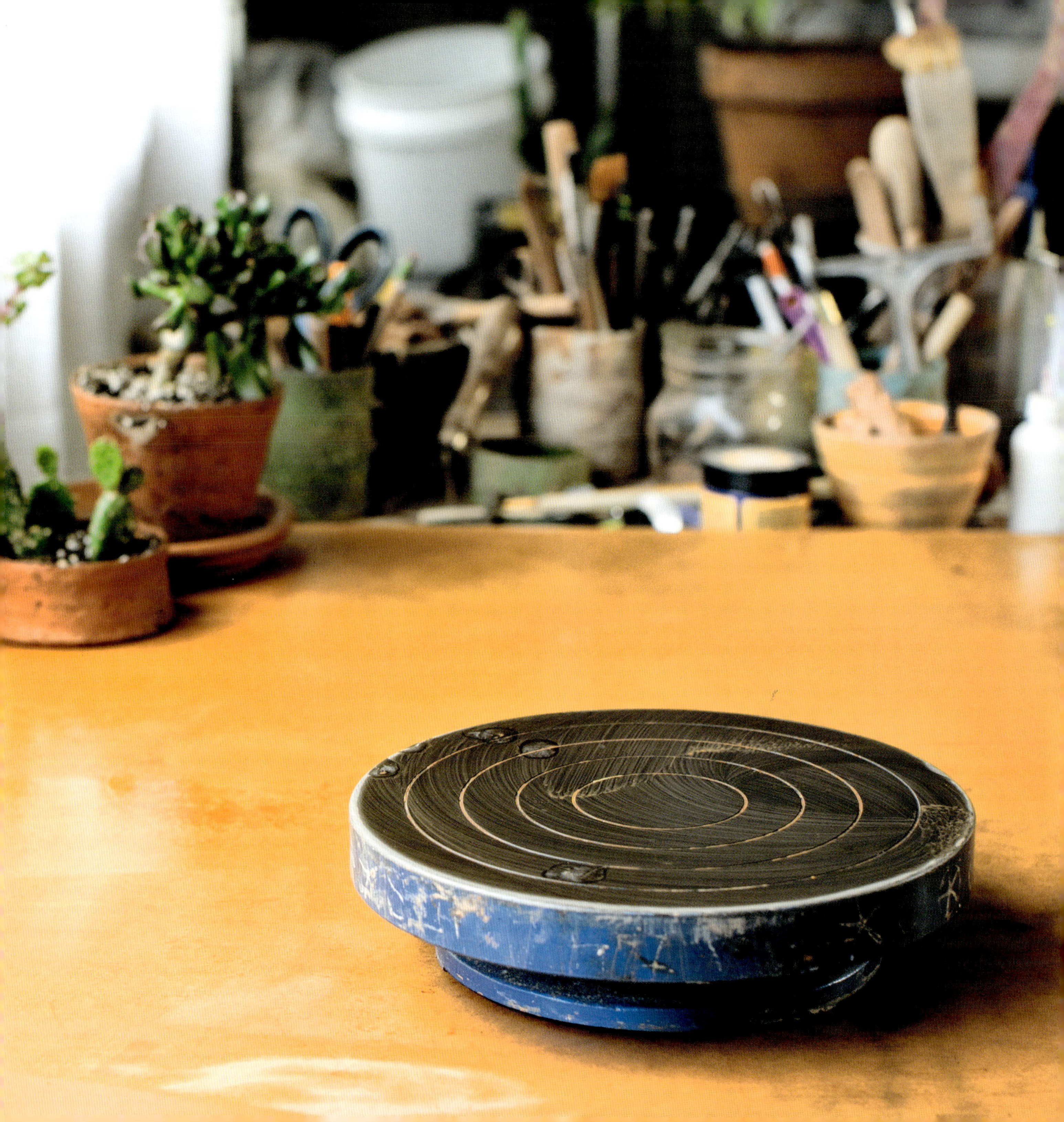

section

1

WELCOME TO THE STUDIO

Although some authors encourage you to read the whole first chapter or section first, I encourage you to skim this information and then come back as needed. The best part of the clay journey is the making part. So get your clay out and get to the making! If you find yourself in the middle of a project and something is mentioned that you don't understand, hopefully you'll find the answers in this section. Yes, there are lots of new words, definitions, and skill explanations, but don't let them intimidate you! You don't need to memorize any of this, and many of these ideas will become embedded in your foundation of knowledge as you move forward in clay. My hope is that the information I'm providing here will help you navigate the complexity of working in clay. Your interest and practice will guide you down a path no one can predict. There are projects that will refer you back to this section; think of it as the instruction manual when you get to the parts that are difficult. Clay has its own language, and this section is the key you need to start deciphering it.

BODY AND MIND

I admit I did not have healthy work or personal habits when I found clay, and for the first few years I pursued it with a blinding passion. Unfortunately, I ended up doing a lot of harm to myself. I learned hard lessons when my mental and physical health suffered. I reached a breaking point where I almost gave up my clay career. From the outside, it might have looked like I was thriving in my profession (teaching workshops and selling ceramics), but I was miserable, unhealthy, exhausted, and had another year planned like the past one that had just broken me. Something had to change, and it wasn't the clay—it was me. I realized my personal well-being wasn't even on my to-do list. I had used the excuse that I didn't have time for things like eating right or exercising. I realized it wasn't that I didn't have the time; it was that it wasn't a priority. That realization helped me sort out what my priorities should be.

I changed things dramatically, putting my well-being first, making changes to my personal life, and implementing new boundaries around my clay practice and career. Once I made these changes, there was no going back. My life and my work life got right-sized, and I am 100 percent better for it. I hope you will take a few of my suggestions in the spirit they are shared. Armed with basic information and good habits from the get-go, you will keep coming back to your clay practice happily and healthfully. I want you set up for success, and taking care of yourself is priority one.

Body

When you are hand building, it's important that you work from a place of comfort, stability, and knowledge. In developing this book, it is important to me that you know how much I value your effort and participation in clay and, ultimately, the commitment you have made to yourself. There is safety and trust here in these pages for you. When people embark on a creative journey, it is truly an investment in themselves. Growing and connecting to a creative practice is one of the things that makes life worth living, in my experience.

If you drop in to your local studio, keep in mind every studio setup is different, and they are often not set up with comfort, ergonomics, or the differently abled in mind. Setup is often centered around equipment, tables, shelving, and how many bodies can fit. Community studios can be physically uncomfortable, as tables and chairs may be the wrong size for your body or wrong for how you like to work. Equipment is designed to be one size fits all. (I still haven't met the person for whom it fits perfectly!)

With more than twenty years working in clay, traveling far and wide, and through trial and error, I learned what will keep my body and brain happy in the studio. In this section is the knowledge I have gleaned along the way, questions I have asked myself, and behaviors that have helped keep me healthy and sane. As we are all different, take what works for you and leave the rest. As with anything, if you have concerns with your own body and your physical and mental practice, consult a trusted resource.

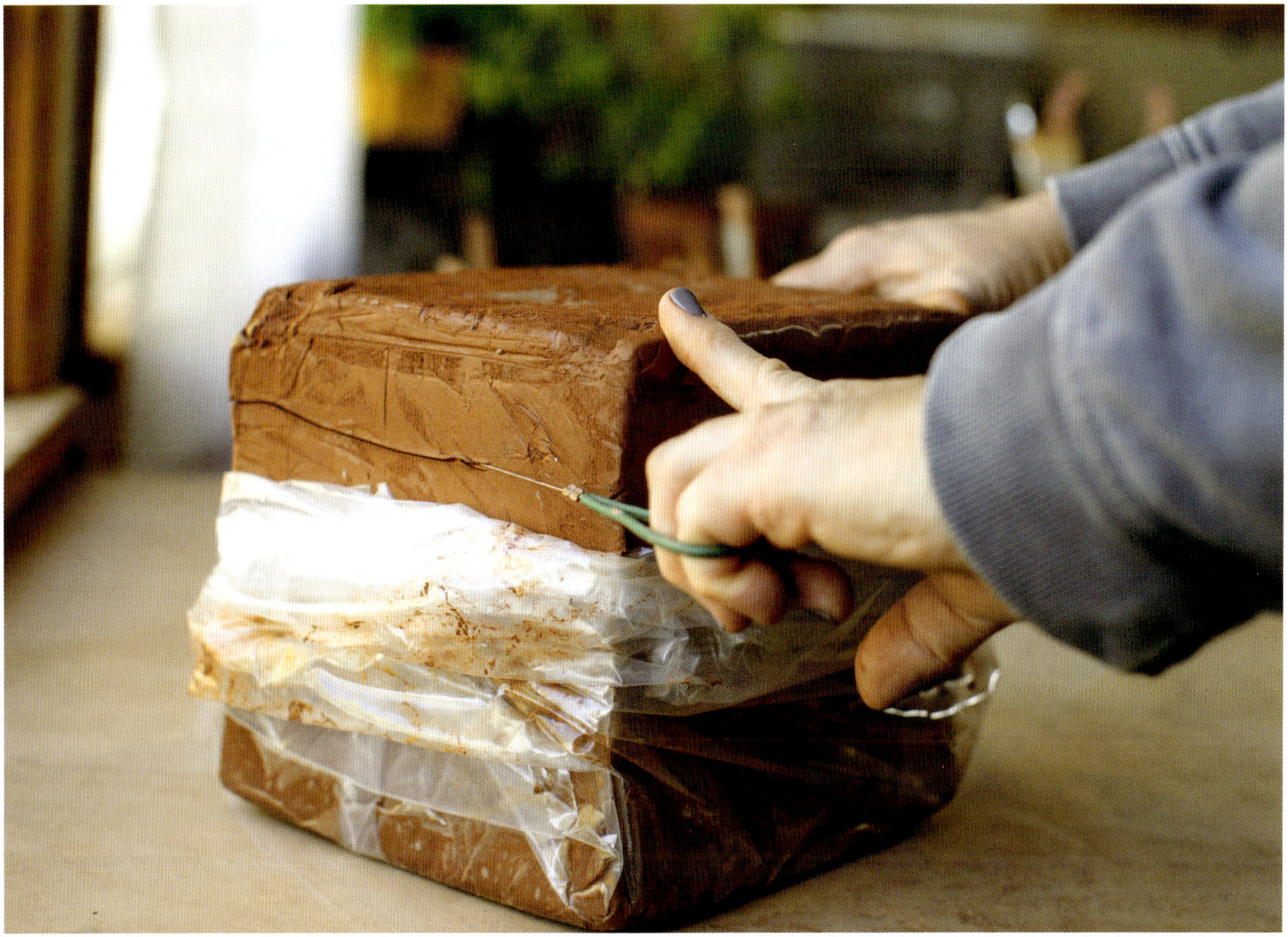

NOTE *Besides physical conditions and materials, there are toxic attitudes and practices that can come along with shared spaces. Racism, sexism, ablism, elitism, and entitlement are all things we have not escaped in the ceramics field. Sometimes, because of the nature of a small business, those behaviors have been left unchecked. We, as a community, have a very long way to go toward inclusive and equitable spaces. There has been a pay-your-dues mentality when it comes to those -isms, and even learning ceramics information and technology, meaning those who came before suffered so those coming after should as well. I reject that practice. Find your community (even if it's just in these pages). Don't let the fact that it is not perfect stop you in your creative journey.*

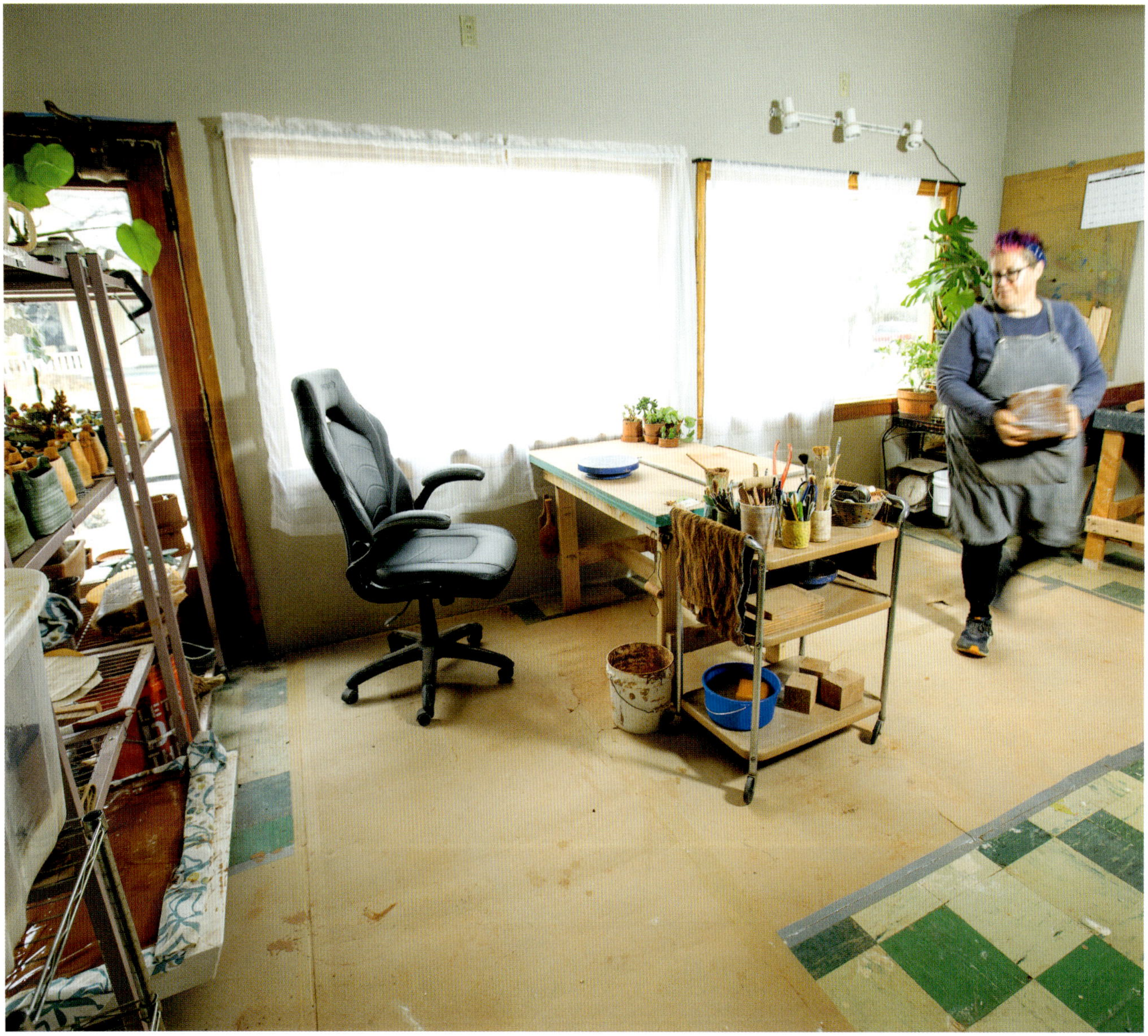

Studio Setup

If you are setting up your own space, or even if you are part of a community studio, these are a few things to think about when prioritizing your comfort and well-being. Ask yourself this series of questions. The answers will steer you toward finding a good space to work and identify what modifications you might need to be comfortable.

- Do you want to work alone or alongside others?
- Does a community space have clear community guidelines and safety practices? A good practice is to talk to members in the studio before you sign up and get a feeling for the attitudes around the studio.
- What is the vibe of the place? Trust what your body tells you.
- Is there a studio manager? Are classes available? What are their policies for hiring teachers? Is there diversity in the teacher and student population?
- Do you want to sit or stand while working? Can you set up tables? Do the tables in the space suit your working needs?
- Do you want to invest in buying equipment and tools? This can be done slowly over time. Most of the time you will be able to find someplace to get your work fired for a nominal cost. I ran a successful business selling pottery *without* a kiln for more than a decade! It is doable.
- Is there heat and air-conditioning? (Clay as a material should always be stored in temperatures above freezing.)
- How is the lighting? Is it natural light or are you in a basement/warehouse with only fluorescent lighting?
- Do you have space for some shelving? Is there storage for your clay and tools?
- Will you have to carry heavy bags of clay up and down stairs?
- Will you have to transport greenware?
- Can you comfortably get around the space? Are there any obvious hazards?
- How much space do you really need? (This question is so simple but so important. I notice folks always taking up a lot of space, but I have realized I can make do with my corner of the table and a small cache of tools perfectly well. Space is nice, but don't overdo it!)

Best Practices (Inside and Outside the Studio)

EXERCISE, EAT WELL, AND GET YOUR REST

Trigger warning! We are inundated with ridiculous amounts of diet culture nonsense. My advice is to be well. I have had my own journey with diet and exercise, and it would fill up a novel (a messy, heartbreaking, trauma-filled novel). My journey now is about well-being. Those hard lessons I mentioned before have helped me know what works for my body physically and, most important, mentally. It has taken a lot of work to get to where I am with my well-being. This is more important than anything else in my life. It is how I show up and care for myself, which is reflected in all the things I do out in the world, including my studio practice. Know that how you care for yourself will affect how you are able to work in your studio. I encourage you to find a balance and rhythm in your self-care routine that incorporates your studio time. Being creative and finding flow in your creative space requires freedom from distraction, and taking care of yourself shouldn't be the distraction that impedes you—instead, it should support you in the journey.

NOTE *Stay hydrated! This is a really important factor in both studio and non-studio life. There have been so many times when I forget to drink water while working. I end up battling a headache and fatigue and lose my ability to focus on details. I usually leave the studio because I am miserable. Keep that water bottle nearby, and hopefully your studio has a bathroom!*

BREATHE

One of the most effective ways to reduce stress is to do some box breathing. It is really simple. Breathe in (four count), hold (four count), breathe out (four count), hold (four count), repeat. This practice, or some variation of it, can greatly reduce your anxiety and stress and increase your focus. I try to remind myself to take some deep breaths whenever I find myself tensed up or just doing nothing, such as sitting in traffic or sitting at my studio table contemplating my next move. Many people normally breathe quite shallowly; however, it is great for our bodies and mindset to do some deep breathing, even if it is just a minute or two a few times a day. Give it a try.

TAKE BREAKS

Don't be afraid to take a break. Some of the best advice I received from a mentor was that time spent out of the studio can be more important than time spent in the studio. This is how we refresh, as well as get new ideas and experiences that we can draw on for our art practice. Grab a coffee with a friend, take a walk—taking a physical and mental break can help change your mindset, and reconnecting with your body can add to your productivity and focus back in the studio.

CONSIDER POSTURE

Whether you sit or stand while working, we all have postural tendencies. We tense in concentration or hunch to get closer to what we are doing. We hold ourselves in all kinds of uncomfortable ways. When working, try to be mindful of your body. Discomfort is your body telling you there is something wrong. Common complaints by those working in ceramics spaces are lower back pain, neck cramps, and carpal tunnel symptoms. Watch how you pivot, hold your arms and hands, and stand or sit. Remember, you are moveable in this situation; notice your body and see whether you can move to better suit your workspace. In my studio, I am always adjusting the height of my chair, or even my table, while working to keep myself in a comfortable space. Working with clay can be tiring and difficult, especially in the beginning. You are working and developing new muscles—both mental and physical. In the excitement and passion for this new journey, there is a danger of exhausting or hurting yourself. Be sure to rest and recuperate.

You'll find recommended stretches on pages 18 and 19, most of which are what I call "opposite work." They help you open yourself back up after all the hunched or closed-in postures you'll get into while working. If you can remember, drop your shoulders, move your hands and fingers around, and stand up and move at a minimum of every hour.

MIND YOUR HANDS AND SKIN

When working with clay or glaze, we frequently wash our hands. Clay also draws moisture from your hands, which can be rough on your skin (especially in the winter months). Find a good lotion; I prefer barrier-type creams, as they help protect my hands while I work and last a good while. Avoid direct contact with the caustic materials sometimes found in some clay or glazes (perlite or wood ash are a couple common ones). These can cause burns to the skin when mixed with clay or glaze. There are other materials usually found in raw state in a glaze lab that you should also avoid direct contact with; they should be marked clearly. Check the resource section under the online databases—the ones to do with glazing will have a list of hazardous materials.

Stretches

HAND STRETCHES

I recommend doing these stretches intermittently throughout your studio time, more often if you are just beginning. So much of what you are learning will be building new muscles in places you may not have been using before. Also if you are cramping up or easily fatigued, take a few minutes every hour to take care of your hands. Take a break and give yourself a little hand massage.

STRETCH YOUR BODY

At a minimum you should get up and walk around every hour. I suggest a series of stretches as part of your studio practice. For each person this will be different. Age and mobility are big factors in your range of motion. If you want to keep using your body freely, practice some restorative stretching after and during your clay sessions. The goal is to get your spine activated and the blood flowing back to all your extremities, especially if you have been hunched over a studio table. If you have a full day in the studio (eight hours), take a midday break and move your body. Create a short studio routine for yourself. If you have the space and time to create a full stretching routine, great, but the studio is not usually a place you want to be on the floor. Create a routine that is quick and easy to remember. It should be a way to maintain, loosen, and open your body back up after sitting or standing in a making session.

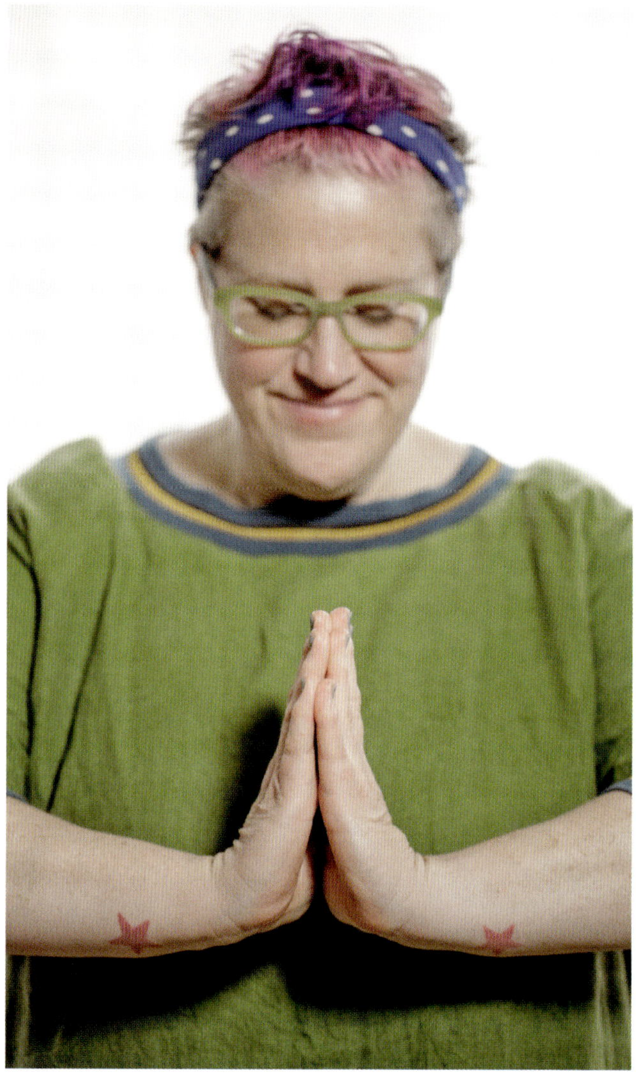

Hold hands in prayer fashion, a little away from the body and gently twist hands (tips of fingers) towards your body. You should feel a gentle stretch. Hold for 30 seconds.

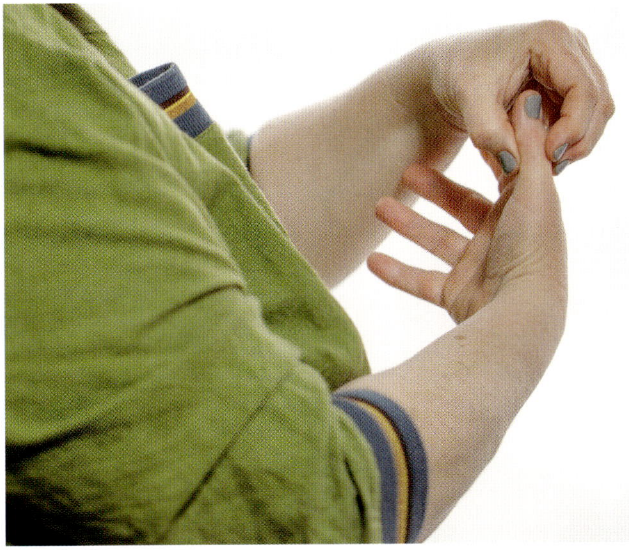

With gentle pressure, use your hand to articulate your fingers and thumb on the opposite hand, working both away from the heart and towards the heart. Repeat for the other hand.

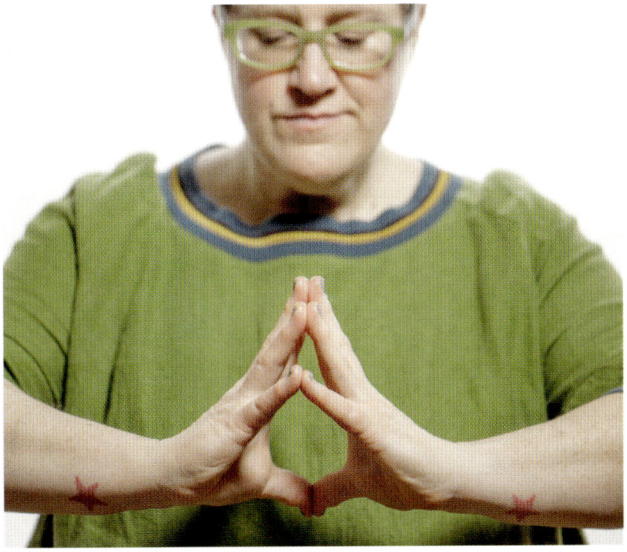

Place fingertips together, spread out a bit, and gently press fingers together. Then, bring your palms together. Move them together and apart.

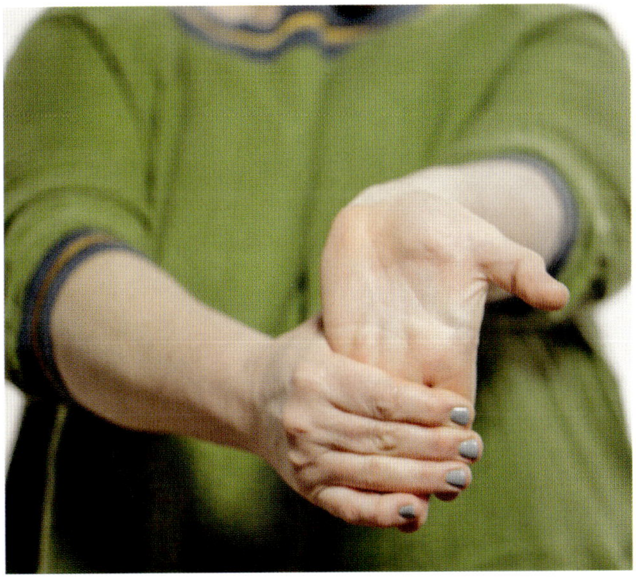

Extend your arm in front of you palm up. Use your opposite hand to gently stretch the hand down. Hold for 30 seconds. Repeat for your other arm.

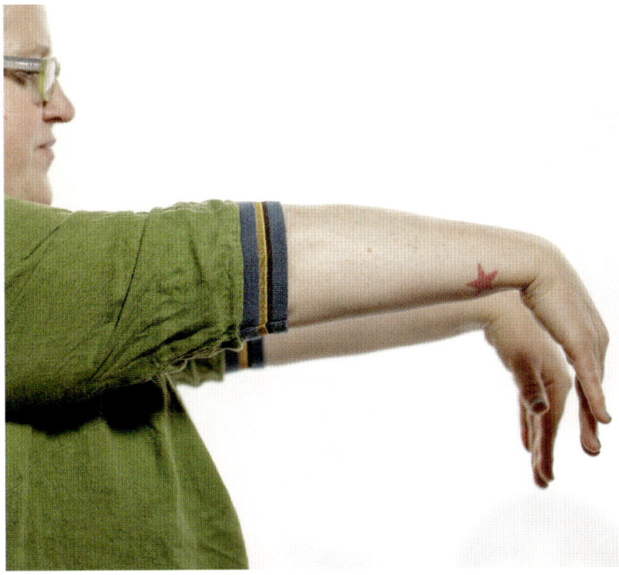

This is the "zombie arms" stretch. Extend both arms in front of you, and fold hands forward. Hold for 30 seconds.

Mind/Mindset

The passion of learning new creative skills can take us a long way down the making path. I want to touch on bumps on the road you may encounter. Things happen, and life priorities get in the way of your art practice. Perhaps you have some failures in the studio that deflate your energy and your desire and ability to get back to the studio. One of the most difficult things in any studio practice is getting started. When we have limited creative time, starting can be especially difficult if you are the type of person who needs momentum. The start-and-stop moments of life sometimes prevent us from pursuing our creative practices. Even though I call clay time my job, I face distractions and my own tendency to procrastinate. It's human nature.

RECOGNIZE THAT YOU ARE THE MOST IMPORTANT PART OF YOUR STUDIO PRACTICE

Without you, nothing is going to happen. Set regular time aside for yourself to be in your studio (even if that is at your kitchen table). Take that commitment seriously. If you don't have time to break out all your clay gear, draw in your notebook, read some of the projects in this book, or find the next thing you want to make when you have the space and time. Show up for yourself when you say you are going to. Doing so helps your clay practice become a regular event. It also shows family and friends that you are making time for yourself in this particular way. Remove distractions if you can. Leave your phone in another room or off your body. If people are distracting you, plug in your headset and listen to some music. Make a bubble around yourself so you can find some focus and energy to play with clay.

BE OPEN TO THE POSSIBILITY OF FAILURE

Failure is a part of this process. This book and the projects in it are about skill building. They are meant to slow you down and help you focus on each of the small steps to get you to a finished object. These fun, playful projects will help you build foundational skills, but they also may be challenging, and some will test the limits of your patience. Clay is a medium that engages the moment. It wants your time, your energy, and your focus—and if you don't give it those things, it will teach you some difficult lessons. Every person brings a different set of skills; your hands are different than mine. The functionality of your body is different. How you interpret the photographs will vary. Be patient with yourself and the process. You are going to work to solve the creative problems in front of you. Remember, you are the adventurer here; you chose this journey.

HAVE A WELL-BEING CHECKLIST

Part of the reason you have chosen this path is because it is fun and joyful, but in that joy can also be struggle and challenges. At some point, you might throw your hands up in defeat. Rest before you give up or quit. I have found if thing after thing isn't working and I'm just getting angry, frustrated, and disappointed, it's time to get out of the studio. Go out and experience the world. Think of this practice as research. What do you enjoy? Take pictures, try new things, find new hobbies or interests. When we engage with our interests, we can bring that engagement back to a studio practice. In the studio, practice is what helps build and develop our skills, this also applies to practicing mindfulness in our time outside of the studio. (Checklist ideas: Did you eat? Are you distracted? Are you tired? Did you exercise? Do you need a walk in the sun?)

HOW TO USE THIS BOOK

I like to think of all ceramics knowledge and skill as a pie, and that whole pie is way too much for me to eat. Just as I am never going to sit down and eat a whole pie, I will never know all there is to know in the clay realm. I only fancy myself an expert in one tiny sliver of the clay knowledge pie, and I have been working in that sliver for the past twenty-plus years.

This book and the projects within are your beginning introduction to ceramics. My goal is to give you a taste of some of the possibilities of clay. The galleries are meant to show you a small glimpse of what's possible with hand-building skills. I want to add to your toolbox of skills while trying to excite your creative mind. Not every project will be your kind of project, and that's okay. I urge you give them all a try: you will learn some new skills, and maybe surprise yourself with a new interest. (I did when coming up with the projects for this book. I would have never imagined how much fun it was to make little clay creatures. I had a blast, and it engaged a whole playful part of myself I didn't realize was just beneath the surface of my self-imposed seriousness!) This is your adventure, so you can always skip ahead to a section that really sparks your interest. That excitement is a great place to start.

It's about the Journey

My last thought is just a general philosophy you might keep in mind. This clay thing is really about the journey and not the destination (or object). When we make things, in the early days we can sometimes get caught up in the objects, which is totally understandable—it's a celebration every time you open a kiln. Don't forget that we spend more time making and remaking (the journey), and in thinking only about how to achieve an end goal (the destination), we can lose sight of just how important and meaningful that making (journey) time is. It is a privilege to carve out studio time, to spend your moments in a creative endeavor. In reality, we quickly move on from the shiny, beautiful thing we have created to make the next object, because there is joy in the making. Just remember to enjoy those moments sitting at your table, lost in the making—it is a rare and beautiful gift.

With that in mind, go forth and enjoy. Remember to have fun. Remember that failure is part of the process. Remember to rest. Be present. Enjoy your clay adventure!

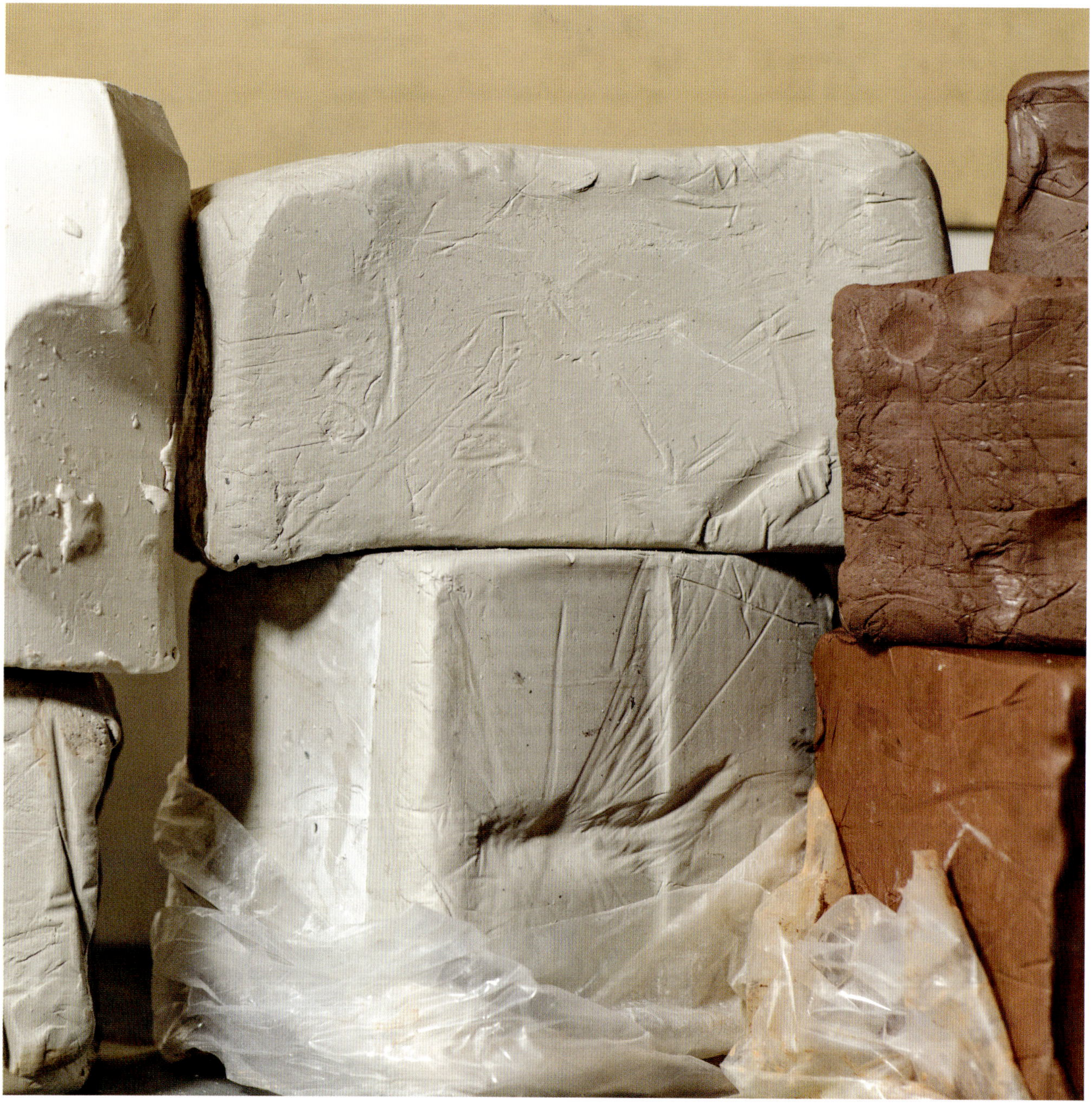

There's just something satisfying about cutting a fresh piece of clay straight from the bag!

CLAY

Clay is where we start. If we were painters, it would be a blank canvas. To start, I recommend you try *all the clays* that excite you. Like with everything in life, you will find your preferences—some aesthetic and some technical. The magic of making is not in the clay; the magic is in me and you. My dexterity and competency with clay comes from years of playing around with many different clays, learning the various properties and rules for certain clays, and most important, from knowing how I prefer to work with clay. We all have tendencies that become apparent when we work. By choosing certain types of clay to work with, you can lean into your strengths and increase your chances of successful outcomes. That "magic" comes with trial and error and experience.

In the beginning of this clay journey, you might run into a language barrier. In grad school, we would sometimes gather for a dinner party, and it inevitably happened that one of the grads would start talking clay, and you could almost hear the inward groan of the significant others in attendance. Just like any subculture, the language around the topic can seem very mysterious and technical and, at times, alienating. In this section, I want to give an overview and foundation of the language around clay and its properties in layman's terms, so you don't get lost when folks start talking clay.

Clay chemistry is not what excites me . . . I love making. I am not a clay technology person; I learn what I need to and leave the rest until I have a need to learn it. If the technical stuff excites and interests you, there are lots of resources out there for you. I feel lucky to have had two kinds of teachers, one of whom had amazing technical knowledge and interest. He forced me to learn enough to ask smart questions and problem-solve when I had technical difficulty. The second was a teacher/mentor who wondered why I was spending all my time making clay instead of making *with* clay. He helped me get out of the bog that can be the technical side of ceramics. Although there is a place for learning the technical stuff, you can easily head to the clay store, grab a bag of clay, and start making! Part of this journey is to find a balance between the technical and the artistic and how you want to participate. My hope is that with a cursory understanding of the language used around clay spaces, you will have a good foundation to start understanding what is possible with clay, and the confidence to navigate deeper, if you so desire.

You have probably experienced digging in the dirt or maybe walking near a river and finding some clay: it presents as sticky, slimy, and very compact dirt. Although technically clay, this is not what we work with in the modern studio practice. Today most commercial clays and clay recipes are formulated to have more *plastic* qualities, making the clay very workable in most hand-building or throwing situations. Historically most clays were what we call *short*—they lacked some of the materials that make the clay more elastic (plastic). The difficulty of working with shorter clays is why most early pottery was made with hand-building techniques, as it was not possible to stretch the clay (as desired with wheel throwing) like we do nowadays with most commercial clays.

Cones

You may have heard folks throw around the term "cone" and some number that may or may not have made sense, such as "cone 6" or "cone 04." *What the heck are cones?* you might have wondered. Long before thermocouples and digital readouts, cones were used to read the temperature inside kilns. We still use them today. Pyrometric cones are of ceramic material that soften, bend, and eventually small pieces melt and when exposed to heat and time soften and bend, according to the silica and alumina rations in the cones. Cones are placed in a kiln near a peephole and are checked visually throughout the firing process. (Never look into a kiln without proper protective eyewear.) Although most kilns have thermocouples and digital readouts now, it is good practice to have witness cones in kilns to verify whether the kiln has reached the correct temperature for your clay body and glaze.

Some electric kilns are set up with a cone sitter, where a small cone for your goal temperature is placed. Once the goal temperature is hit, the kiln shuts off; cone sitters are a great safety feature to save you from overfiring. For gas or atmospheric firing, cones are more commonplace. You need to know the current temperature range and when to adjust it.

Learning to fire kilns is very daunting—it is a raging inferno in there! If you are interested in learning more about electric, gas, or atmospheric firings, there are many book resources out there. I also advise finding an experienced teacher who is willing to teach you. Kiln firing is something that requires practice and problem-solving, so having firsthand guidance is really the way to go. For our purposes, I want you to understand that cone numbers, such as cone 6 or cone 04, refer to a predetermined temperature range, and it is important to know in what range you are working regarding clay and glaze. My practice has been geared toward working in electric kilns; they can work in all the temperature ranges, so there are lots of options, and electric kilns tend to be very accessible and ubiquitous in most ceramics spaces.

For more information on the actual temperatures in Celsius and Fahrenheit and what a cone chart looks like, look up an Orton cone chart.

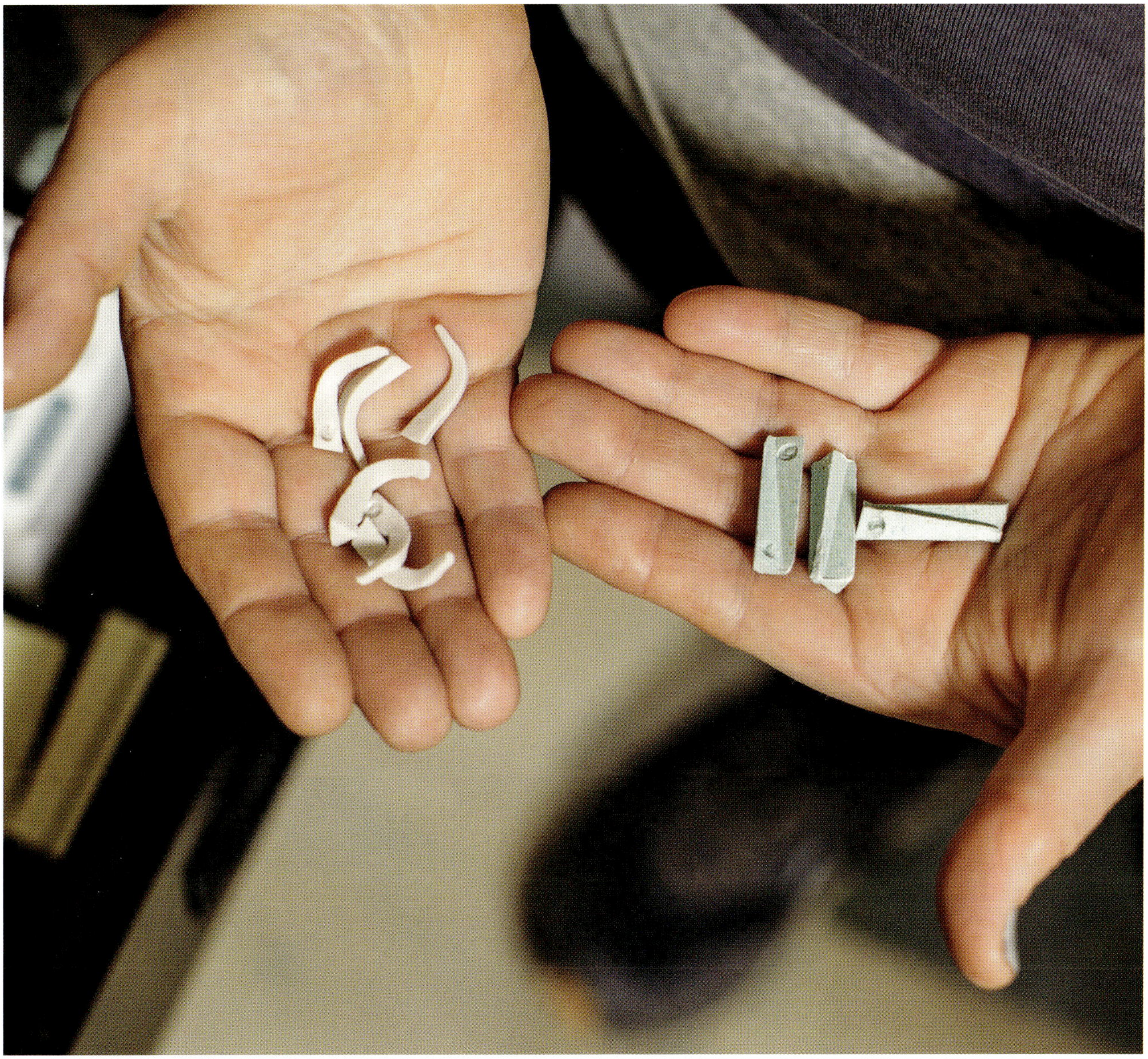

Cones before and after firing. These are cone 5, you can see a small stamp at the bottom of the cone that has a number in it indicating the cone or firing temperature. These were fired in an older test kiln with a cone sitter, when the cone starts to get soft and bend the kiln shuts off and the firing is finished.

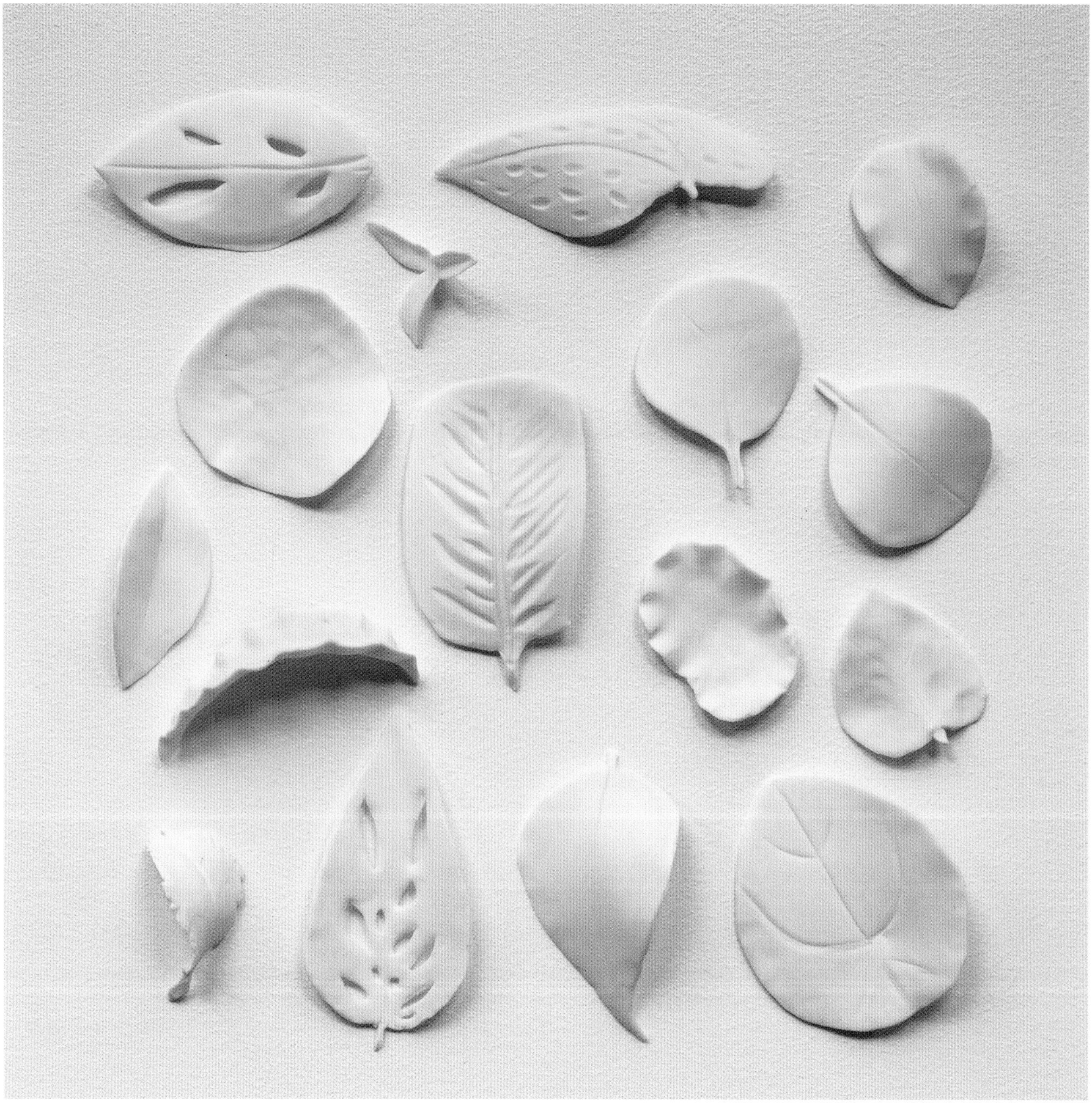

The bright white clay you see in projects such as Flora (page 66) is porcelain.

Types of Clay

There are three basic categories of clay: earthenware, stoneware, and porcelaneous.

EARTHENWARE

Earthenware is ceramic ware made of slightly porous opaque clay fired at low heat. A common misconception about earthenware is that it is always red, or that all red clay is earthenware. Terra-cotta planters are what spring to mind. Earthenware clay can be red or white, depending on the types of materials used to create the clay body. One of the main drawbacks of earthenware clay is that if it is fired over 04 it turns into a puddle or bloats or some other undesirable outcome! Another quality to consider is that earthenware remains somewhat porous after it's fired, meaning it will still absorb water. I call this feature punky. Earthenware is not vitrified clay; once a piece is fired to completion, a vitrified clay body will ring if you flick it with your finger. If you perform the same action on an earthenware pot it often sounds hollow or makes a "thunk" sound.

One of the great qualities about earthenware is that it's usually quite smooth in texture. Traditionally, earthenware has been used for flowerpots and cookware, most notably. Earthenware's openness means it has the ability to expand and contract in heat, which makes it a very good clay for cookware. Some of my favorite pots in the world are Spanish earthenware cookware. One of the perks of this low-fire clay body is its ability to develop brightly colored glazes at low temperatures.

Earthenware is a great clay and has lots of wonderful attributes, but also a couple of drawbacks. Because of its porosity, it can break down more than other clay bodies that are more vitrified, or impermeable to water. That bit of punkiness means the fired clay body can chip more easily, and regular use can wear down the strength of the clay. The fact that it's porous means whatever glaze you use on it needs to be non-crazing (no breaks in the glaze surface) and nontoxic, especially if it's going to be used for food service. If it's not going to be used for food, a wider variety of glazes can be applied. Another drawback is that earthenware tends to not have very good greenware (unfired pottery) strength, meaning it can become brittle when it is drying and bone dry.

STONEWARE

The next type of clay, and I dare say a most versatile clay, is a stoneware body. This clay body typically has grog (basically crushed-up bisqueware, defined on the next page) or sand (variable mesh) added to it. This changes the particle size and density of the clay. Varied particle size can help with the greenware and fired strength of the clay and its workability. The varied particle size makes stoneware bodies wonderful to hand build or throw. This style of clay is usually mid-range to high-fire clay and comes in all kinds of colors (think earth tones). Stoneware has great greenware strength. Because these clays fire in a hotter temperature range, they are typically all fired to vitrification. This makes a piece less likely to be good bakeware because there's no expansion and contraction when heated. It is great for making all other functional ware and sculpture work. It is also more likely to be used in atmospheric firings.

PORCELANEOUS

Porcelain is typically the whitest clay and contains the finest particle density, making it possible to achieve amazing thinness and strength. It is available in mid-range to high-fire porcelain bodies. Depending on oxidation or reduction, during firings, you'll get either a yellow or blue hue. This clay body is used not for cookware, but it is really wonderful for dishware and sculpture work. It's a beautiful material and fun to work with.

One of porcelain's amazing attributes is its ability to achieve translucency, meaning you can see shapes and light through it. Translucent porcelain is thin and has been fired at high temperatures. It is also extremely strong and versatile, used in dishware and even in space shuttles!

Get ready for a challenge, though. Porcelain can soften and warp during firings. It is prone to developing cracks. If you choose to explore porcelain, be patient as there is a learning curve. Porcelain can be challenging to work with, but its beauty is rewarding.

Reclaimed Clay

× × × × ×

Reclaimed clay is previously used clay, such as unwanted greenware, trimmings, and remnants, that has been saved. It can be mixed with fresh dry materials or dried out and reconstituted to be used again.

States of Clay

GREENWARE

Greenware refers to any clay object that has not been fired yet and is still in its raw state. It can be broken up and slaked down and made into workable clay again.

Greenware Strength

× × × × ×

The term "greenware strength" is used to describe drying clay. As clay dries, its workability decreases, and as it becomes bone dry, the clay object is at its most fragile. How that clay withstands the drying process is greenware strength. Some clays have great greenware strength; you can put a clay object on a shelf, and it just dries. Stoneware-style clays are a lot less fussy than an earthenware or porcelain body, which can sometimes become brittle as they dry. Greenware strength, and your own preferences (and tendencies), should be considered when determining your preferred clays. See the section on drying and plastics for clays that need a bit of babying (page 50).

BISQUEWARE

Bisque or bisqueware is how we refer to clay objects once they have gone through the first firing. A chemical change occurs, changing clay into ceramic material. This means that it can no longer be broken down into a raw, workable clay material. This is also the point when glazing happens in most ceramic work. The clay is much less fragile than when it is in its greenware state, but it's still porous, which makes it perfect for applying glaze.

GLAZEWARE

Glazeware is the finished product of the ceramics process. Traditionally and simply put, glaze is a mix of chemical materials suspended in water that is applied to bisqueware and then fired to completion based on the clay and glaze temperature requirements. Those chemicals change to become a glass on the surface of the object.

Untraditionally, glaze surface can also mean any kind of coating on your ceramic work. Room-temperature glaze: paint! After your final firing, paint or other materials like flocking can be applied. Usually this is used for sculpture or nonfunctional work. This is more in the realm of mixed-media surface design.

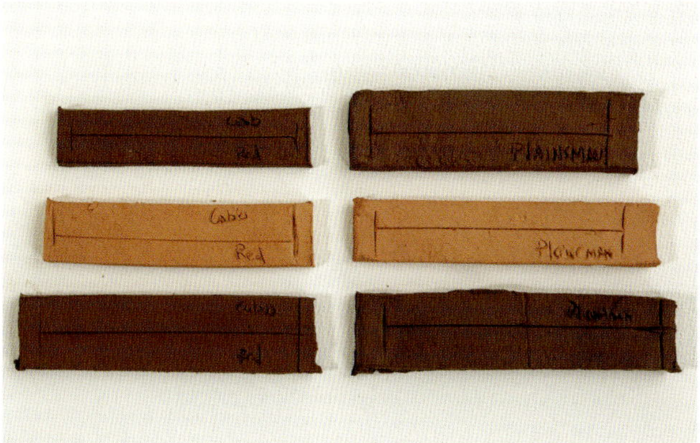

CLAY SURFACE: FIRED UNGLAZED

It is possible to leave clay unglazed and fired to completion and have a food-safe/vitreous surface. This is dependent on your clay; some clays fired to completion are still porous and, therefore, are not recommended to be left unglazed for food/functional purposes. Often, raw clay surfaces are found in higher temperature ranges (i.e., cone 5 and above). Usually, stoneware or porcelain clay bodies are your best bet when leaving a surface that will come into contact with food. For sculpture, almost anything goes—just make sure your clay is vitrified and strong enough to survive installation and transport.

NOTE *A word on shrinkage. Every clay body shrinks as it goes from its wet state to greenware to bisque to glaze fired. Most clays have a shrinkage rate of around 10 percent, plus or minus. It's something to think about, but not worry about. If you are curious, make some shrink bar tests. Roll out a small slab, measure out a 5 inch (12.7 cm)-long line (ten ½ inch [26.7 cm]-long segments), and make vertical marks at the ends. Then fire to the desired temperature and measure it again. That is a really quick way to find out how much your clay shrinks.*

Vitreous

The term "vitreous" refers to the density of the ceramic material. All the materials in your clay have come together (melted, chemically bonded) to form glass. Or, your object has basically become a rock!

Workability Stages

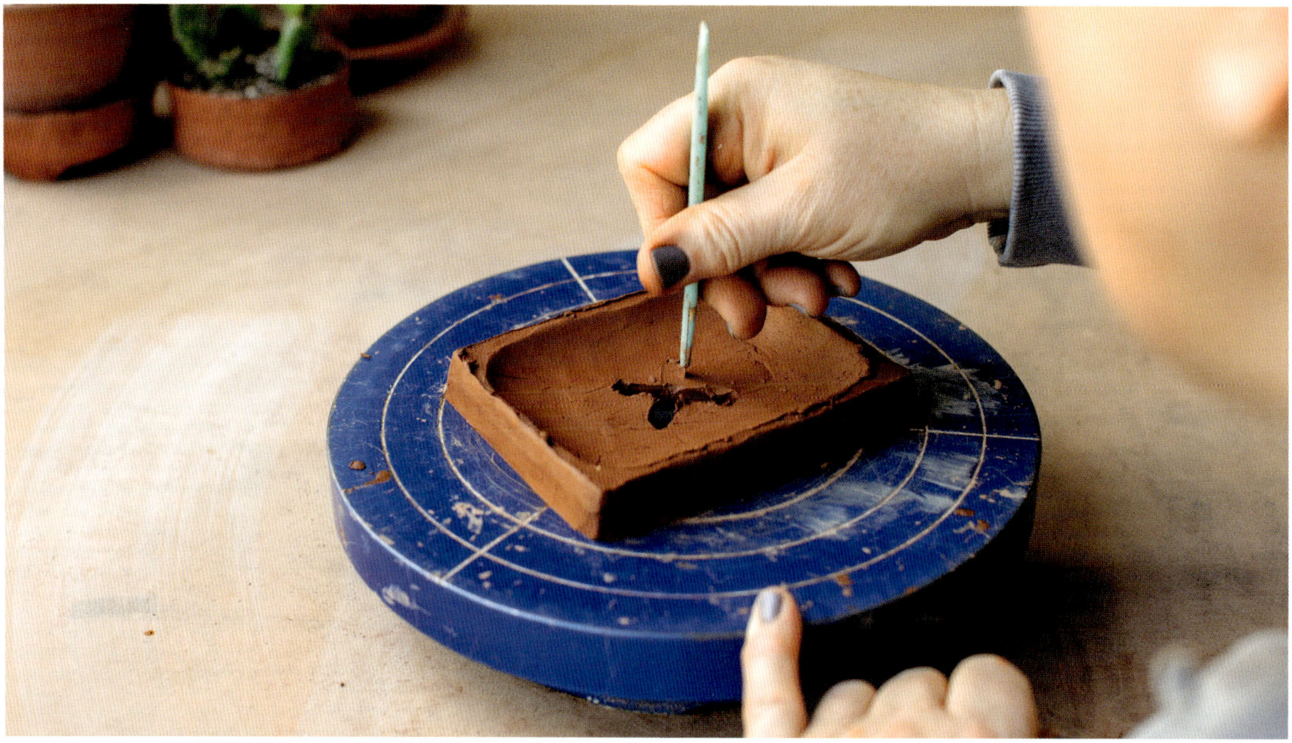

Learning what's possible at the various workability stages is something you'll master through experience. The good news is this means projects will get easier and easier with practice!

SOFT/MEDIUM LEATHER HARD

This stage is when the clay remains extremely workable, but it is firmed up enough to softly hold its shape. In the ceramics world, we often use types of cheese as a descriptor for clay. Imagine a ball of mozzarella that, if cut into a single slice, can be bent so the ends almost touch without it breaking, and when released, it mostly snaps back to its flat shape.

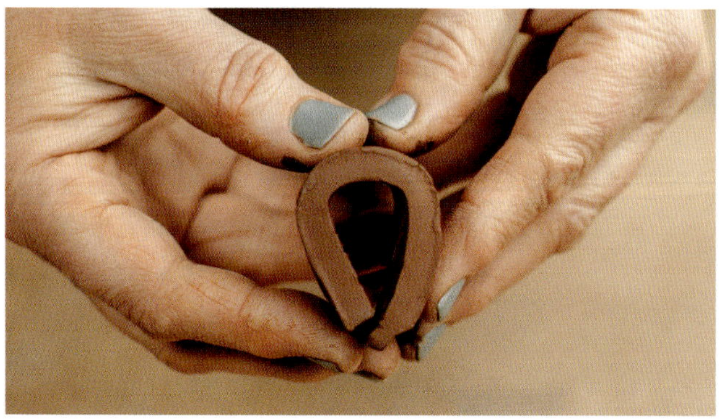

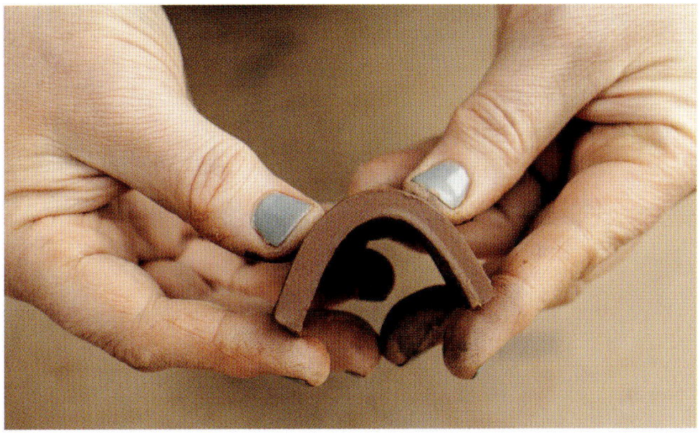

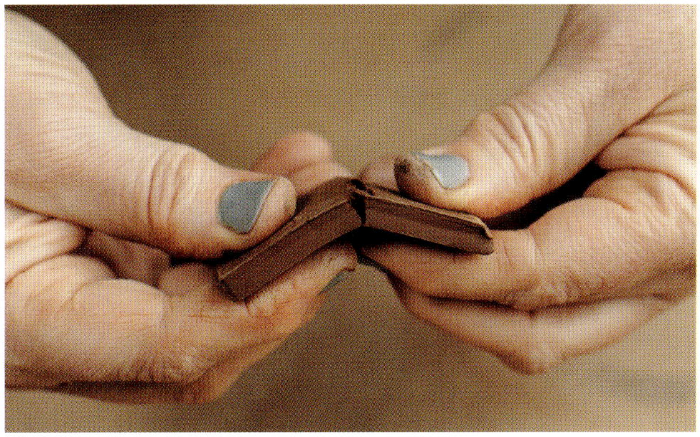

LEATHER HARD

This is the last stage of workability. Imagine a hard cheddar cheese. If you try to bend a slice, it snaps in half. This is the stage when a lot of refinement will happen, as the clay is set in its form and only surface manipulation can occur. It is also still possible to slip and score (see page 49) like-temperature pieces together. They often need a little bit of care during the drying process. You don't want to add fresh clay directly to leather-hard clay; it will often not stay together, and this is how cracks happen. Remember the clay has dried significantly at this stage (and shrunk), so fresh clay, which still has a lot of drying to do, will shrink at a different rate than the leather-hard object. Using like temperature to like temperature of clay is the best chance of success.

BONE DRY

In the bone-dry stage, the clay is no longer workable; at its most fragile and is ready to be bisque fired.

TEMPERATURE

This is a Sunshine word. I use it often to refer to the wetness of the clay and the workability. It comes from my perception and understanding of the clay going through a temperature change as the water leaves the clay (as it dries). It is at room temperature when sitting in a bag ready to be worked with, even though it feels colder than room temperature (due to the water in the clay), but it is the ambient temperature of the room. It starts to get warmer as you work with it, from your energy and body heat. It also starts to dry the moment it leaves the bag. When the object is finished and put on the shelf to dry, the water migrates to the surface and evaporates, and the clay starts to feel cold. It keeps feeling colder and colder as it dries until it is bone dry and becomes the ambient temperature of the room again. To test this, hold a piece next to your cheek at different points during the drying process. It is a good practice, when learning to load a bisque kiln, to test the pieces before they go in the kiln—they should feel warm (room temp) against your skin. If they feel cold, leave them on the shelf until the next firing.

Health Hazards

Clay in its wet state clay is mostly inert. But there are a couple things to keep in mind. Mold can be present in wet clay, especially if the clay has been sitting for awhile in a bag. Also, recycled clay can be filled with skin particles, hair, or particulates floating around the studio. Much of those particulates will grow mold, fungus, or who knows what—again, not a science person. If you are prone to skin allergies, be mindful of what clay you are using. I know folks who can work in latex/nitrate gloves. I don't find them comfortable or easy when working with clay. Instead, I tend to use more barrier creams/lotions to protect my hands. They help a little and are especially important in the winter.

Some raw material ceramic ingredients can also be hazardous. It is recommended when working with dry ingredients in clay or glaze mixing to wear a respirator. Most ceramic supply stores will have them available. Remember to change the filter cartridges regularly if using a lot and store in a dust-free container. Studios with access to raw materials should have hazardous materials marked. Check the list of online resources (page 168) to find lists of particularly hazardous materials.

A serious health hazard in regular studio life is silica dust. This is problematic if it is airborne and breathed into the lungs. Serious health problems (such as silicosis) can result with long-term exposure. The following are two easy safety precautions:

- DO NOT sand or scrape bone-dry clay. It can be very tempting to try to save work that has unexpectedly dried out or that you forgot about on a shelf. When you sand it when it's dry, you create a lot of dust particles. You may be willing to risk it for yourself (with a mask on), but it is a bad habit. Remember, if you are in a shared studio, there are people in the studio who are there every day, all day long, and there's a lot of dust that can be created daily. So be mindful and a be good ceramic neighbor and avoid this practice.
- Keep your work area clean. Try to clean up your clay debris as you go, especially if it is still in a greenware state; it can easily be swept up and put into a reclaim bucket or trash. The best way to clean up is to use water and a sponge to clean your tabletop. For the floor, try not to sweep or only spot sweep with a small brush and tray. Mop with water to get the fine particles. Each studio will have protocols in place; be sure to follow those safety guidelines. If you are in your own space, make up your own guidelines and keep to them. There is nothing like red clay footprints tracked around your house to know you have been playing with clay, and what was a simple cleanup job just turned into a much bigger problem!

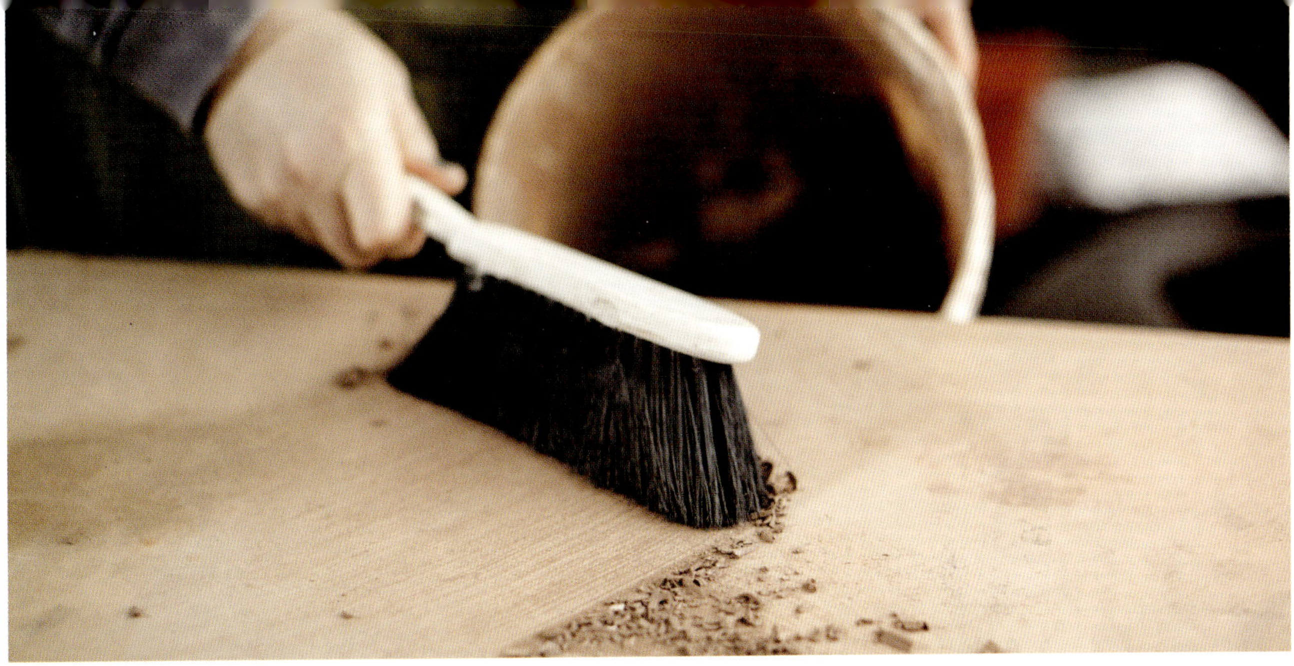

A few best practices for cleaning up. Sweeping up bits and pieces at the leather hard stage can easily go into a reclaim bucket.

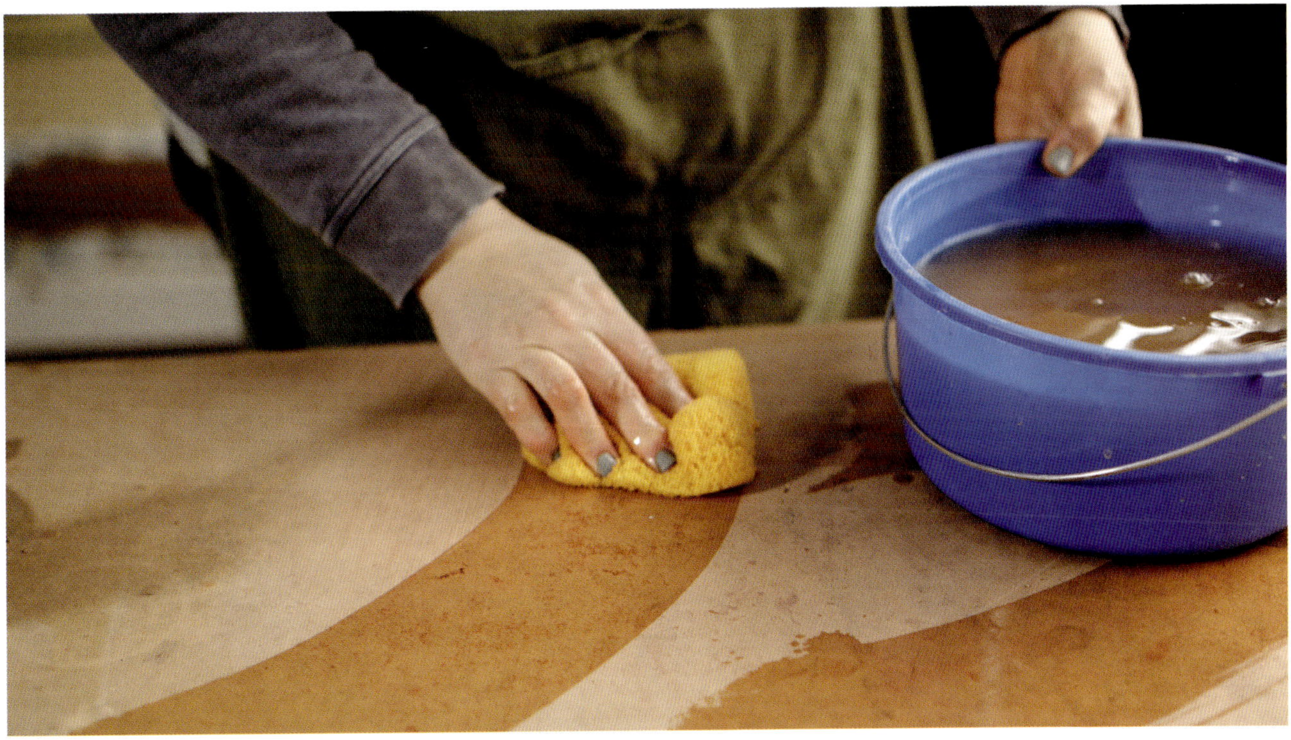

Using a sponge and bucket of water is the best way to clean your space and avoid creating a dust storm.

TOOLS

Sometimes not having the right tool keeps us from getting started. How often have you been about to get something started and then realized you need something to get that chore or project off your list? How about the home project that requires seven trips to the hardware store? It is beyond frustrating. I don't want that to be your experience playing in clay.

I am frequently asked about my tools or what my favorite tool is in my collection. We ceramic folks tend to be tool addicts. Although I have a few essential tools, and definitely a few I rely on heavily in my clay practice, I realized something a long while ago when I was asked to write out a response to a question about what my most essential tool was in the studio. My answer was *me*. I am the most important tool in my studio. If I don't show up, *nothing happens*. Just like the magic is not in the clay, the magic is also not in the tools you use. The most essential tool in your studio practice is *you*!

I want you to remember that when that procrastination chatter starts in your head or when you see a new intimidating skill in this book or demonstrated elsewhere. There are lots of ways to do things and a very few essential tools that will get you started. I have whittled down the number of tools in my studio over the past twenty years. That doesn't mean I don't have a plethora of tools in my studio—I hate to throw them away, as I might need them. Here I have tried to keep the tool list to the minimum types of tools you might need to get started, i.e., the stuff you need to be productive but can put in one box and stash easily when you are not using it. Not all of us have access to studios or the space to set up a home studio. I don't want that to be a limiting factor for you.

We are often presented with images of folks in picture-perfect studios, and lament that our workspace is so shabby. Let me tell you, I have had countless studios over the years . . . some have been picture-perfect, but many more have been less than perfect, especially in the beginning of my clay journey. Early on in my career, I was traveling to three different adjunct teaching jobs, each more than an hour apart from the other, and I didn't have a studio of my own. One of the ways I made that work was to have a "portable studio" in the car—a box with my essential tools and a bag of clay. I could work anyplace I was. I *was* my studio, and the resources I needed could be pieced together within the community spaces in which I was teaching. I promise you can get started with just the bare minimum of tools and some clay, because you already have the most important element: *you*!

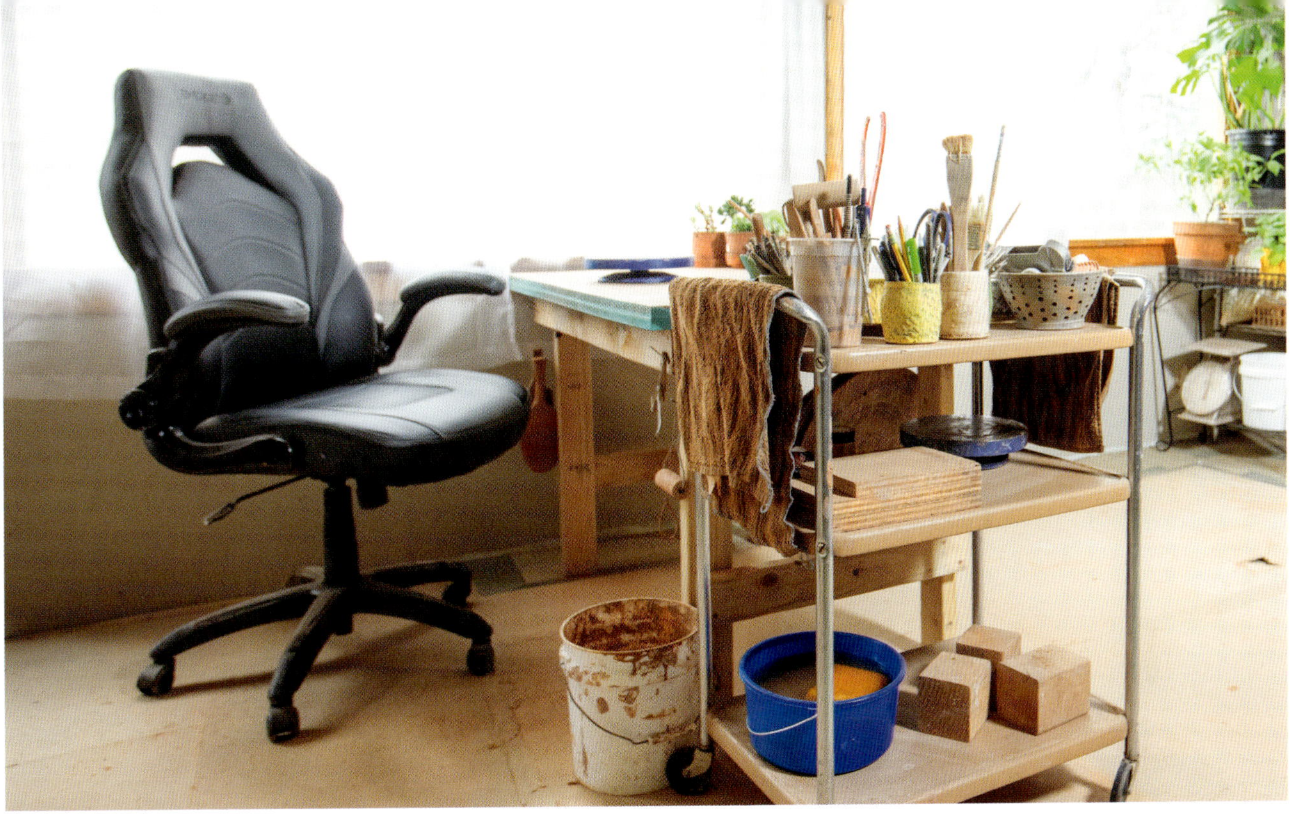

Make sure your workspace fits your body and your needs.

Essentials for the Body

COMFORTABLE TABLE

In the beginning, your good, old kitchen table will work—you want something that is easy to clean. Even a small folding table will work and can easily be stored with your tools when you are not making. Consider putting some craft paper down to protect your tabletop and make it easier to clean up.

COMFY CHAIR

Use a good chair you don't mind getting dirty. It is great if you can adjust the height and positioning of the chair. I work sitting down; some folks like standing and working—adjust your table height accordingly. If you prefer standing, be mindful of the flooring. You may want to invest in some mats that make it more comfortable to stand for extended periods. Keeping a tall stool nearby might also be a good idea.

GOOD LIGHT

We sometimes assume all light is the same. But if you are sensitive to lighting, it can really affect your mood, eyes, and the duration you can spend in a space. Be aware of your lighting situation and adjust where you work if you can't adjust the light.

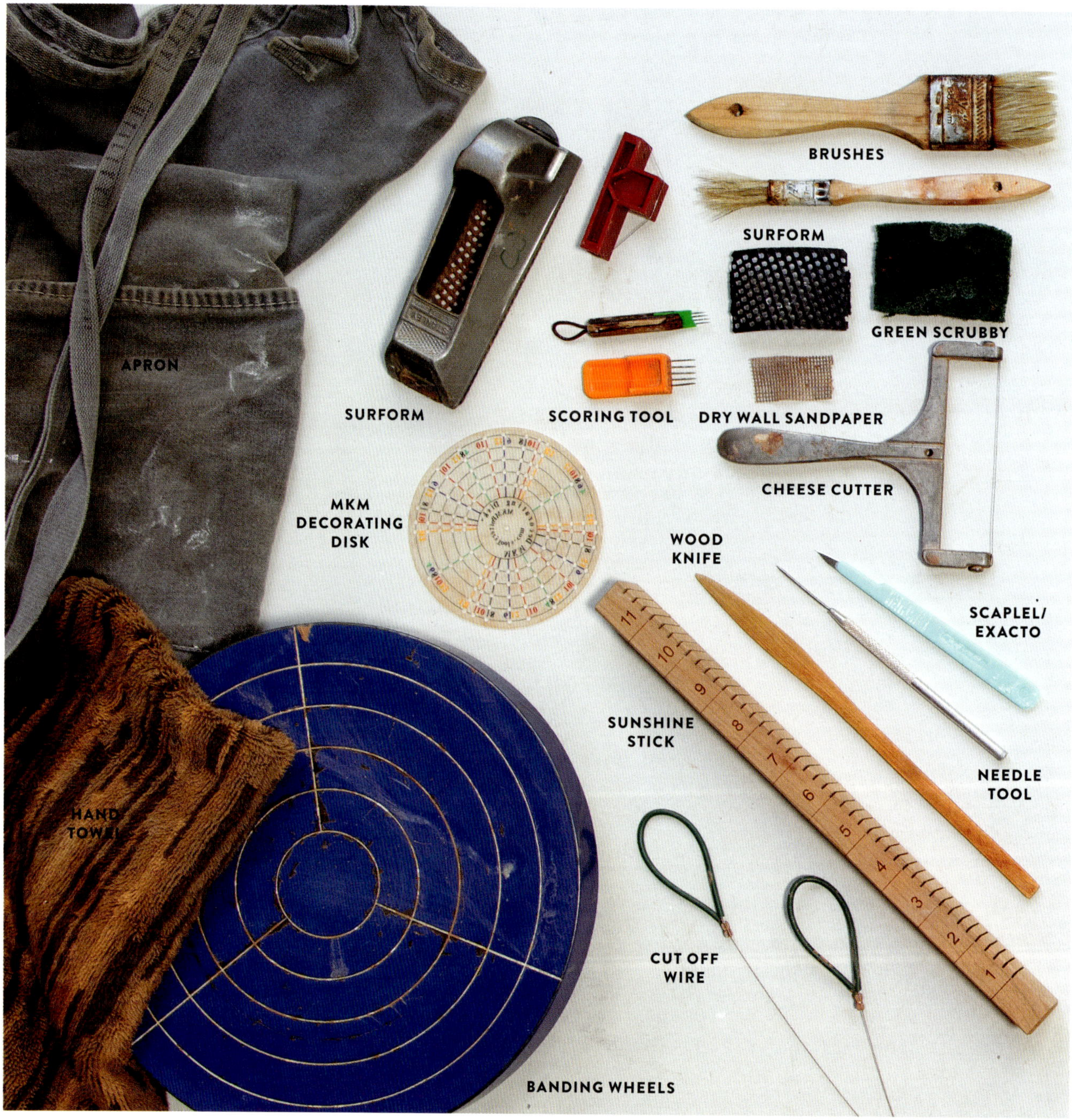
BRUSHES
SURFORM
GREEN SCRUBBY
APRON
SURFORM
SCORING TOOL
DRY WALL SANDPAPER
CHEESE CUTTER
MKM
DECORATING
DISK
WOOD
KNIFE
SCAPLEL/
EXACTO
SUNSHINE
STICK
NEEDLE
TOOL
HAND
TOWEL
CUT OFF
WIRE
BANDING WHEELS

Tools and Materials

The Basic Tool Kit

× × × × ×

For all the projects in this book, I recommend you have a set of tools on hand that I refer to as the **Basic Tool Kit**. Although I will outline additional tools and materials as needed, here's what I consider the essentials: banding wheel, wooden knife, needle tool, cheese cutter, scoring tool, ribs, cut-off wire, and scalpel. You can slowly add whatever else is helpful over time.

BANDING WHEEL: The banding wheel is the best friend of the hand builder. With practice, it is a tool of efficiency and flexibility. When you are just starting, it can seem like a clunky, spinning mess. Slow down and try a few skills, such as centering, keeping the work in the middle of the wheel. It should look still when spinning, that's how you know its centered. Collaring in, after you have managed centering and a bit of coil building. Collaring is using your hands or a rib and the spinning of the wheel to bring the top of your wall more towards the center. Tapering it and narrowing the opening. It takes some practice but is doable, it is a skill more common in wheel throwing. Also, you can center a cup or bowl on the wheel head and slow trimming feet with the aid of trim tools. Use a bat on top if you are not comfortable working directly on the wheel head. Play around, and eventually this insanely heavy tool will be indispensable to your practice.

NOTE *This is the one item in the basic kit that is an investment. Buying it can wait, or it can be made on the cheap with some materials from the hardware store. A good banding wheel will last you a lifetime and make your time as a hand builder much easier, so save your pennies and when you're ready, invest in a nice heavy-duty banding wheel. No need to go big—I have an 8" (20.3 cm) tabletop Shimpo banding wheel that I use for everything!*

BASIC TOOLS

APRON: An apron is very useful for keeping your clothes from getting dirty or stained, especially if you are using dark-colored clay bodies that are rich in iron. Be sure to wash it regularly; you don't want lots of dried clay on your apron creating dust. See the Health Hazards section (page 32) for more information on silica dust.

BUCKET AND SPONGE: A bucket and sponge are essential for cleaning up your space, and the bucket can also be used to store your tools.

WOOD KNIFE: A wood knife is a must-have in my hand-building tool kit. It can be used as a refinement tool and for ribbing and compressing the interior of forms.

SCALPEL OR UTILITY KNIFE: A scalpel or utility knife (such as an X-ACTO knife) is a helpful tool for cutting and trimming clay.

TRIM TOOLS: A refinement and reductive carving tool originally used for "trimming" feet on a potter's wheel, is a must-have.

METAL RIBS/PLASTIC SHERRILL RIBS: Having a few different styles of ribs on hand will help you master the ribbing action. Ribs come in all shapes and sizes and are surprisingly handy for cleaning up your work, compressing the clay, and texture application—they are a general must-have in the studio. Sherrill Mudtool ribs are a brand of plastic ribs that come in various shapes, and the colors indicate the firmness. I really like the yellow and green in shape 1 and 4. Also a small, red, shape 0 is really handy.

MKM DECORATING DISK: Measuring tool to use when dividing up makes for carving or decorating round objects.

CHEESE CUTTER: If I was to tattoo a tool onto my skin, this would be it. Unassuming in design, this is a wonderful tool for doing edge work, leveling off the clay, and getting clay out of the bag. It takes some practice to use, but when students watch me with my cheese cutter, they say it's like I draw in the air with it.

CUT-OFF WIRE: Useful for cutting work off your banding wheel or getting clay out of your bag, this is an important tool to have.

SCORING TOOL: This is a really small but important tool used for making hatch marks that make it possible to create strong connections between clay attachments (e.g., attaching handles to scoops).

SEVERAL BRUSHES: Brushes are essential for glazing and applying water for attachments. Dry brushes are great at removing burrs and loose bits of clay on work.

NEEDLE TOOL: A needle tool is great for cutting out clay shapes. It's not, I repeat, not a scoring tool, but it can be used as a surface decoration tool.

ROLLING PIN: Any kind of wooden rolling pin will work. I really like a pastry rolling pin (more like a large dowel). It offers a bit more length than your traditional rolling pin. If you are applying pressure with a regular rolling pin, you can have issues with the handles bending, as there is metal rod running through the center. Traditional rolling pins are more commonly used for cookies or pie dough, which has a lot more give than clay.

RULER: A general studio tool, a clear, wide ruler is handy because of its straight edge, but it's also essential for making templates.

SUNSHINE STICK: This tool works both as a ruler and a leveling cut-off tool, when used with the cheese cutter.

HAND TOWELS: I use old bath towels cut into smaller tea-towel sizes. They're good for cleaning up and drying your hands. Be sure to wash them often.

HELPFUL TOOLS FROM YOUR LOCAL HARDWARE/ CRAFT STORE AND DIY TOOLS

PROPANE TORCH/HEAT GUN: This is a great tool to have on hand, and it's not a huge investment. I prefer the torch, as I pay attention to fire. With the heat gun option, I burn myself, the table, ware boards, plastic, and the floor. Be aware that the heat gun is intense, and the heat lasts a bit longer than the torch. It also lays flat when not in use (hence the burning everything), whereas the torch tends to sit upright on a base. Use caution and be aware of your surroundings when using either tool. **[NOT PICTURED]**

DRYWALL SANDPAPER: Drywall sandpaper comes in large sheets. Cut off 1" x 1" (2.5 x 2.5 cm) sections, crumple up to remove the grit, and it's ready to go.

GREEN SCRUBBY SPONGE: Cut 1" to 2" (2.5 to 5 cm) strips of this sponge to have on hand.

MISTER (SPRAY BOTTLE): Check out Flairosol mist bottles. They create a fine mist of water and spray more evenly than a traditional spray bottle (but those will also work). **[NOT PICTURED]**

SURFORM: Grab one from the hardware store with some back up blades. This tool is traditionally a rasp used in woodwork.

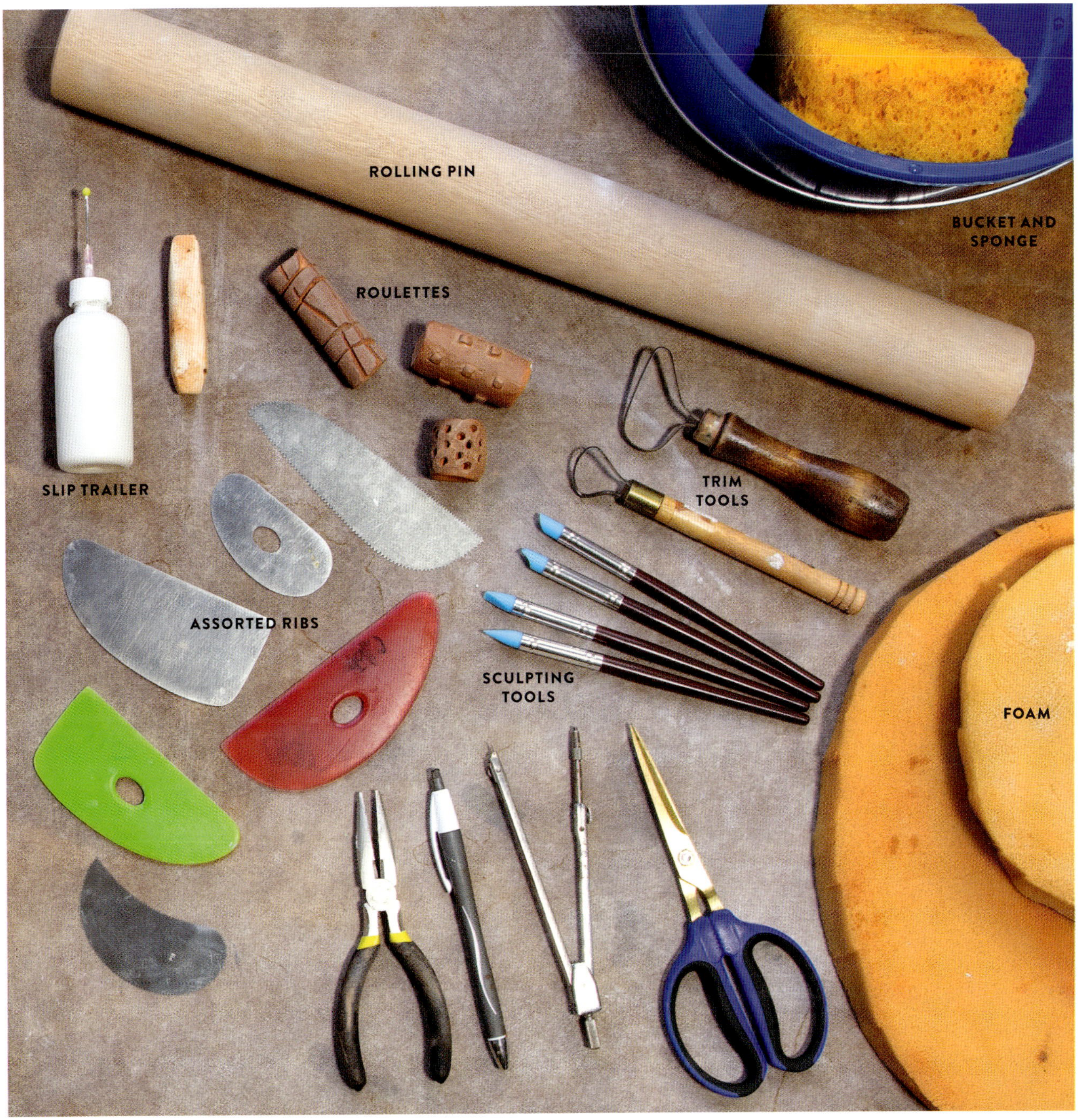
ROLLING PIN
BUCKET AND SPONGE
ROULETTES
SLIP TRAILER
TRIM TOOLS
ASSORTED RIBS
SCULPTING TOOLS
FOAM

DRYWALL BOARD/DIY WARE BOARDS: Some hardware stores have ready-made 3' (0.9 m) squares, which is awesome! If not, a regular-sized drywall board will go a very long way. I bring a utility knife with me to the hardware store to cut down the board to more manageable pieces to fit in my vehicle to get it to my studio. (Remember to place duct tape on the edges of the board to keep plaster from getting into your clay.) Same goes for plywood ware boards; have the hardware store cut them down to size—into thirds usually works—so you can get them home.Then you can cut them down for your specific needs. It's a good idea to cut them to similar measurements, which helps for storage as well as placement on shelving. Ware boards are used to make on, transport, or store your work. Kind of a mini table to keep you works safe and stable. They can come in a variety of sizes, ones that you make on will be smaller than ones you use to store work. But it is a comfort thing, make ones that fit your making style, and your storage and shelving space. I have roughly 15–25 different ware boards in the studio, that is after 20 years of accumulation. Drywall boards are typically larger, 3" x 3" (7.6 x 7.6 cm) squares, and used for wedging or rolling out slabs. I usually have a couple for different clay bodies, they get tossed out after the paper starts ripping off and plaster is exposed. Don't leave wet clay on drywall boards for extended periods of time to extend the life of the board.

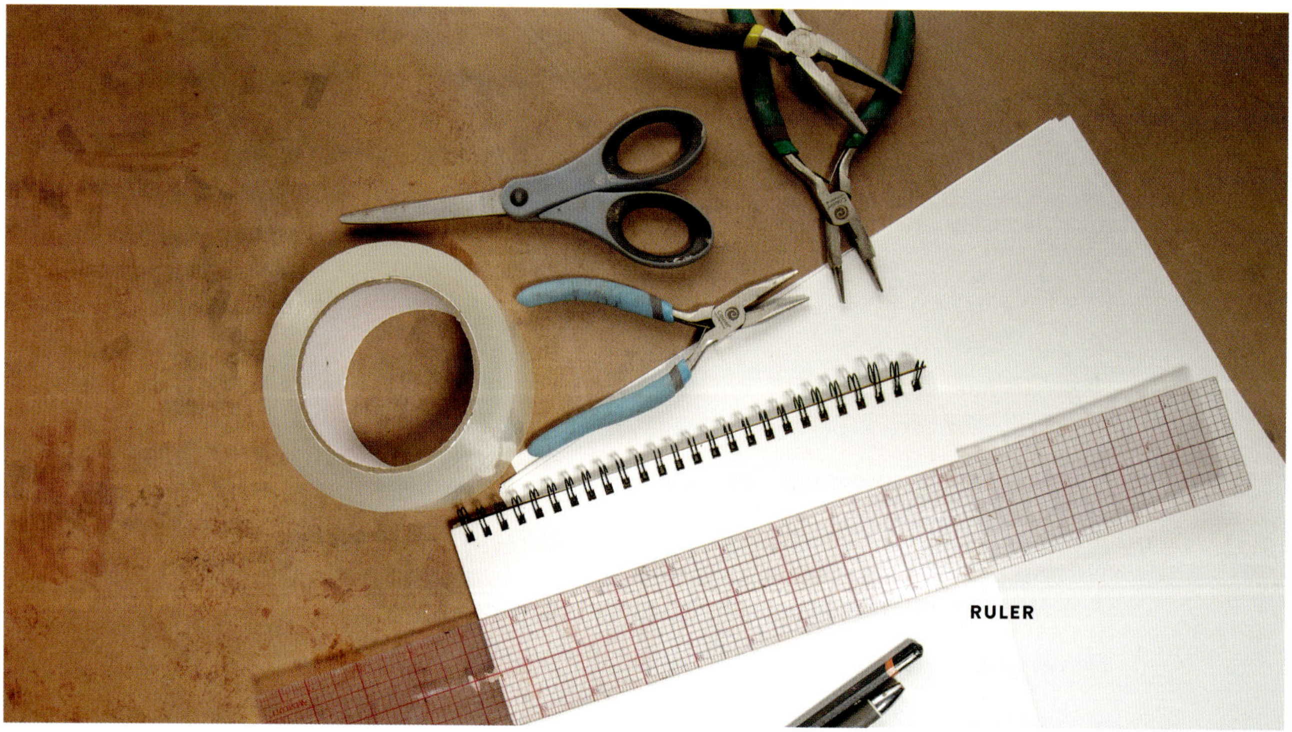

These are a few things you might need for making templates, and a few different types of pliers make playing with wire a bit easier.

FOAM: Pick up some foam from the fabric store. A 1' (30.5 cm) square that is 1" to 2" (2.5 cm to 5 cm) thick will make a great resting surface for work. You can cut it into a circle shape (the size of your studio bats) with a pair of scissors. It is always handy to have a couple of pieces of foam around... you never know when you might need them.

PENCIL/PEN, PAPER, SCISSORS: These tools are all handy for working out ideas and designing templates.

TAPE: Clear packing tape or masking tape is always handy in the studio.

PLIERS: I have a large toolbox in my studio with an assortment of tools (hand drills, screwdrivers, wrenches, Dremel tool and bits), but for the projects in this book I reached for several needle-nose pliers, which are handy for shaping and cutting wire.

EPOXY/MOLDABLE GLUE, SUCH AS SUGRU: *Optional.* Epoxy is sometimes used to piece together work after the firing, or even on some tools with unwanted sharp edges (rasps). There are lots of types of epoxy. PC-7 is a heavy-duty, two-part epoxy that is great for strong structural applications. Products such as Sugru (a colored epoxy-type material) are more decorative and elastic feeling. Explore the hardware store to get an idea of what might work for your needs.

DRILL BITS: I have a dedicated set of drill bits specifically for clay use. Once they have touched clay, they are often not great for other applications, as they become dull and worn down by the clay. I have used the same set for a decade in my clay practice. Find an inexpensive set and label it for clay use. If I don't use the bits with a drill, which is totally an option, I add some epoxy to the ends to make them more comfortable for hand use.

TOOLS NEEDED FOR FIRING PROJECTS IN THIS BOOK

FIRING STILTS: Firing Stilts are basically a tripod of Kanthol/Nichrome wire in which you can balance work during a glaze firing. Typically used for work that has glaze on the bottom like the Scoops or Reamers projects. The marks left behind can be filed or dremeled off. Firing Stilts can be purchased, or you can make ones with Cone 6-10 clay and Kanthol/Nichrome wire.

NICHROME OR KANTHAL WIRE: You'll see Nichrome and Kanthal wire photographed in a few of the projects in this book. They come in several gauges and will survive the firing process. Not all wire will survive the heat of the kiln. Be very cautious of wire not labeled for ceramic use.

Some of the tools in this list are readily available in community studios. Borrow what you can. It is really nice to have your own set of tools once you know what you like. Pay attention to what you use and what feels good for your hands, and the tools that are essential to you will present themselves.

KEEPING TRACK OF YOUR TOOLS.

Label your tools with your name! You will see from a lot of the images in this book that even though I have my own space, my tools all have my last name on them. When I teach workshops, my tools tend to walk away; folks like to try them out—no problem with that. But I would miss some of them greatly. Tools, besides being useful, can have sentimental value. Some of my tools were gifts, or I made them and they are specific to me and my needs. Writing my name on them with a permanent marker helps me keep track of them and leaves no question to whom the tools belong. They are an investment in your studio practice and tell the story of your journey, so keep hold of them!

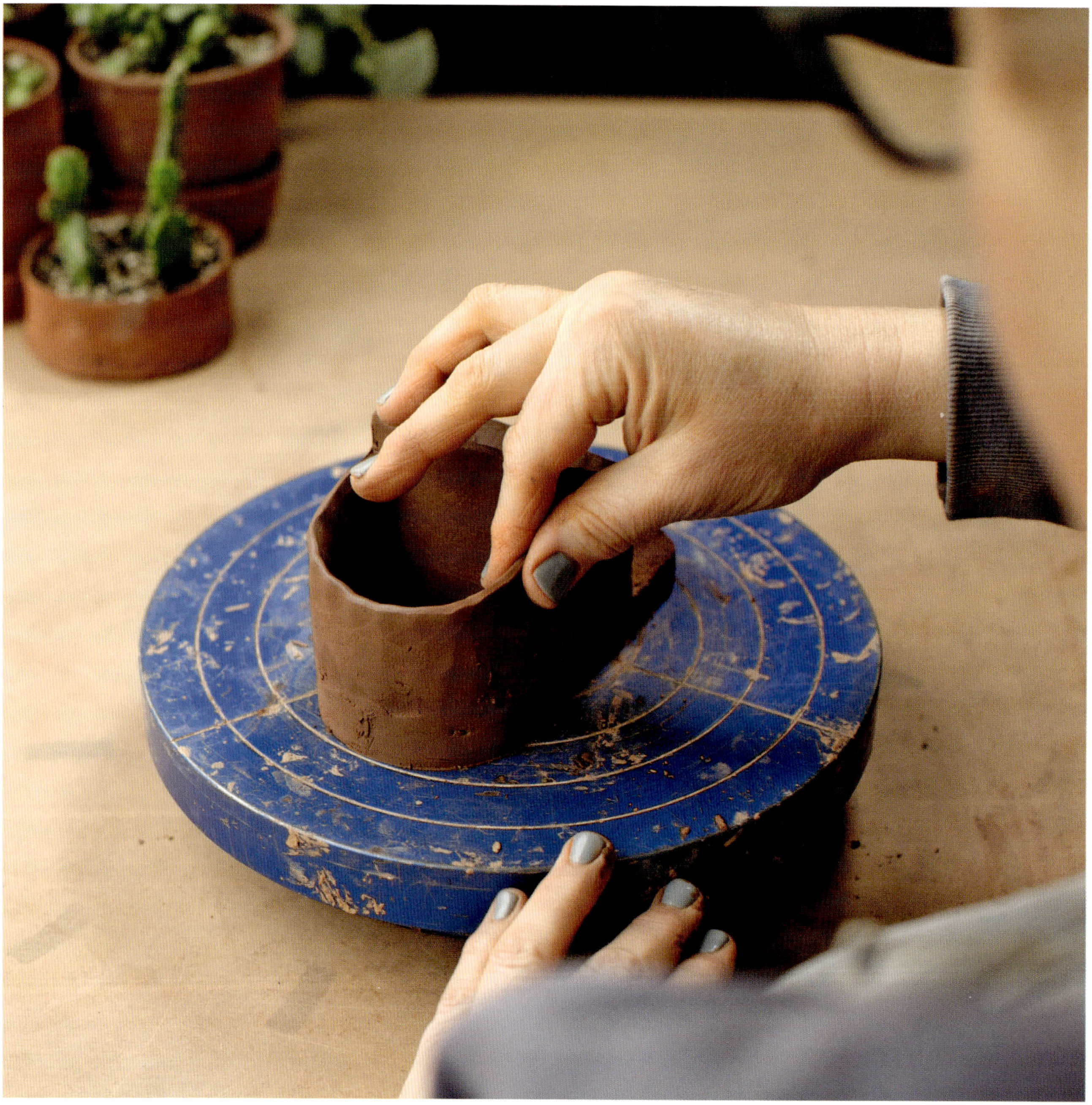

Edge work can dramatically change the look and feel of a project.

MISCELLANEOUS TERMS AND CONCEPTS

When you first start working in clay, it can feel like you signed up for a foreign language class and didn't realize it. There are so many new terms and ideas that it can be difficult to understand. Don't worry—you will learn as it applies to you. If you are anything like me, if you don't need to know the information, you won't commit it to memory. When your interest starts to grow, and as you gain more experience, the more you will hold on to the information you need!

What follows are some of those terms and concepts that don't link directly to a specific foundational skill but are used often in reference to making with clay. This knowledge will help you navigate this new world of clay.

NOTE *If I've covered a term in another section, it will not appear here (e.g., for states of clay information, turn to page 28). Also, I have tried to link connecting terms and concepts to foundational skills. Turn to page 45 for more information.*

ADDITIVE: Additive refers to any process in which clay is added to an object. An easy example is scoring and slipping a handle to a mug. Most hand-building techniques are additive: coil building, slab building, and so on. Also, any accoutrements, such as handles or knobs, are additive, as well as greenware decorative techniques, such as underglaze or slip.

DESIGN: This is a big concept in a tiny word. In the context of clay and making, it can refer to both form and surface development. It is frequently used in reference to the function of objects, but it can also be used in discussion about abstract sculpture. There are lots of books and essays out there on theories of design. You can dive deep into the education of the design world, if so inclined. For this book, we mostly use this term with regard to using *your senses* and *your aesthetic eye* to develop a pleasing, useful, (fill in the blank) object, be it functional or abstract.

EDGE WORK: Edge work refers to how you choose to finish an edge. It can be soft or tooled, meaning you can use your fingers or a sponge or a sharper tool, such as a scalpel or cheese cutter. All edges (termination points) should be considered and refined, but it is a choice left to the maker. Time and practice will help guide your aesthetic choices.

PINCHED EDGE: This refers to using your fingers and thumb to finish the edge of a form, leaving a softer, less sharp look to the lip of an object. This technique can be used directionally to give a very different effect to the edge of an object, making it appear more open or more enclosed.

TOOLED EDGE: Tooled edge refers to a finished edge with sharp, clean marks made by an implement, rather than a softer edge that has been obviously worked by hand.

GRIDDING: Gridding is the practice of using some kind of measuring tool (such as a ruler or measuring disc) to make lines on your form to create concentric circles or lines. This technique is often used to decorate or cut out shapes in an object.

REDUCTIVE: Reductive refers to any process, such as carving, scraping, surforming, or trimming, that removes clay from an object. This term is often used to describe refining shape or form, or as a decorative surface technique.

ROUGH OUT: A rough out is the quick pulling together of a general shape that will be refined later, when the clay is more amenable to detail work.

TEMPLATE: A template, usually some kind of paper shape that begins the building process, helps build a form or provide a footprint for building objects. It can be used multiple times to create the same object. A template often starts as a general idea and is then modified and refined as the object develops. In the prototype stage, it is often made with craft paper and then once refined and modified, transferred to a more resilient material, such as a heavy-weight watercolor paper.

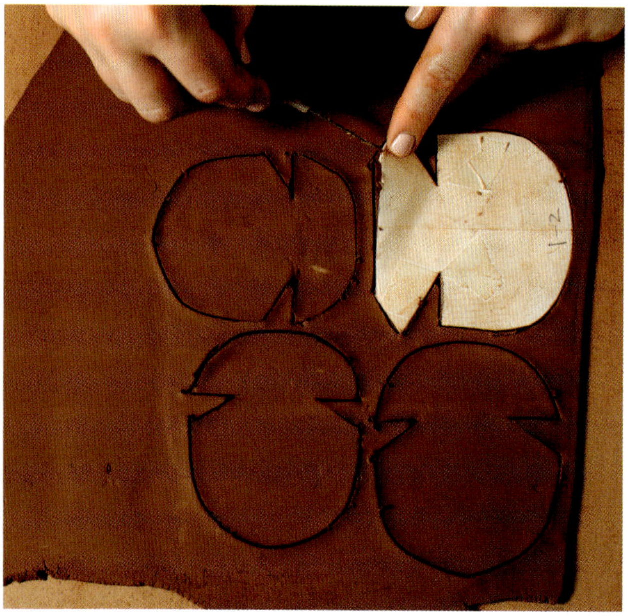

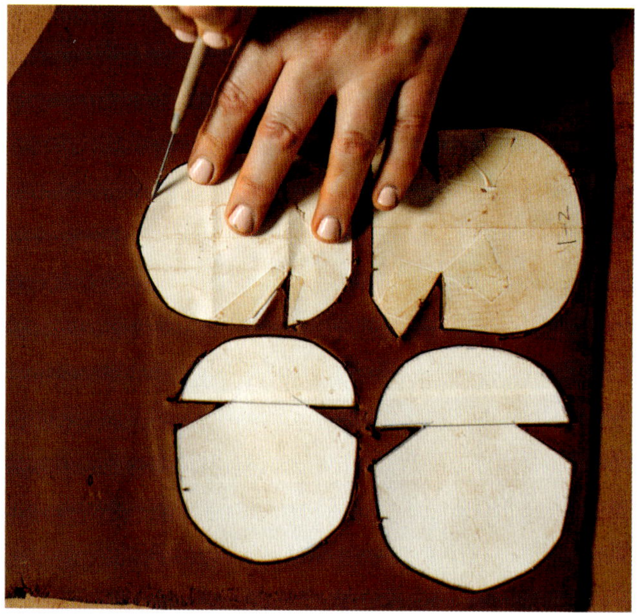

FOUNDATIONAL SKILLS

These are some of the skills you will run across in the project sections of the book. Refer back to these pages if you need a refresher.

Coiling

Using clay straight from your bag, squish out a coil in your hands. Depending on the size of your hand, your coil may vary in size a bit. Aim to have a workable size of coil for your hands, and err on the smaller, versus larger, side. **[A] [B]**

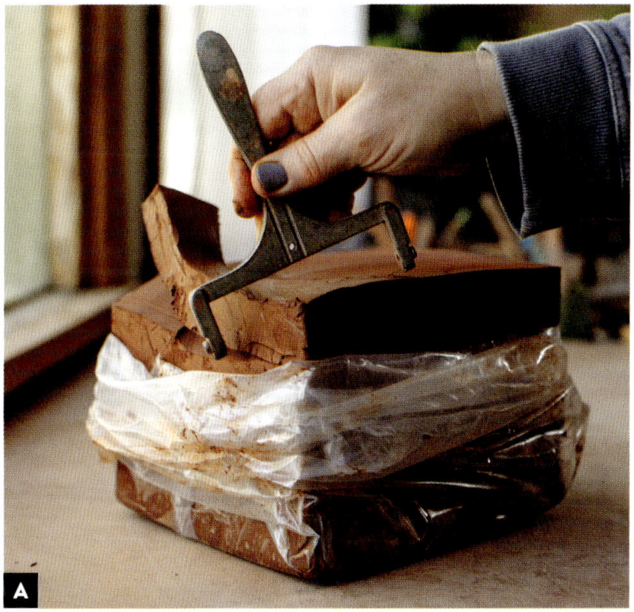

A

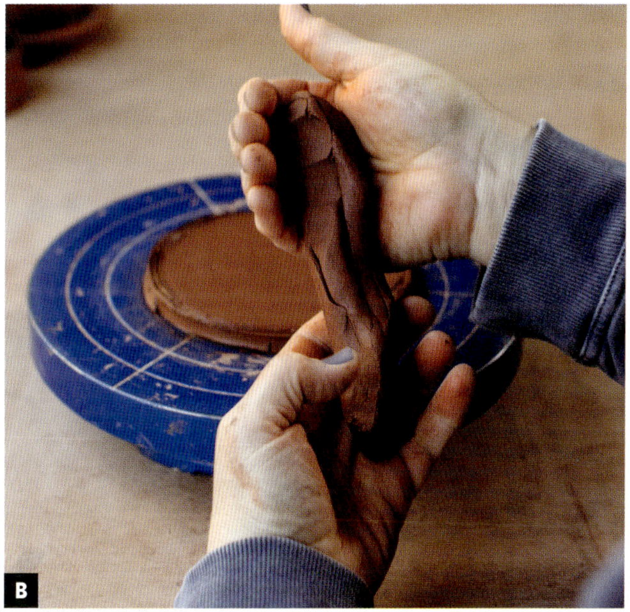

B

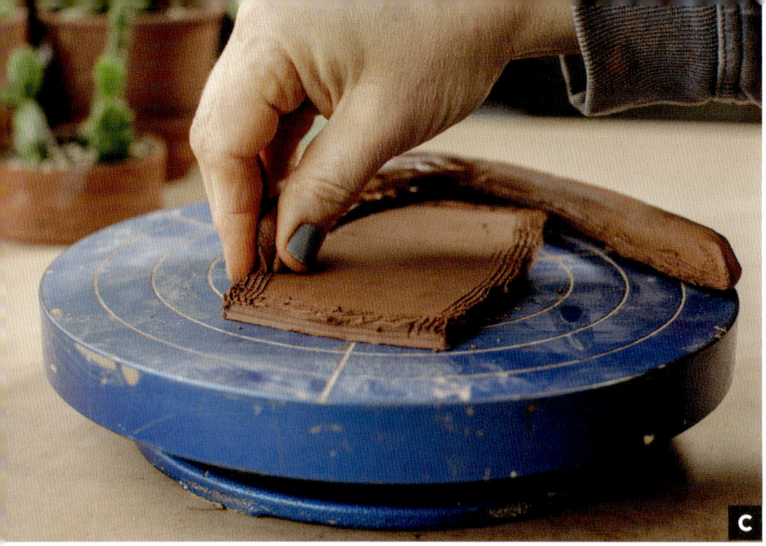

C

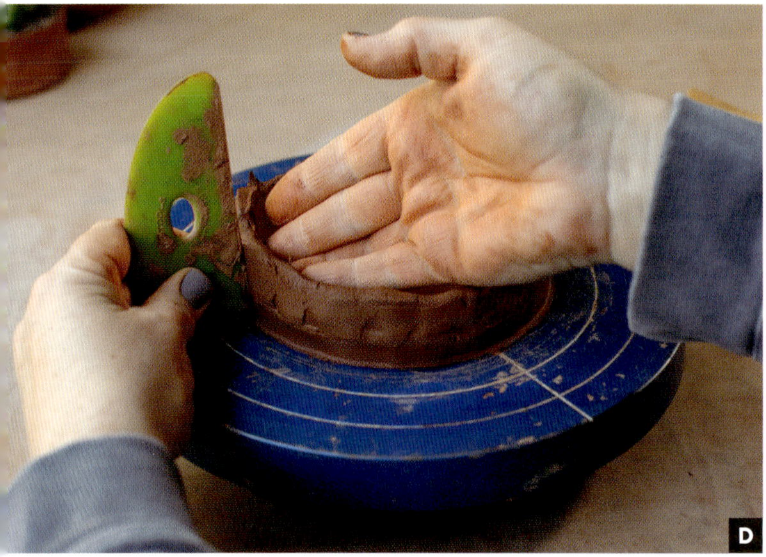

D

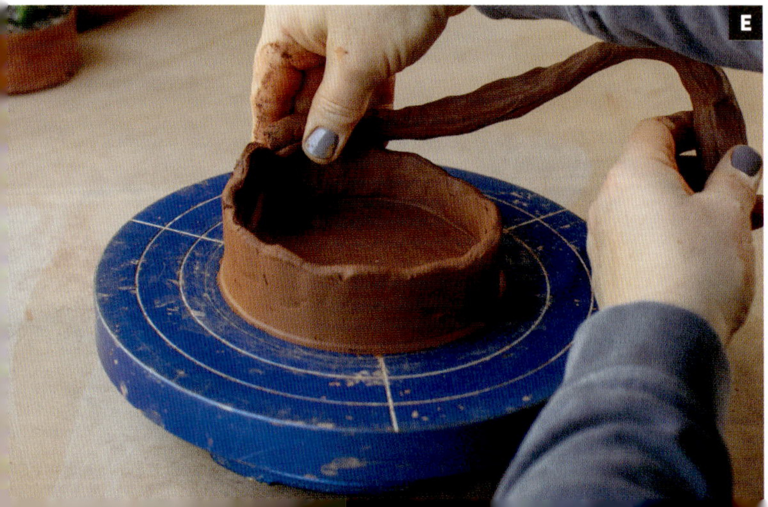

E

Score the coil. Using a paintbrush, wet the scored coil sparingly. (It shouldn't be dripping wet.) With your left hand, use your pointer and middle fingers and thumb to begin to attach the coil to the scored footprint. Work your way all around the footprint and pinch off the excess coil when you meet the beginning of your attachment. Avoid starting at a corner because they are harder to compress and that can lead to cracking. Starting someplace mid-wall is a good practice. **[C]**

Using a right-angled rib, clean up and firm up your attachment on the inside and outside of the form. Pay special attention to the connecting seams. Be sure to use your footprint edge as a guide to maintain the shape. **[D]** The thickness of your wall should be about ¼" (.63 cm).

The goal of this ribbing action is to make sure your attachment is solid, to get the thickness of the wall consistent, and to get your form on point. Do not move on until all three of these goals are accomplished for every coil attachment. This usually take me about three passes inside and out.

Make another coil, following the same method, and aim for the same size as your first coil. Attach the new coil to the existing wall. No scoring is necessary if the clay is the same consistency/temperature. Using the pointer and middle fingers of your left hand on the outside of the form and your thumb on the inside, attach (squish) the coil to the wall; you want about ½" (1.3 cm) of overlap. **[E]**

Allow the coil to grow and twist as you continue attaching it; this is completely normal. Make sure you move in half measures; your thumbprints should overlap and leave a flatter surface. **[F]**

Avoid laying the coil on top of the wall and then squishing down. This distorts the wall, and the low surface area attachment can lead to cracking. It also adds way too much clay to the form, prolonging ribbing, increasing the need for darting (see page 48), and creating distortion in the form.

Overlapping increases the surface area of the attachment, which means it is stronger and less likely to crack.

Rib the form. Use a small metal rib to clean up the inside and outside of your form. Make small ribbing movements in the direction you want your form to grow, working your way around the form inside and out until you are ready for your next coil. The goal is to remove any evidence of the connection seams. **[G]** Continue to add coils in this method until the lowest point of your wall (it will be uneven) measures 4" (10 cm) from the working surface. **[H]**

TIP *While attaching coils and ribbing, you might run into a few problems. See the Skills section on page 45 to troubleshoot.*

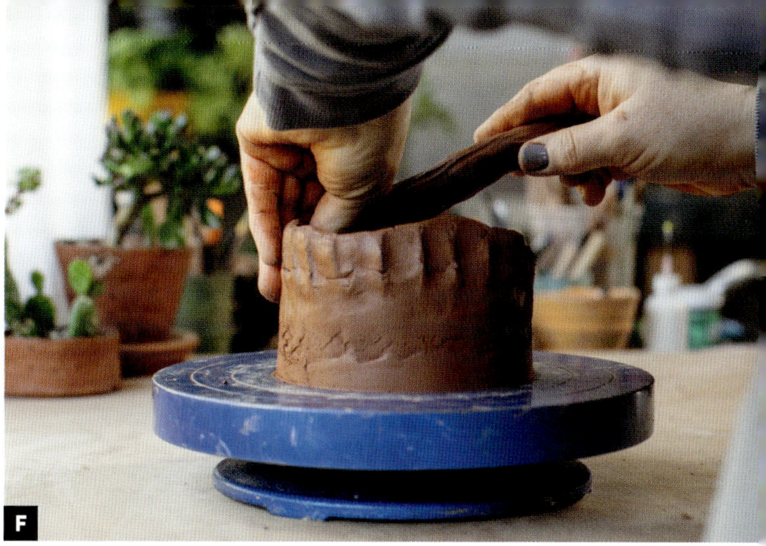

F

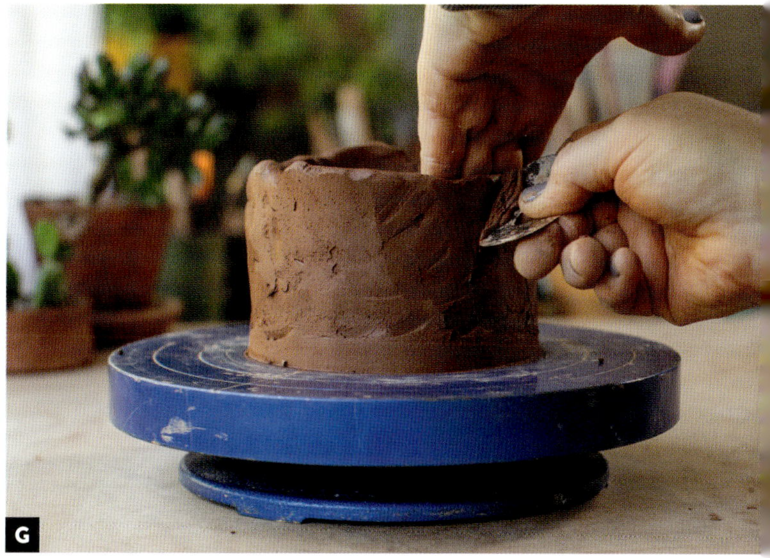

G

H

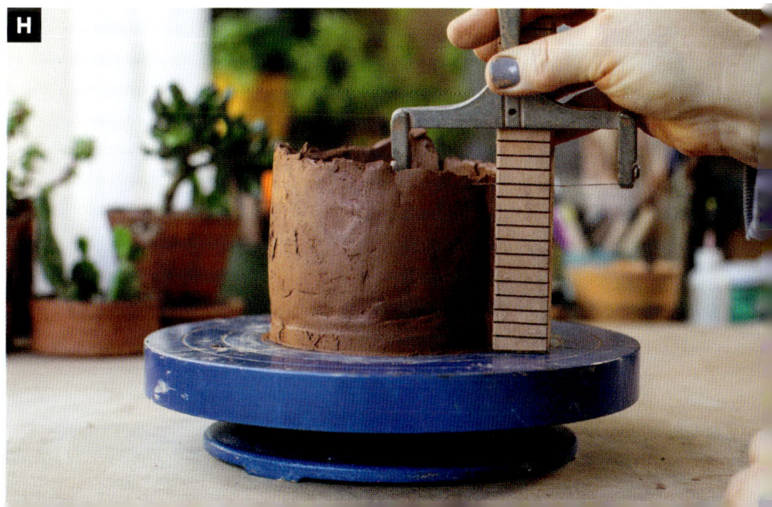

Related Terms to Know

Compression: This term is used often in the ceramic making process when referring to attachments and strong forms. In short, what you're doing when working with clay is making sure the clay particles align to form a strong material. This happens under the pressure of your hand, fingers, ribs, or tools. There needs to be force from two sides. Think of this as if you are making a clay sandwich: rib/clay/worktable or rib/clay/hand.

Darting: Darting is the practice of taking out a triangle-shaped sliver of clay and joining the sections of clay back together. This can change the shape of your object dramatically, depending on the size of your dart. The goal is to bring the object into a more desired form, or even to change the direction in which the wall of an object is heading. Usually darting is a corrective tool/skill to bring a shape back to its intended form. It is often used in coil building but is not limited to this process. **[A] [B] [C] [D]**

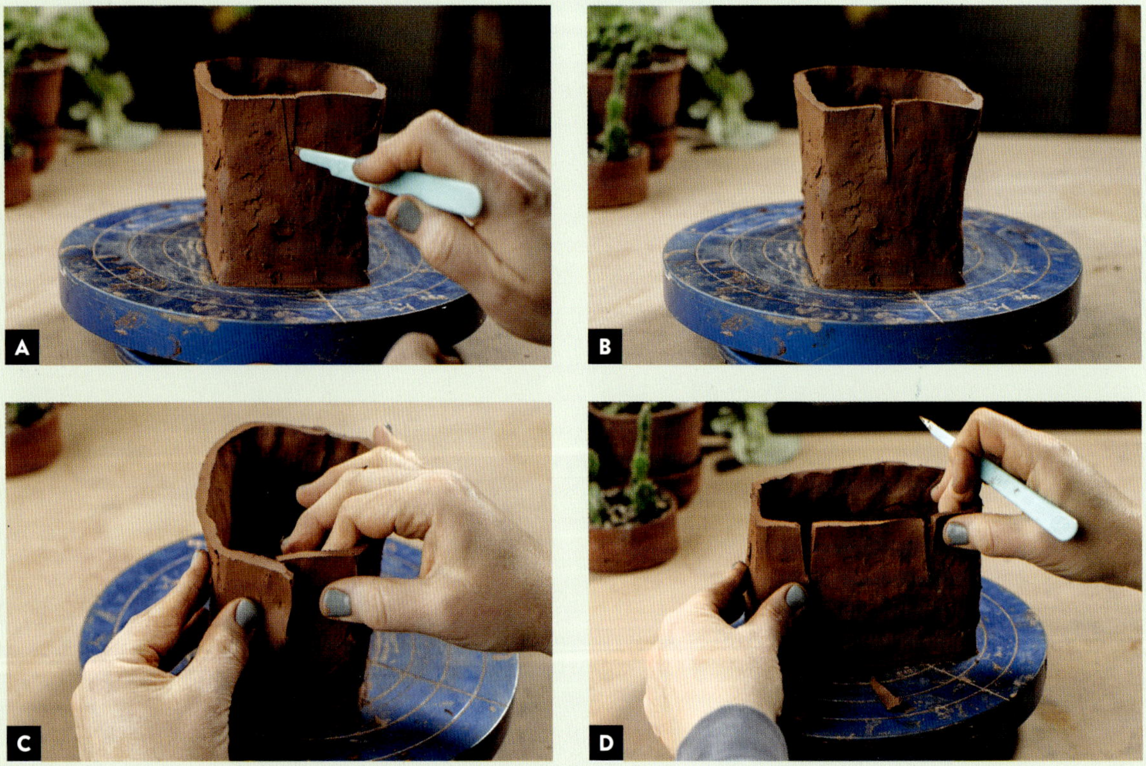

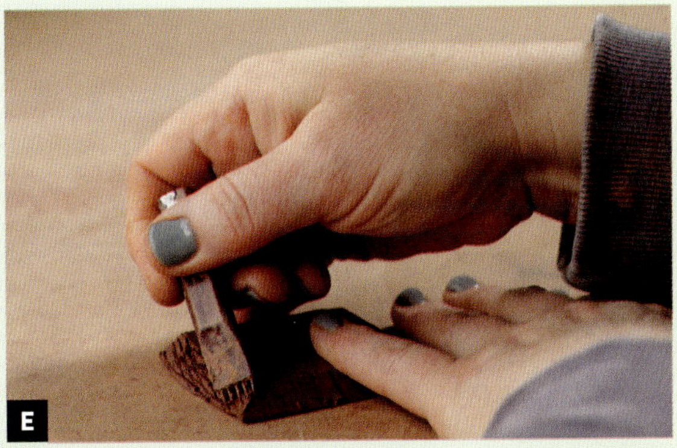

E

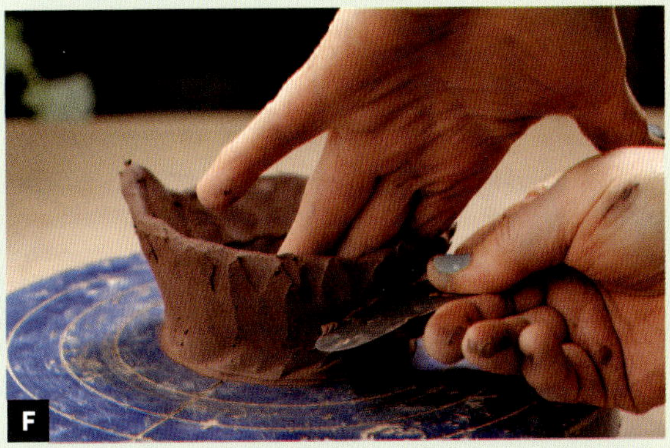

F

Slip and Score: Slip and score refers to using a sharp multi-pronged implement (see above image) to rough up the clay surface where two connecting points will attach and applying either slip or water to one side to create a wicking action that allows the clay to bond. The wicking is most effective when water is applied to the wetter piece of clay to be attached to a form that is more set up, i.e., dried slowly and evenly. **[E]**

Note: *There seems to be two camps in the clay world: the slip camp and the water camp. I am of the water camp. I keep a small cup of water and a dedicated brush to apply my water on my worktable. That water has a bunch of clay in it because I sometimes scoop up the small dry bits of clay on my table and put them in my water cup. (So, really, I have clay-infused water.) What I don't like about slip is that it fills in the score marks, but I do find that slip is sometimes helpful when working with different clay bodies, especially porcelaneous clays. Use your best judgement and experiment—you will discover what works for you.*

Ribbing: Ribbing refers to using any kind of rib or wood knife to compress the walls or clean up the seams of clay objects. The goal can be to smooth or create texture. Remember to support the ribbing action with counterpressure from your hand (the clay sandwich: rib/clay/hand). **[F]**

How to Dry Your Pieces

Dry your clay pieces slowly and evenly, always avoiding directional air (from a heating source or a fan), as this can cause your object to dry unevenly, which can lead to warping and cracking. Drying slowly can mean leaving a piece out in the open air of your studio or under plastic. Every studio climate is different, and some objects need special care when drying. Pay close attention to your environment and how the clay reacts. You may save yourself some heartache if you have some plastic handy. Following is my guide of what to use and when, but first a word on plastic, which you'll be using to cover your work.

USING PLASTIC TO PROTECT YOUR WORK

Not all wrapping plastic is created equal. I often see old clay bags used in studios, but although these bags are great to store raw clay in, their stiff nature tends to mar freshly made work. I also often see large black trash bags in use. Although these will get the job done because they are soft and large enough to wrap whole ware boards, you can't see through the plastic. This can be a problem when you are working in a community space and storing your work in a generalized area, because your work may be hard to find again or easily accidently damaged by a neighbor or even yourself as you put work on the shelf. Plastic shopping bags, while ubiquitous, are one of the worst plastic bags for wrapping work. The plastic is so thin that it "breathes," so objects you intend to work on later become too dry.

My best recommendation is dry-cleaning plastic. It's soft, not breathable, clear, and it comes in large sheets and is reusable forever (maybe not forever . . . but close!). Hit up a dry cleaner or friends who have clothing dry-cleaned—a few sheets last a long time.

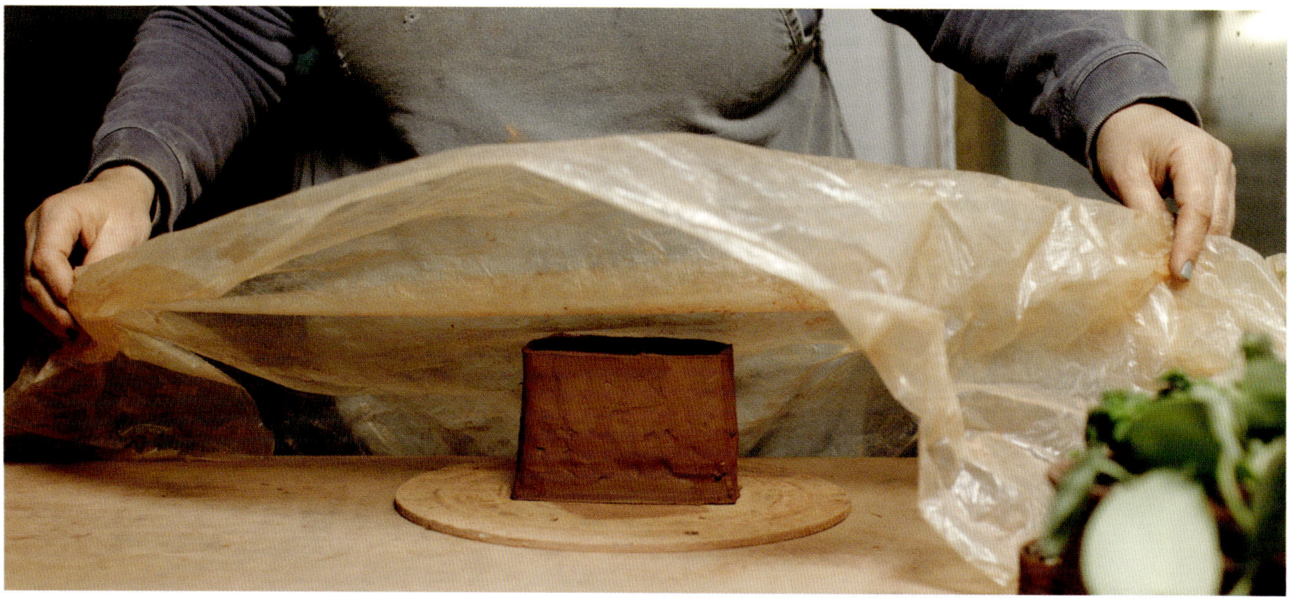

PLASTIC WRAPPING METHODS

UNDER PLASTIC OR GENTLE DRAPE: Place your piece under gently draped plastic when you want to slow-dry it but protect it from any directional air that would dry the form unevenly. You can do this as soon as you are finished with a piece, or you can let the piece become set up (dried slowly and evenly) a bit before draping it. Gently draping plastic over a piece is the closest step to leaving it uncovered.

WRAPPED IN PLASTIC: The goal in wrapping your work completely is to allow the work to set a smidge but also remain workable so that you can return and keep working. An example is a large vessel that needs to be made in sections, or a piece with several parts that will need to be scored together at the right stage. Wrapping it in plastic allows you to keep the clay workable, while allowing it to set up at the same time.

DOUBLE-WRAPPED IN PLASTIC: Double-wrap your work when you know you need to come back to your project and don't want any chance of it drying out. Using this method hopefully keeps the project the exact same temperature (dryness/wetness) as when you wrapped it. When double-wrapping work, it's a good idea to place it on a bat or ware board, as you can wrap the board and object together with plastic without damaging the object. My bats are plastic or Masonite, and my ware boards are plywood. AVOID wrapping work on a plaster bat; it will suck moisture out of the work way too fast. Once the work is wrapped up tight once, mist it with water just enough to see some condensation on the plastic. Now wrap it again in plastic, trapping the moisture in there. This is really handy if your time in the studio is intermittent, and you need to make sure your work remains workable after several days away,

SHEET DRAPE: Not much work in this book will benefit from sheet draping. This method is often used for larger pieces that need to slow dry and remain covered and protected from directional air, but still have air flow. Sheet draping is one of the better ways to slow dry work in more humid climates.

NOTE *If you would like to see how I make a damp box, check out my YouTube Channel: Sunshine Cobb Ceramics. I have a quick tutorial posted there.*

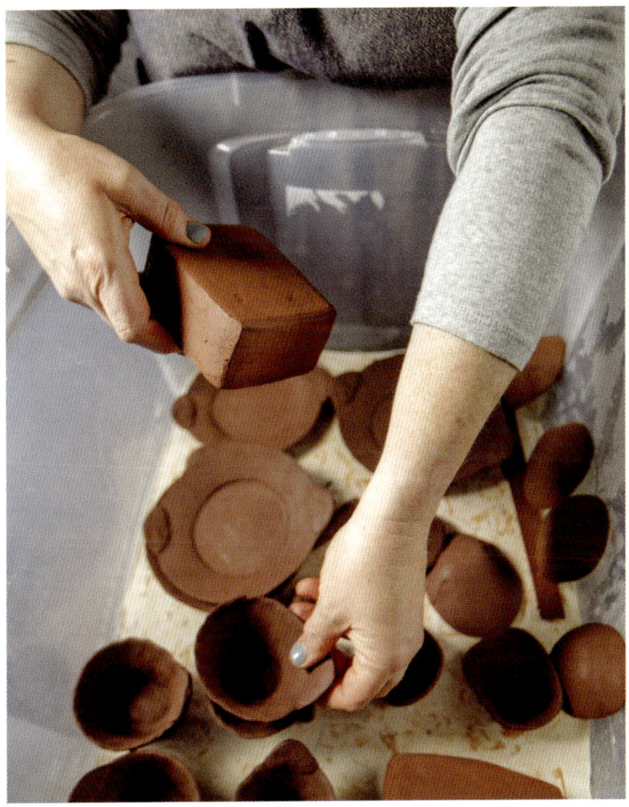

Rolling Out a Slab

This is one of the most important skills to learn. Like making pie crust, you're going to have to practice a bit before you get it right. Following is a list of items you need for rolling out clay slabs.

DRY RELEASABLE SURFACE: I use large squares of drywall board on my workbench or table. Make sure the edges of the drywall board are covered with duct tape; if the plaster gets into your clay, it will pop out of the clay during the firing process and leave holes or cracks in your piece. (My tabletop is MDF wood and is a good releasable surface, but it will warp and break down if water is left on it for prolonged periods.)

ROLLING PIN: I prefer a pastry-style rolling pin (no handles)—it's like a very large dowel.

PAINT STIR STICKS: You'll need a few paint stir sticks or a couple of yardsticks cut in half—something thin and flat that is stackable, so you can adjust the height of your slabs. You need an equal amount for two sides of your slab. I make do with two large and two small paint stir sticks.

CLAY: Clay fresh from a bag is easiest to learn with!

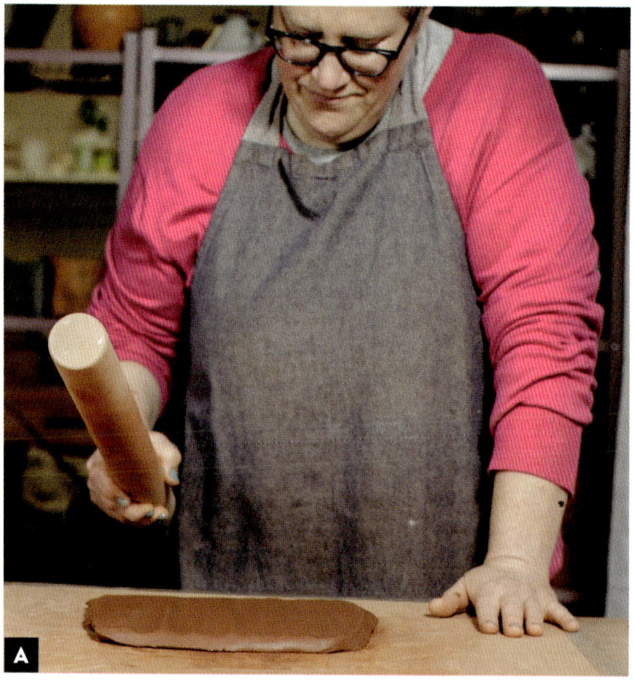

A

STEPS

Before getting started, ensure you have a clean drywall board and rolling pin.

Cut off a section of clay, about 1" (2.5 cm) thick. Place the clay in the center of your working board and, using the rolling pin, gently roll the clay, working from one end to the other. (If you cut out a large, thick piece, you may need to gently pound out the clay, using the rolling pin like a hammer on the clay in overlapping motion, just until the clay is thin enough to start rolling.) You will be making several passes, so don't push down super hard. Just stretch a little at a time. **[A]**

After each pass with the rolling pin, lift the clay and give it a quarter turn. This does two important things. First, it separates the clay from the working surface, which makes it easier to stretch and roll with the next pass. Second, it ensures the clay shrinks in every direction evenly. It may sound strange, but clay has a memory—if it was a slab, it remembers it wants to be flat; if it was a pinch pot, it remembers how and in which directions the fingers pinched the clay. So, if a slab gets stretched in only one direction, it often leads to excessive shrinking in that direction. If you have assembled an object with multiple slab cutouts, that could lead to warping and cracks. **[B]**

After a few passes, lay your paint sticks next to the right and left sides of the clay at the desired thickness of clay; the rolling pin should reach both sides easily. Continue rolling, lifting the clay off the surface and giving it a quarter turn with each pass. The sticks will be your guide to know when the slab is even and has reached your desired thickness. **[C]**

Time to compress. Spritz the slab with a little water and, using a stiff rib, make overlapping passes across the slab in three different directions: horizontal, vertical, and diagonal. Gently lift the slab on one end and flip it over and repeat on the other side. This ensures your slab is well-worked, compressed, and will remember it is a slab. **[D]**

Your slab is ready. Here are additional tips:

× If your slab is large and difficult to move, use thin plastic to coat the slab and then flip it, or flip it between two boards.

× Remember to keep your slab flat as much as possible; it will remember if you twist and contort it when you are moving it, which will cause problems down the road.

× If you cut out templates, be mindful that once you pull the piece from the board, you may need to re-cut the shape, as it may have stretched a bit. This is totally normal.

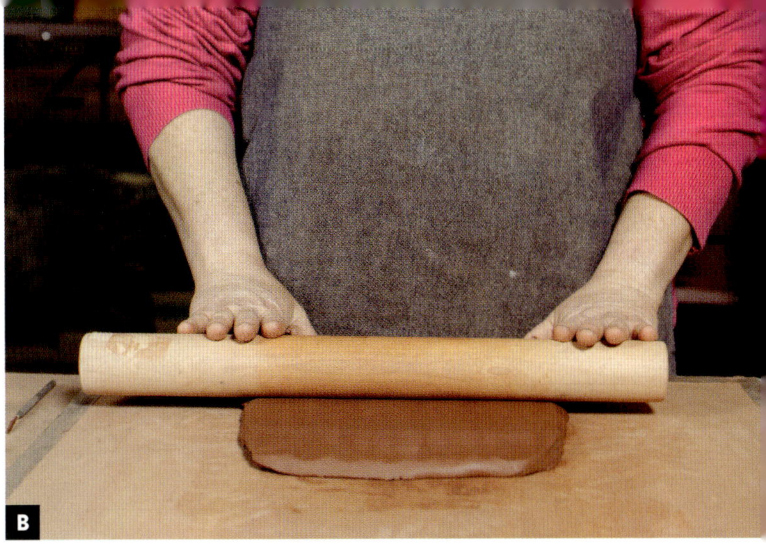

B

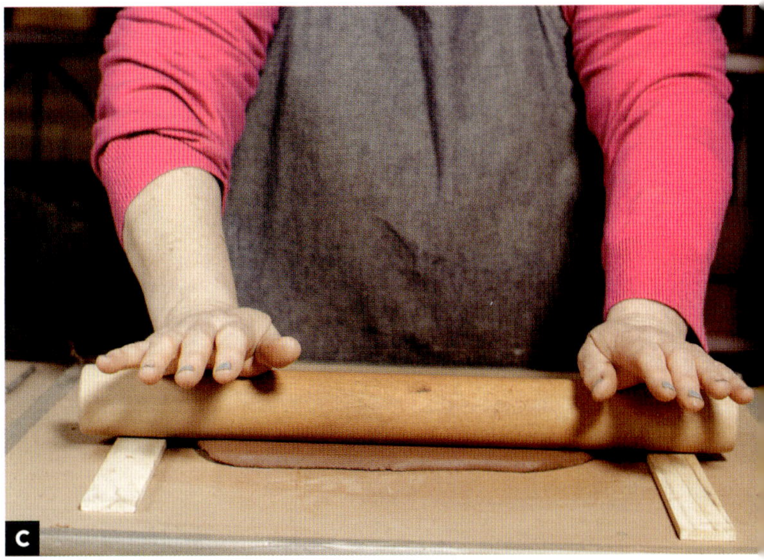

C

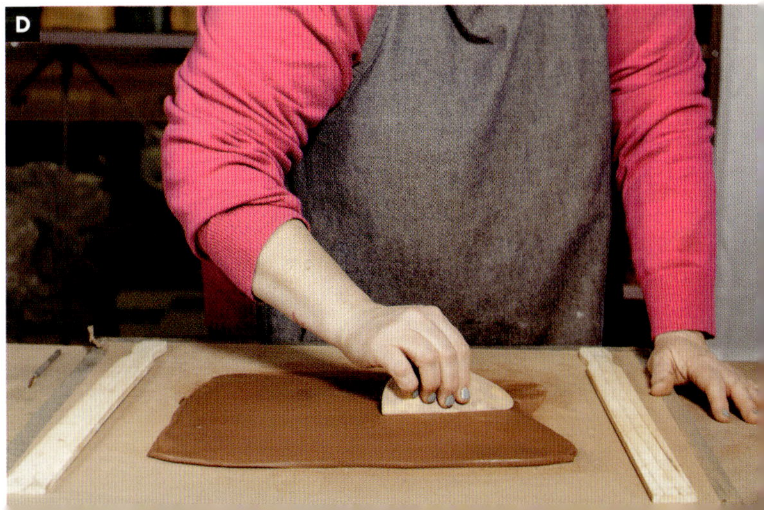

D

Related Terms to Know

Cleaning Up Seams or Attachments: Cleaning up the seams entails using a rib or other tool to take away any excess clay/slip/score marks and reinforce your seams or attachments. This is done in part to ensure a strong connection, but it is also part of the craftsmanship. It's the dotting of the i's and crossing of the t's of the ceramic making process. This step is essential in slab building and handle attachments.

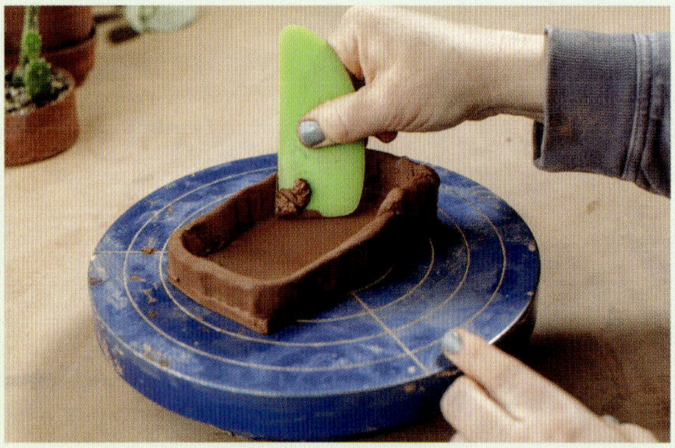

Beveling: Simply put, beveling is cutting an edge on an angle. This technique is used in slab connection points to increase the surface area of the connection, therefore making it stronger.

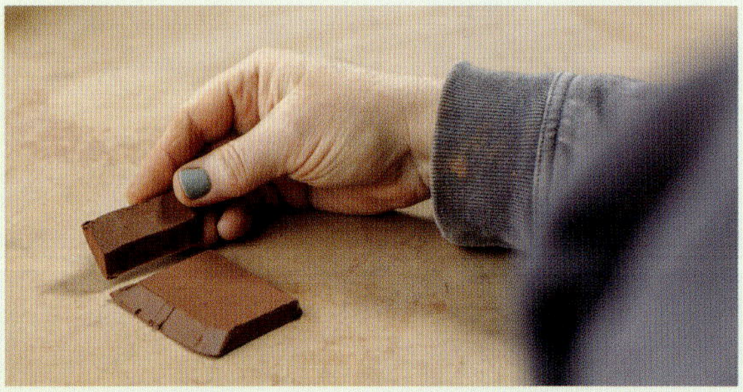

Wedging: Wedging can be difficult to learn in the beginning, but it's important to know how and why we wedge clay. What I hear often is that wedging takes the "air" out of the clay, which is true and not true. When learning to wedge, you will invariably wedge air bubbles into your clay. As you get better, you will wedge air bubbles out of the clay. But the actual goal of wedging is to align all the particles in the clay in the same direction, and to make sure the clay is an even consistency (without any dry parts). This makes the clay much easier to work. We never know how long that clay has been sitting on a shelf. So, we wedge our clay.

Wedging is a whole practice, and it can be hard on your body, so I've learned a method that saves my wrists. I call it slap wedging. Take a section of clay, cut it in half, and layer it. And repeat. Doing this over and over will create a lot of very thin layers. The result is no bubbles, aligned particles, and even clay consistency. It's much easier on your body. You can also take a larger amount of clay for more traditional methods, making prep for projects a bit quicker.

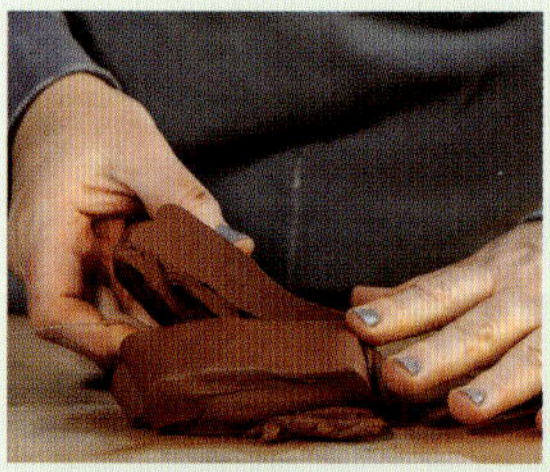

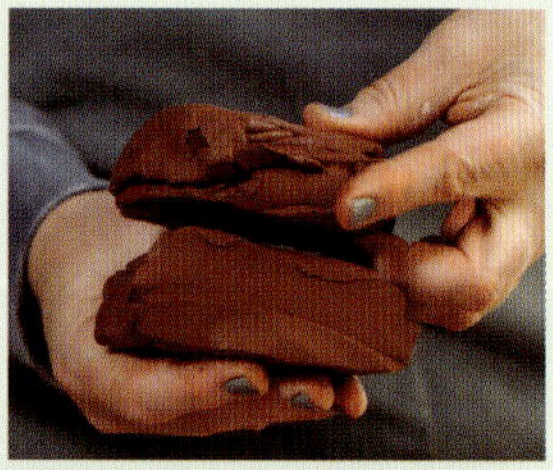

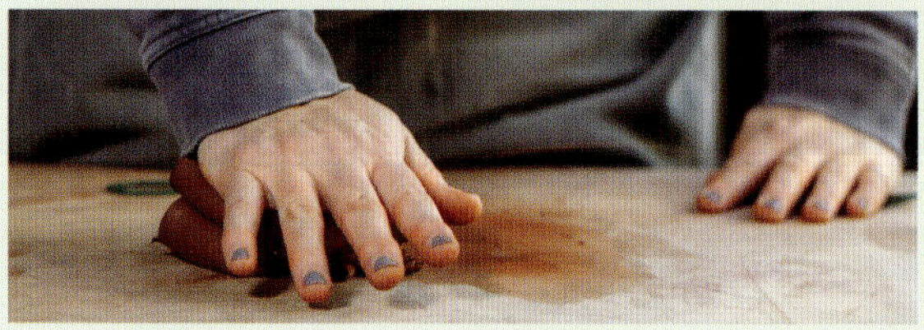

SURFACE DEVELOPMENT

Unloading a glaze firing can be like opening presents on your birthday with so many unexpected surprises. Sometimes it's the worst possible outcome. I have unloaded whole kiln loads directly into the dumpster after some glaze and firing fails! Although I considered including a few glaze recipes and a firing chart in this book, ultimately my feeling is that the beginning of a journey in clay is something one book isn't supposed to do start to finish. Diving into glazing is overwhelming, even to the seasoned professional. Glazing is an art unto itself, and I am still learning.

I have been using the same commercial glazes in my personal work for the past ten years, and recently a couple of my glazes stopped working predictably. Once you think you have things figured out, your interest takes you in a new direction, or maybe materials change and what worked no longer works the way it did. This change has nudged (actually shoved) me to start testing and developing new glazes for my work. Color and surface are very important and create a lot of feels in my body. Glazing and surface development are a very slow and methodical part of the clay journey involving so much testing and so much failure. They are ultimately rewarding, but hard to do when you are in love with the making process.

In this section, I want to share a few ideas about where glazing may take you, as well as a few pieces of advice I wish I knew when I was starting out. I'll also try to point you in the direction of some additional resources available to you.

NOTE *For the finished work you see in this book, I used either commercial glazes, underglazes, or no glaze at all. All the work was fired either to cone 3 or cone 5. Specific glaze information can be found in each project, so you can get an idea of how the finished object was achieved.*

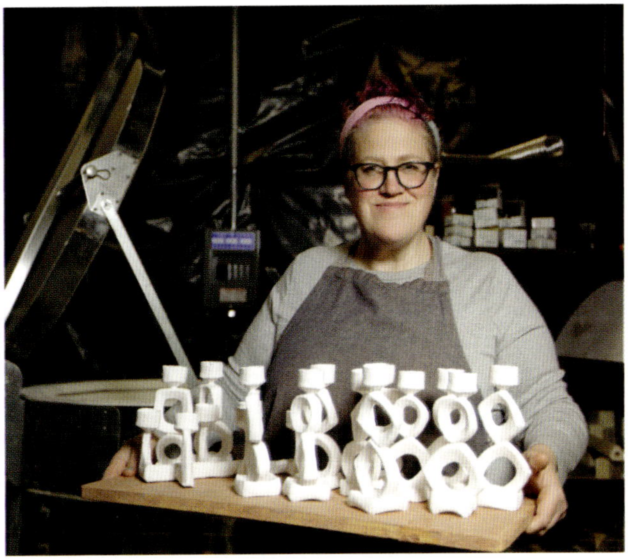

Glazing Tips

KEEP A GLAZE JOURNAL

My first bit of advice is to take copious notes when you are glazing! Create a dedicated notebook for this purpose. Draw a little picture of the object to be glazed, note which glazes you are using, and detail whether you do a 1-2-3 count when dipping, or how many layers you paint on. This will help you duplicate your successes and learn from your failures. Keeping notes will also help you locate your work on shelves loaded with multiple people's work, as you have an idea of what and how many pieces you are searching for!

This process may seem tedious, and you may decide to ignore my advice... but I warn you, these words may come back to haunt you if you ignore them. We all know what's it like to think we will remember some important detail, but then we forget. This isn't just a new-potter issue. At some point while writing this book, I grabbed a bucket of what I thought was a liner glaze and lined a whole kiln load of my pots. It turned out to be a bucket of slip a friend had given me to try. If I had double-checked the bucket label and taken notes about how I was applying it, I probably would have caught the mistake quickly. After throwing all my ruined pots in the trash, I reminded myself to take notes—and also to label all my buckets clearly. Lesson learned, again! I occasionally forget to practice what I preach, and the clay process is a cruel mistress. The reminders are harsh. Also, there is nothing so frustrating as getting an amazing object out of the kiln with no idea how to duplicate the results. Take notes—it will prove handy, I promise.

MAKE SOME TEST TILES

It is always a good idea to have your own set of test tiles, made with the clay you are using. There are many test tile shapes; figure out which one works for you. I like to have a box of bisque test tiles handy for when I'm ready to test glazes. I usually commit to making fifty to one hundred at a time. They will last me a good long while.

After making test tiles, it's a good idea to make a larger object, such as a slab cup or something simple and quick. This helps you understand how the glaze looks on a more 3D object. It is really helpful to know how the glaze and clay interact in a more representational way than on a test tile—it's always surprising how different a glaze can look on an object compared to a small tile.

DON'T PUT ALL YOUR EGGS IN THE SAME BASKET

Whether you are working in a community studio or have a small kiln at home, glaze a few pots at a time. Glaze spaces and ceramic supply stores often have test tiles hanging from the walls. Besides being overwhelming, they are sometimes misleading. That little square of color may not translate to your object as you imagine it will. Talk to other folks in the studio about the glazes you might have access to. Ask a studio manager or class instructor for guidance. Chat with the people at your local ceramics shop about commercial glazes that would work for you in your firing range. Don't blindly trust that a glaze will work for you. Test the glazes on a few objects before you glaze all your work. Glazing is chemistry in an art space. This means there can be a lot of misleading or downright incorrect information and glaze recipes. Testing is essential to the glazing process. Glazing for food safe wares has very different requirements than glazing for sculptural work.

Here's a quick note on asking folks about their glazes and/or techniques: Some people are happy to share what they have learned to some degree. The clay community prides itself on sharing knowledge. However, glazing takes a lot of practice and development. Hours and hours of trial and error to get successful results. People have a right to keep some information to themselves. Especially if they have developed their own glazes or techniques that they rely on to sell their wares. Don't take it personally if someone doesn't want to share their hard-won information. There are many resources for you to glean and develop your own skills and techniques. Check out Publications and Artists Resources (page 168). In this book for a few places to start. Don't be afraid to ask for help, but don't expect everyone to be able to help you. You need to do enough of the work and research to be able ask good questions!

SPEND TIME ON YOUR GLAZING PRACTICE.

Glazing is sometimes treated as an afterthought, and then folks wonder why they are not getting awesome results. In order to get good at glazing, you have to spend as much time glazing and testing as you do making the objects. It is easy to get lost in the making process—it is perfectly normal and part of why we chose to explore clay! Truthfully, making things is where I would most like to spend my time. There will come a time when your bisque-fired work starts to fill your shelves and you need to do some glazing. Please make time to glaze.

What took you weeks, or possibly months, to accumulate shouldn't be glazed in a few hours. The results may disappoint you if you treat glazing as an afterthought. I know you want more for your finished pieces than just glazing them in a rush or in a thoughtless fashion. You need to commit the time to think about what you want for your objects. Research ideas and glaze possibilities and collect images of what interests you. Pick up some glaze books or look at some ceramics magazines (see Publications and Artist Resources on page 168). Even Pinterest or a Google image search is a good place to look for possible glaze ideas.

Take images of your work and do some coloring on them. Go old-school with a printout and some crayons or, if you're hip to the technology, make some digital magic. Know what you have access to or what is within your scope of ability to test your ideas. Make some test tiles or test objects to go through the process. Save your favorite pieces until your research and testing matches your vision for your work. I sometimes think we procrastinate thinking about glazing because we are afraid to be disappointed by the results. We live in the joy of making and we delay the inevitability of the finished object and a possible negative outcome. I guarantee if you don't devote some energy to glazing, it will be a negative experience. Approach the process with baby steps; the time commitment may surprise you. In the end, you will learn about the glazing process and, more important, what interests you for your own work. You will experience more positive than negative outcomes and hopefully a vison and direction for your own work.

GETTING STARTED

Using studio glazes or commercial glazes is a great place to start. You need to learn as you go. Applying glazes takes practice. Understanding what appeals to you in the variety of glazes will vary. You can work slowly toward honing your palette and getting consistent results. When you are ready, you can move toward a deeper understanding of glaze and surface treatment.

One of my favorite glaze books is *Ceramic Glazes: The Complete Handbook* by Brian Taylor and Kate Doody. What I think is great about this book, besides being organized by color (which is awesome), is that they ask the contributing ceramic artists to contribute glaze recipes and ask them *why* they use the colors they do for their work. While we are often seeking a specific color, there can be a lot of thought behind *why* we are drawn to certain colors or surfaces. The glaze journey, while tactile and visual, can be emotionally driven. I often respond to glaze tests with, "Mmm, this doesn't feel right," and then a huge "*Yes!*" when it connects with me in the right way. I want my surfaces to connect to people, and because I don't work narratively (with imagery), I focus on color and surface to draw people in. I have found that is more of an unconscious emotional connection.

Look for and collect images of non-ceramic surfaces you love and that inspire you on your quest for the perfect surface treatment. This can lead you down a path that digs a bit deeper than the "I like blue" conversation. When you are ready, you can take that leap into glaze chemistry and color theory. Check Publications and Artist Resources in this book (page 168). There are several books listed and an online class taught by Rose and Matt Katz that I recommend as a great next step if you hunger for more glaze knowledge. Happy test tiling!

GALLERY

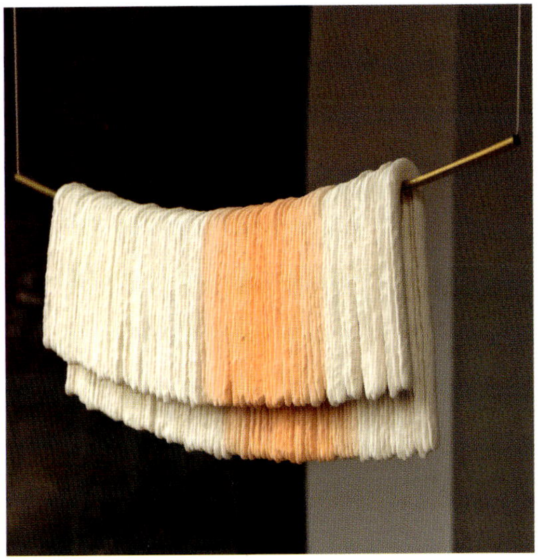

Amanda Salov, *Morning Light*, pinch and assemblage.
Photo Courtesy of the Artist

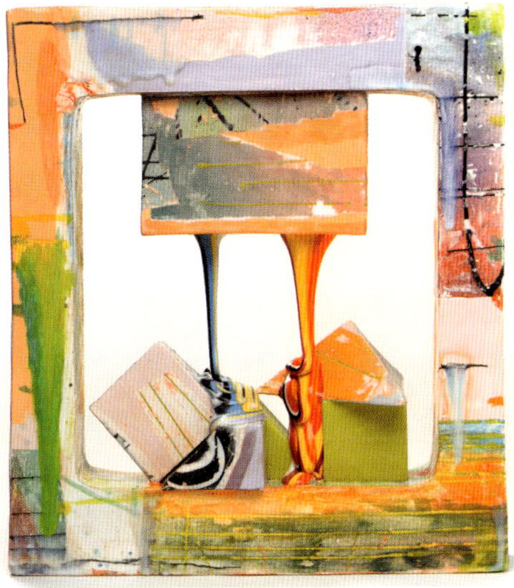

Lauren Mabry, *Molten Veil with Irregular Forms.*
Photo Courtesy of the Artist

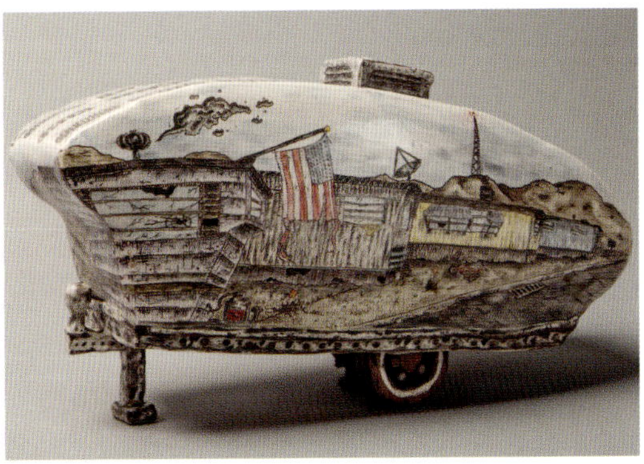

Richard Peterson, *Trailer, 1-800 Leave the USA*, slab built and sgraffito decoration.
Photo Courtesy of the Artist

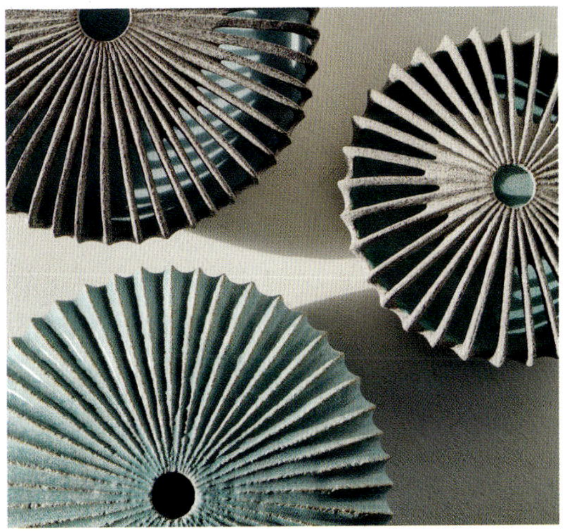

Michele Bianco, *Vessels with Gills*, slab built and hand carved.
Photo Courtesy of the Artist

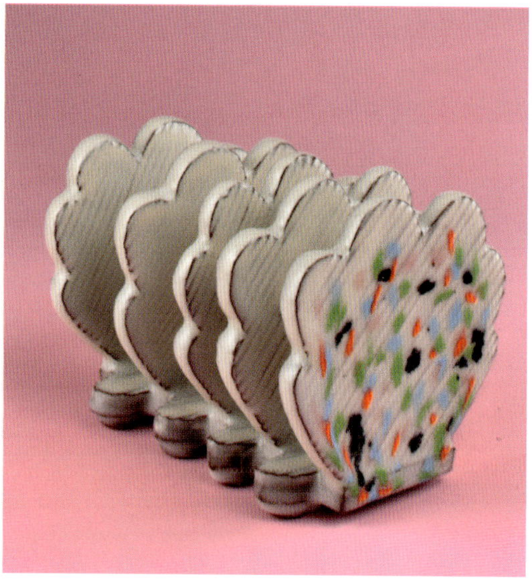

Brian Jones, *Toast Rack*, slab built.
Photo Courtesy of the Artist

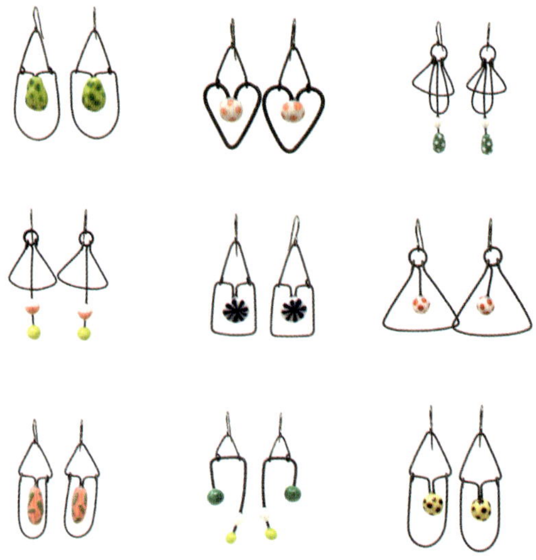

Jennifer Allen, *Earrings*, pinched and hand shaped.
Photo Courtesy of the Artist

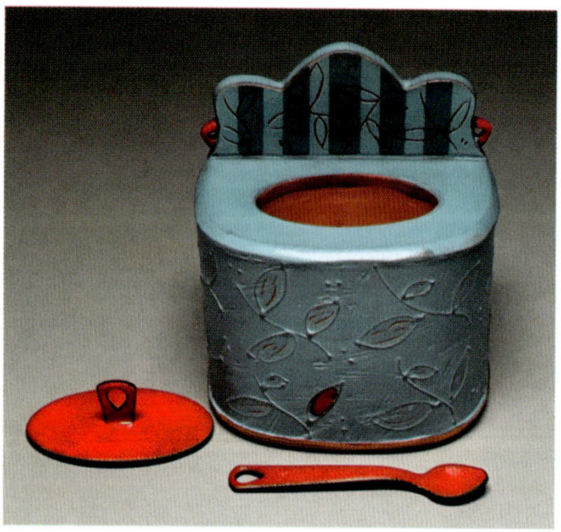

Liz Zlot Summerfield, *Salt Box*, slab built.
Photo Courtesy of the Artist

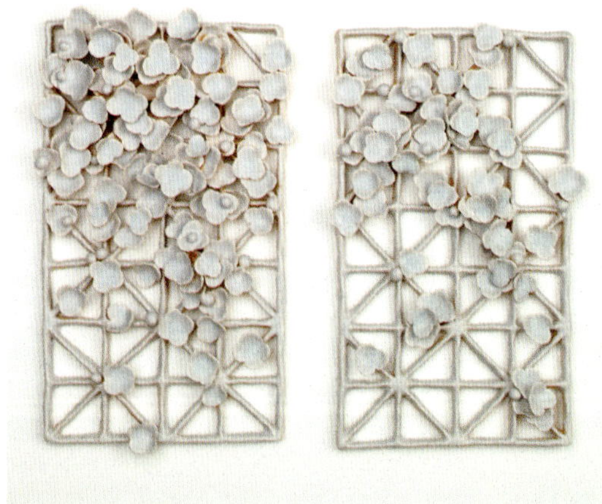

Joanna Poag, *Wallflower: Dirzies*, pinch, coil, and assemblage.
Photo Courtesy of the Artist

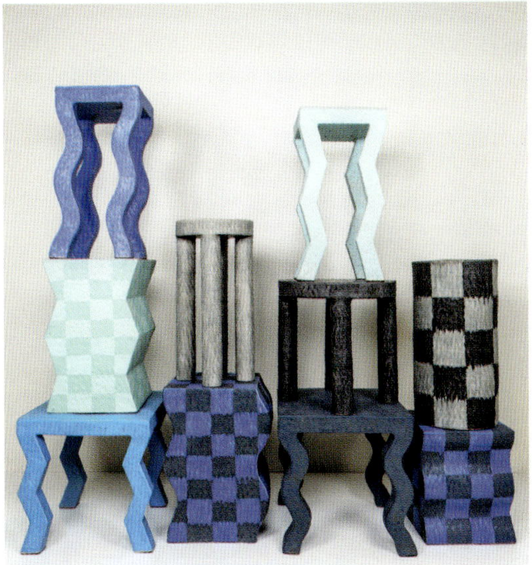

Kelsie Rudolph, *Table Stack*, pinch and slab.
Photo Courtesy of the Artist

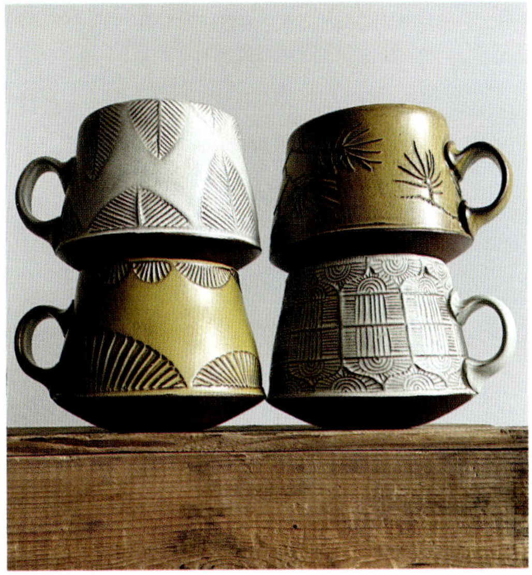

Sarah Pike, *Pike Mugs*, slab built and stamped.
Photo Courtesy of the Artist

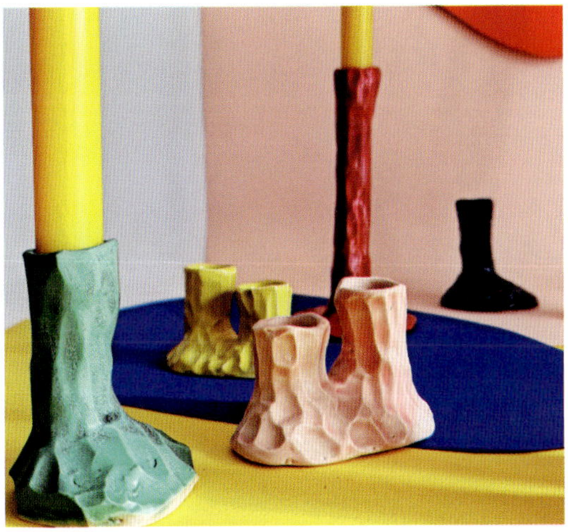

Maria Baleva, *Candle Sticks*, carved.
Photo Courtesy of the Artist

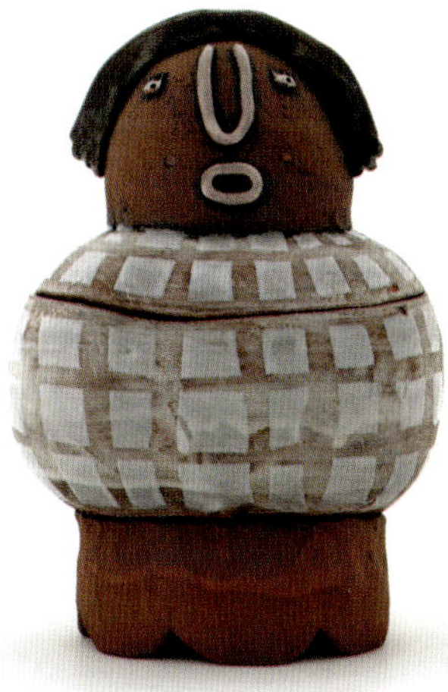

Lynne Hobaica, *Cellar Plaid*, coil built.
Photo Courtesy of the Artist

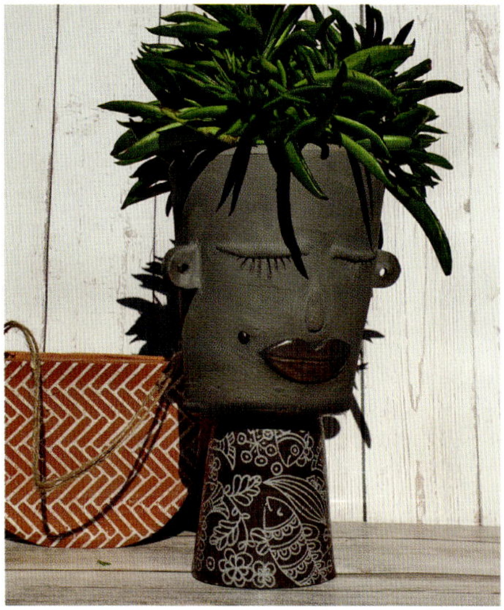

Leonie Allan, *Planters*, slab built.
Photo Courtesy of the Artist

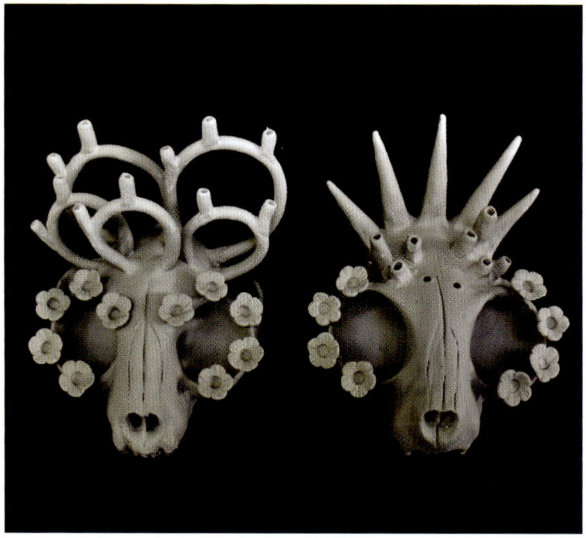

Clairy Laurence, *Cats Skulls 1 and 2*, pinch.
Photo Courtesy of the Artist

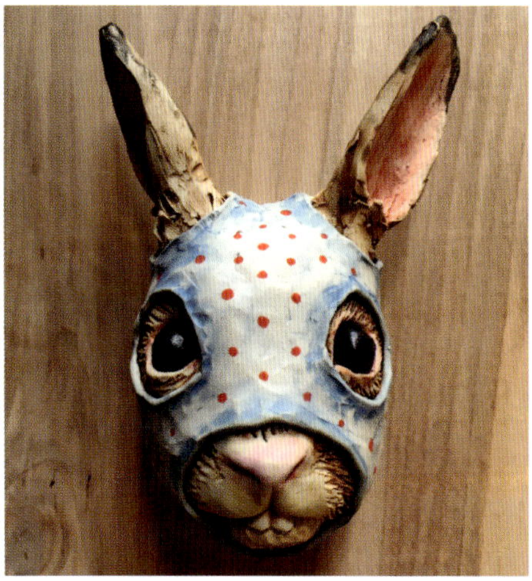

Magda Gluszek, *Luchabbit*, pinch built.
Photo Courtesy of the Artist

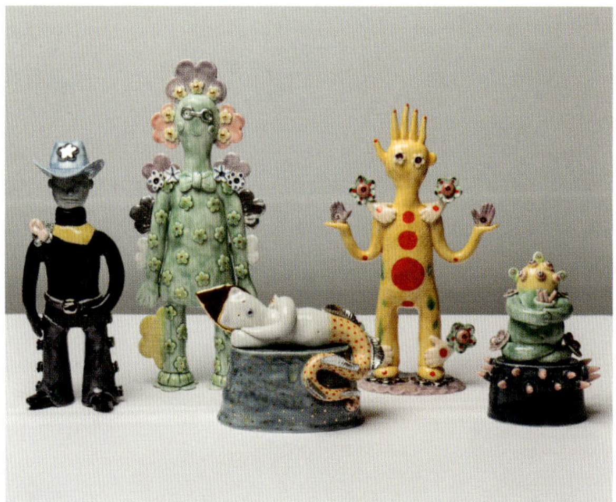

Vipoo Srivilasa, *Wellness Deity Series*, pinch and coil.
Photo Courtesy of the Artist

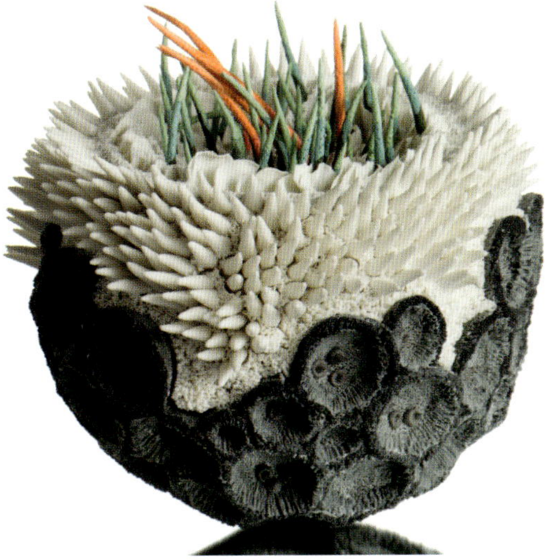

Erum Aamir, *Mirantibus*, rolled, pinch, coil, and carved.
Photo Courtesy of the Artist

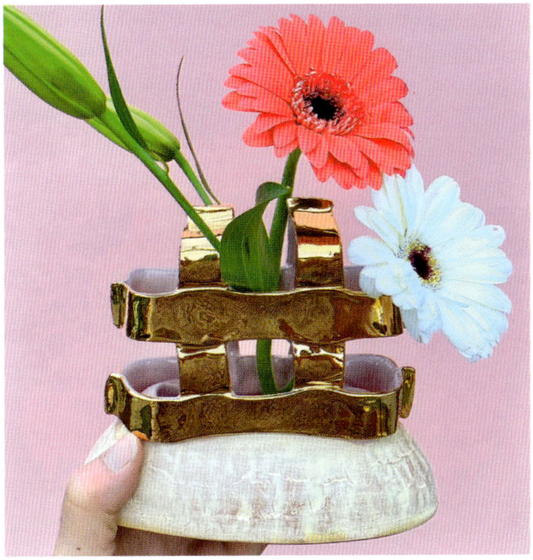

Didem Mert, *Bling Flower Cage*, slab and coil built.
Photo Courtesy of the Artist

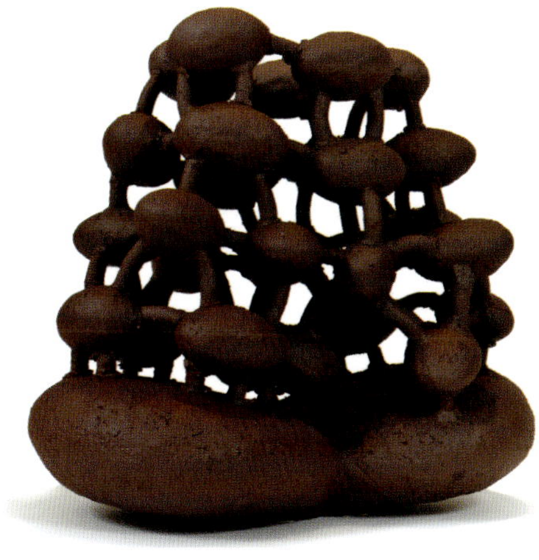

Colby Charpentier, *Cluster*,
assembled from coiled and pinched parts.
Photo Courtesy of the Artist

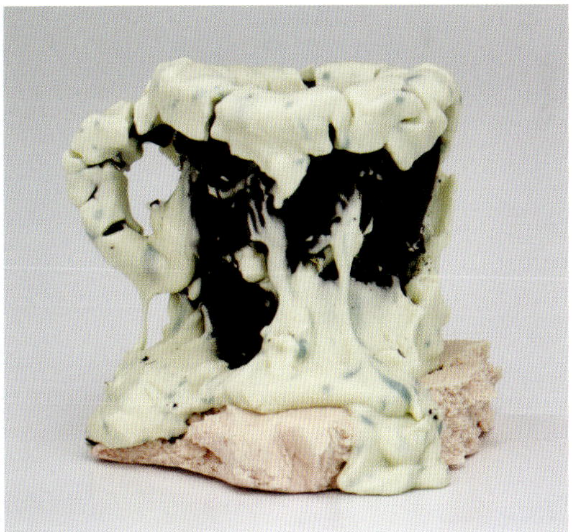

Adam Shiverdecker, *Absurd Mug*,
Kanthal wire frame and clay/glaze melt.
Photo Courtesy of the Artist

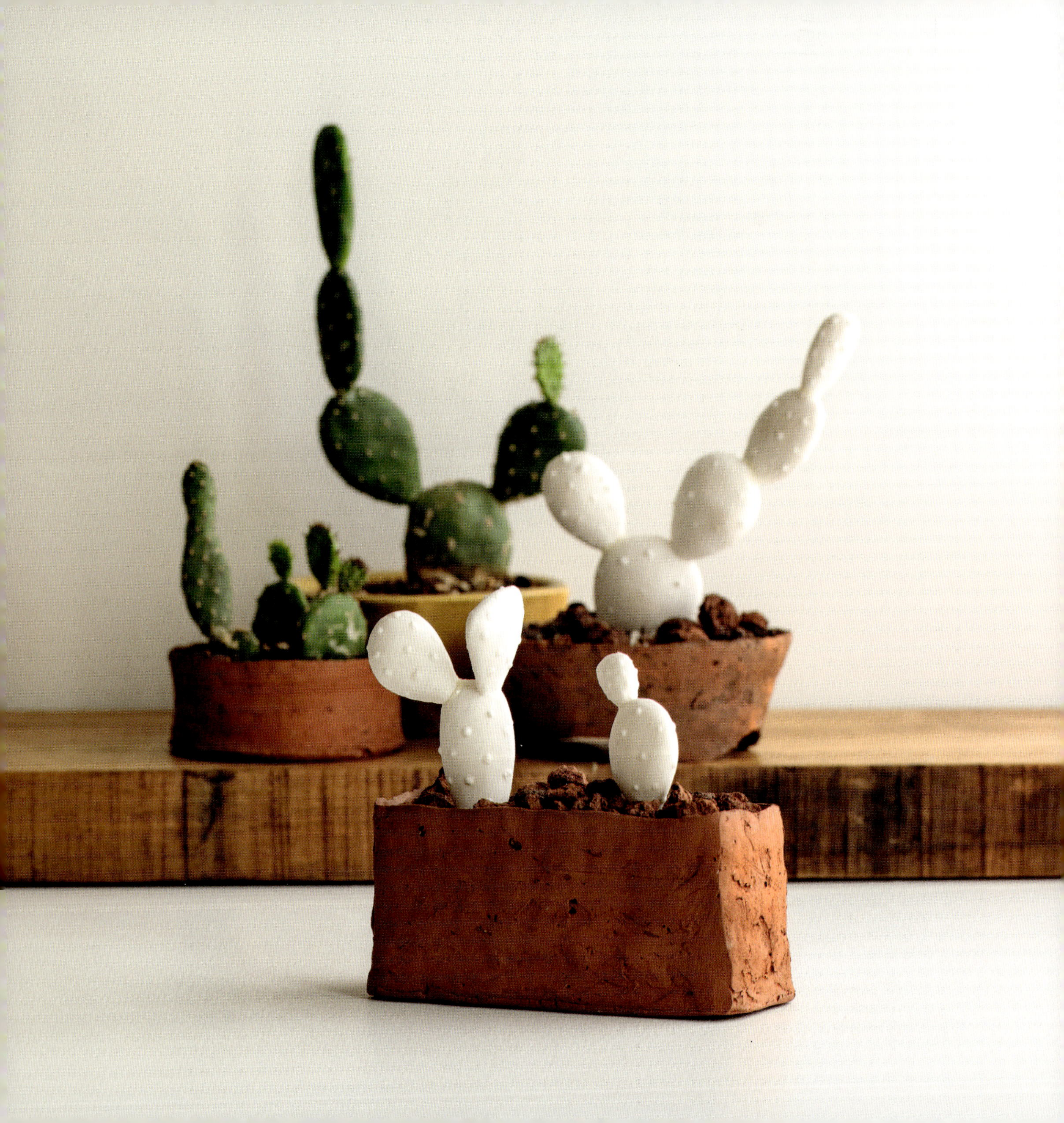

section

2

SCULPTURAL PROJECTS

Sculpture can seem like a fancy and intimidating concept. However, the reality is that once you get past your preconceptions, sculpture is broad and inviting in its definition and application. The goal of sculpture is simply to make work with whatever kind of material in a 3D space. That's it. It can be representational or abstract, large or small, stationary or kinetic. The tricky and intimidating part of sculpture is in combining it with meaning. Believe me, the folks in the museums started just where you are today. No one creates a masterpiece on their first try. Masterpieces are the result of years of trial and error, research and personal investigation, and countless failures along the way. I promise you, your first idea won't be your best idea (really) or—the great fear—the last good idea you'll ever have!

One other important note regarding creativity before we get to the projects: I think we can sometimes get stuck with an identity (or a story we tell ourselves) that we adopt from some childhood experience—you are either creative or not creative. I can't tell you how many times I have been told by folks, "You're so creative," followed by, "I'm not creative at all." Well, I'm here to tell you, a person is not born either creative or not creative. Creativity is fostered; we are given opportunities at a young age to develop trust in our creativity . . . or not. Sometimes our circumstances fail us, and we learn to distrust our creative instincts. As adults, I also feel like there is a misguided correlation between the word "creative" and the word "artist," and that creates too much pressure for folks who want to investigate their creative self. If you believe you are *not* creative (good for you for picking up this book—*you* got this), I ask you to challenge that belief by redefining what "creative" means to you.

In this section I will also be (sneakily) laying the groundwork for you to develop foundational hand-building skills and flex some of your creative skills. The goal is for you to get a feel for clay and see how to work with it in different stages and different methods and familiarize yourself with the tools of the trade. Remember to have fun and take some time to investigate your creative self on this journey. Some research and reflection are part of each project.

Welcome to the playing field!

FLORA

My plant obsession started with my big move from California to Montana. Over my first long winter, I went from having five house plants that first year, to more than one hundred and seventy plants (my sister made me count awhile ago, but I have added a few since then and feel no need to update the number for her!) by my second year. Like any new obsession, it has consumed my waking hours. Any of you who have gotten into plants maybe know this feeling, when you must have all the plants and then, when you have almost all the plants, your favorites start to emerge.

That brings me to the outside garden. Here in Montana, it is difficult to have a thriving veggie garden—our growing season is just too short. It doesn't mean I don't keep trying, just not with a lot of success. That correlates with my investigation into sculpture in the beginning—lots of attempts but without more concrete direction, I met with little success. With clay we can explore objects that do not exist. However, that can be a difficult place to start. One of the best ways to get to abstractions is to work in realism, and find and investigate what inspires and intrigues us in our own spaces.

This project is a double feature. For the first exercise, you will be making a variety of leaves or petals with clay, using real-life flora as inspiration and just your fingers and a couple of tools to help shape and refine the form. For the second exercise, you will be making a "specimen plant" of your choice. (I'll be demonstrating on a succulent/cactus.) This process will involve building solid shapes that are textured/decorated and then pieced together to create a complete plant. These projects are about making an interesting form out of raw clay. We are not relying on slip or glaze decoration to make the shape interesting or recognizable.

Before you begin, collect images, take multiple pictures with your phone, or search the internet for your favorite plants. Plants, plural: Don't just take the first plant you find and stop there. Find several with different shapes and styles. Some may not prove doable or interesting for this project. Remember, your first idea is often not your best idea. The more options and information that you gather will ultimately shape your success. This is the research part of this project, so find several that interest you and take images from multiple angles. You might have access to the real thing and can trace the shape or sketch it. You will be relying on your research to produce a replica in clay. Your firsthand research will provide tactile and complex visual information that will help guide your process to make this project your own.

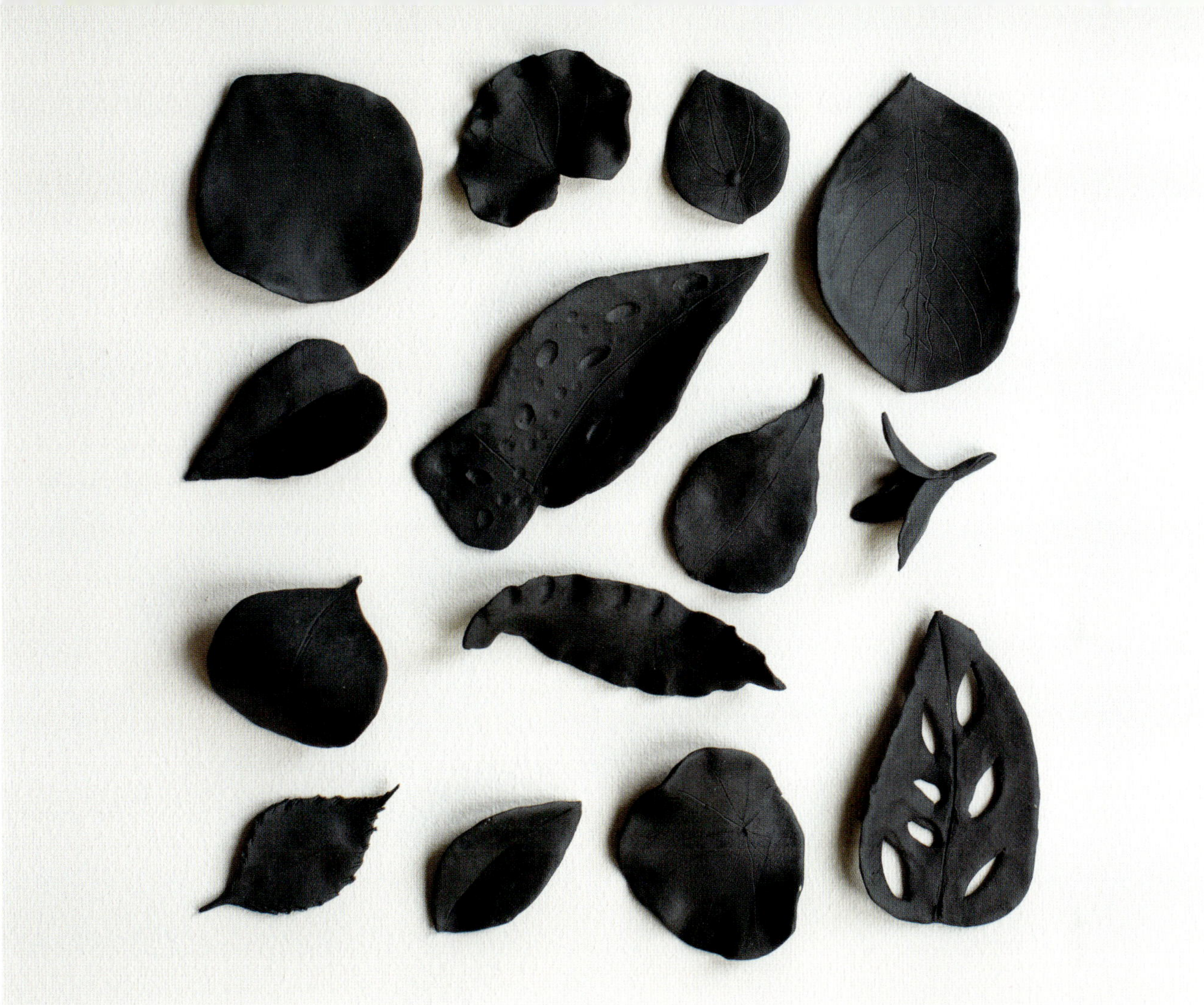

CONE 5, raw porcelain clay, with added black mason stain

Note The clay for this project is a cone 5 porcelain that fires bone white. For some variation you can add mason stain to the clay to develop different colored clay. (Start with small percentages of stain and do some test firings.)

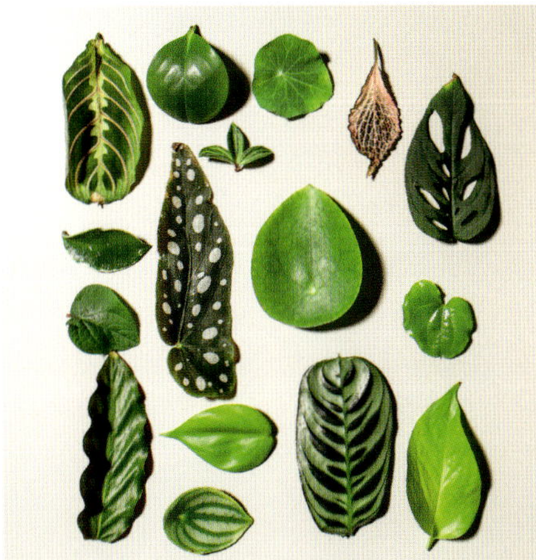

TOOLS AND MATERIALS

Basic Tool Kit (page 37)

Slip trailer

Epoxy

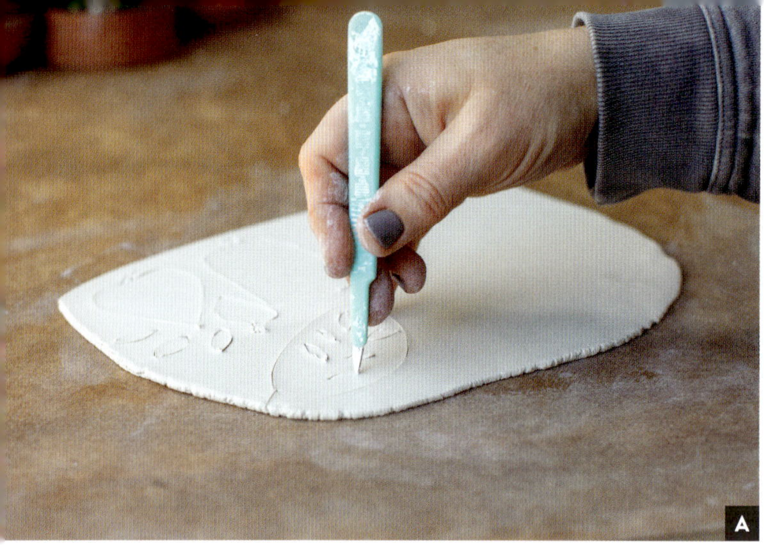

A

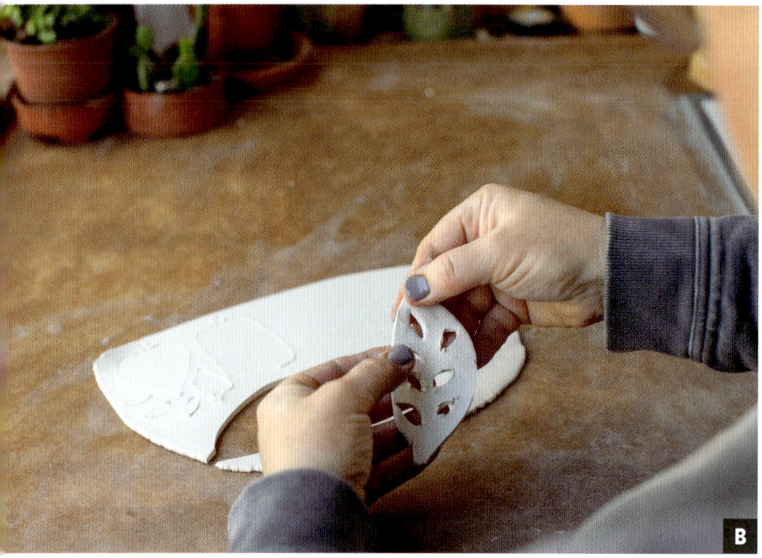

B

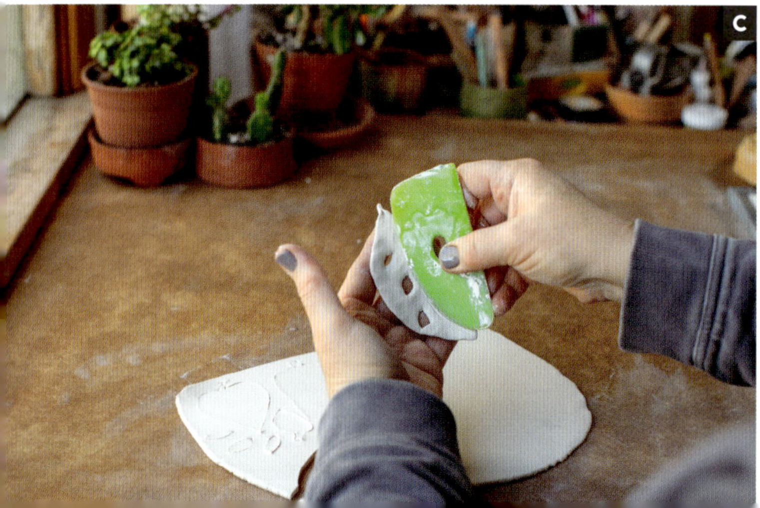

C

Part One: Leaf/Petal

Make a quick template from your own research.

NOTE *Some projects have traceable templates starting on page 162. However, for this project, the purpose of a template is to create a representation of a leaf shape you would like to replicate. Creating a template is important, more so than tracing a leaf or drawing one freehand on the clay, because you can re-use the template if you like the results. (Make sure to write the name of the leaf on the template if that is important to you.)*

Roll a small slab of clay to less than ¼" (.63 cm) thick, and using a needle tool or scalpel, cut out five to ten shapes, tracing along the template to get started. **[A]**

Pull the excess clay up off your working surface and place it back in your bag for another project. Using your fingertips, begin to shape your leaf. Leave the center thicker and taper toward the edge. For this leaf, you want the edge to be papery thin. If you are struggling to get the desired shape, you might have too much clay; a couple options are to cut away the excess or roll the slab again a bit thinner this time, recut the shapes, and start again. Working with thin clay takes some practice. Go slowly and work in stages. **[B]**

Once you have the initial shape roughed out, work on the finer details. This is where some more tools and your reference images come into play. Use a hard-edged tool such as a stiff plastic rib or old credit card to crease and define the spine of the leaf. **[C]** Now let that the form rest and set up. Repeat the process until you have at least five leaves to this stage.

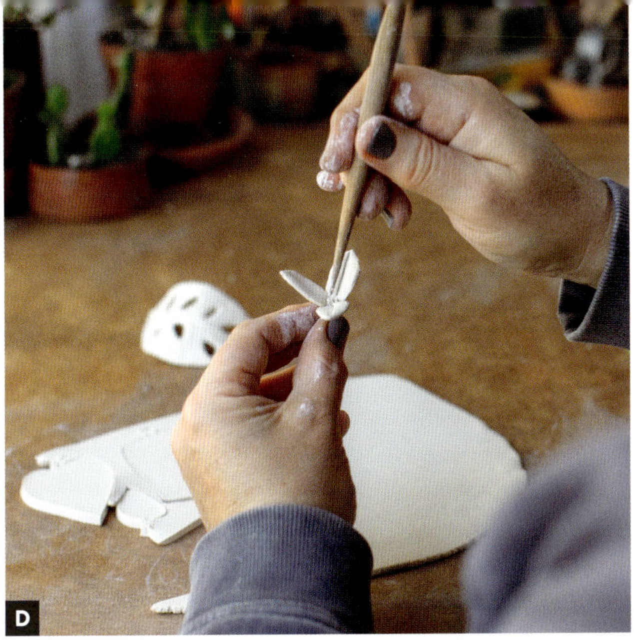

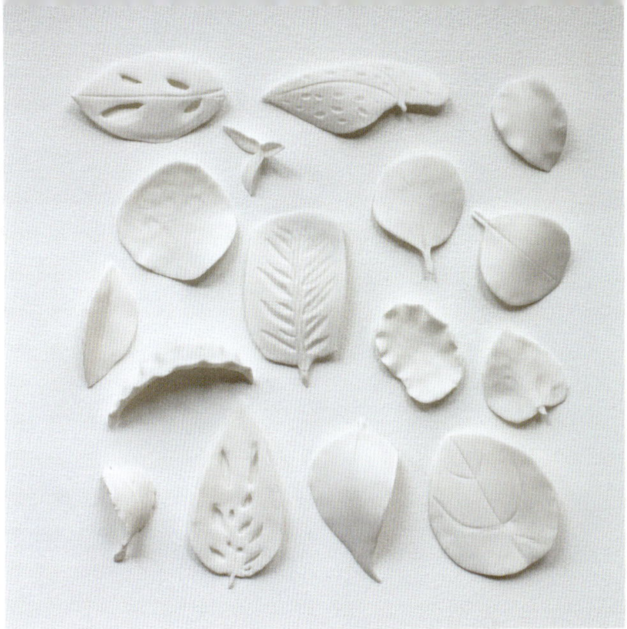

CONE 5, raw (or exposed) porcelain

Now work on refinement. The details are where the beauty of the delicate little petals/leaves come to life. When the forms have set up (medium leather hard), start to make some detail marks. Explore the whole range of minimal decoration to extravagance and see where you are pleased with the results. **[D]**

NOTE *Use an assortment of tools: needle tool, mechanical pencil, soft rubber modeling tool, or ribs. Try them all—find what works for you. Some will feel clumsy or leave marks that are too deep, some will feel right in your hand, and others may need some practice using. Your touch will determine which tool will work for this project and your developing skill level.*

Spend some time defining the marks you sketched out. This process is slow and steady—use the reference images regularly and take breaks if the clay needs to set up to be easier to work on. Through this process you will find a range of dryness or temperatures that you are comfortable working in. Sometimes you need to work with clay that is too soft or too hard to know where your range of workability lies. I recommend placing your working pieces on a soft piece of foam draped under plastic—this will prevent any marks from getting on the hard surface, and the draped plastic will prevent from the work from drying too quickly.

NOTE *These thin little leaves will dry out very quickly and in a bone-dry state will be very easy to break.*

Look over the pieces and clean up any burrs or last details. You might be wondering "What do I do with these?" or "Is that it?" Yes, that is it for the moment. This project is about you working with your hands and developing your eye for details, seeing something and then trying to replicate it. Explore your environment—what sparks your interest? You now have a general idea of what is possible with just a little clay and a couple of tools. Make as many as you want. I'll be saving mine to incorporate into another project in this section. (Hint: You may be interested in checking out the Wall Tile project on page 78!)

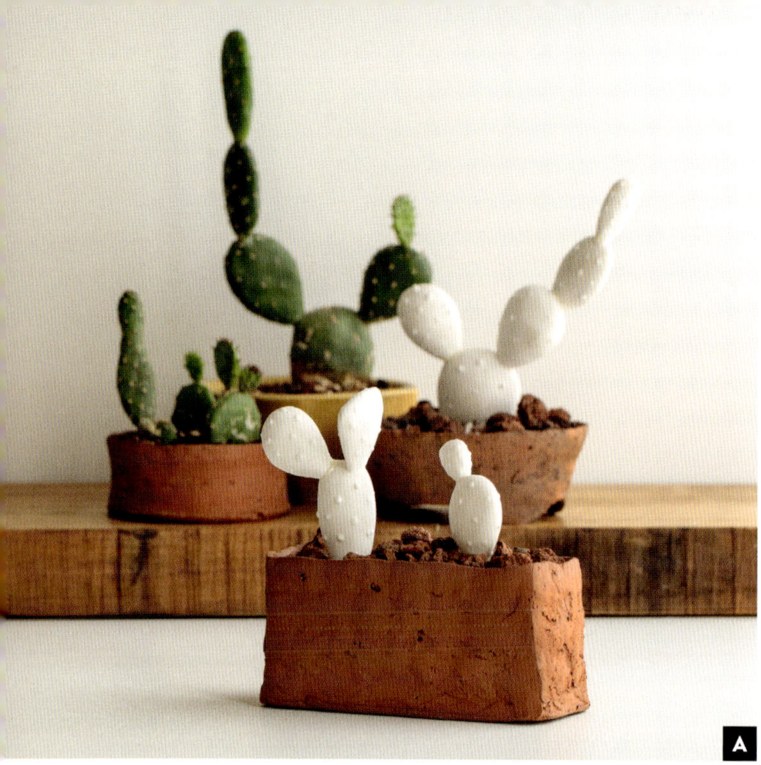

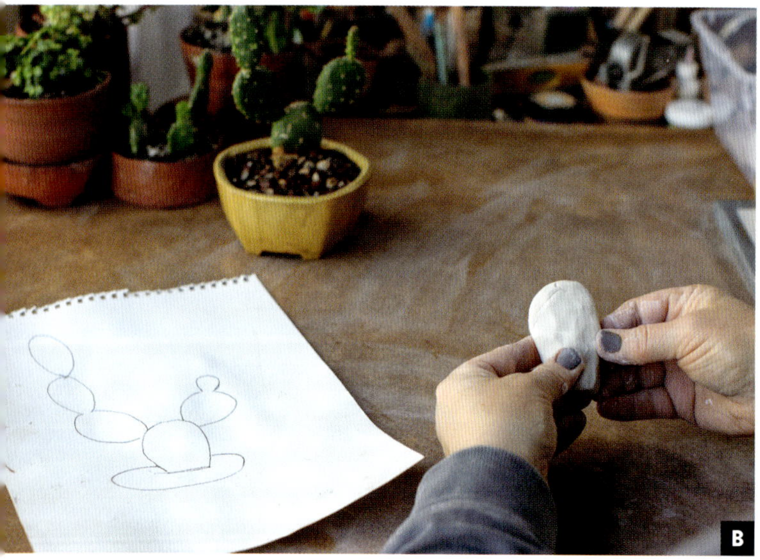

Part 2: Specimen

Think about the old books of illustrations that skillfully captured flora and fauna before we had cameras, the beautiful drawings of a single stem of a plant. That is what you are going to create in 3D. Again, focus on developing shape and texture with only the clay as your building and decorative material. We are not relying on glaze or other colored surface treatments to inform our audience what the object is. This project is designed to be part of a larger installation of a planter and simulated soil. **[A]**

Referring to the reference images for this project, sketch out the general shapes with just a pencil and paper. **[B]** Don't be scared: this is for you to have a generalized understanding of the scale, positioning, and shape of the pieces of the cactus form.

Working with solid, roughed out shapes, use your drawing to get the shape and scale as close as you can. Remember you are working in 3D; these shapes have a weight and fullness about them. Let them set up to leather hard.

Make a small slab base, ½" (1.3 cm) thick and roughly 2" (5 cm) across, with a hole cut in the center large enough to allow the sculpture to rest inside the shape. This will be fired with the form and attached after the final firing using epoxy.

Clean up your base. Once it is stiff enough to hold without bending, use a green scrubby to soften the edges. This part of the object will not be seen in the final presentation of the piece, but it is good practice to make sure all edges are "finished."

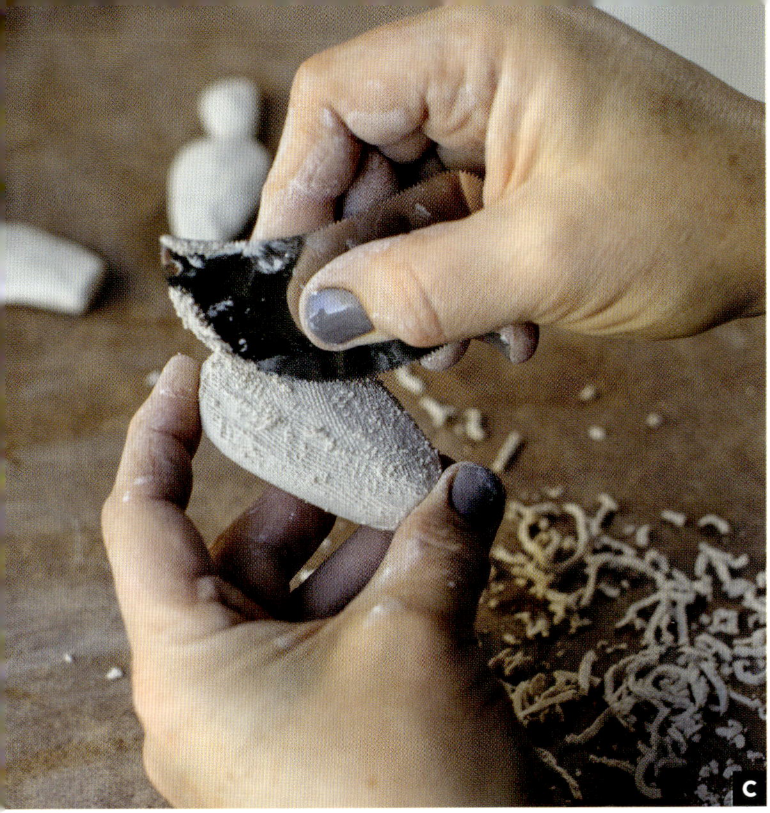

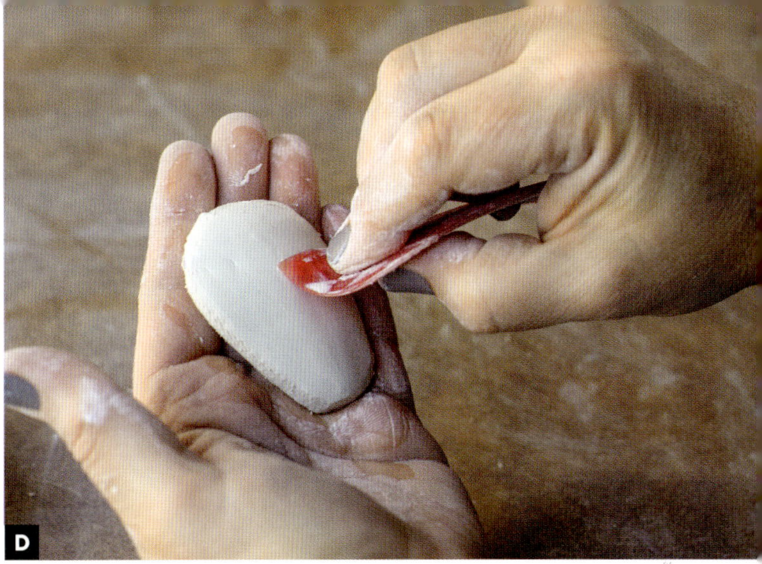

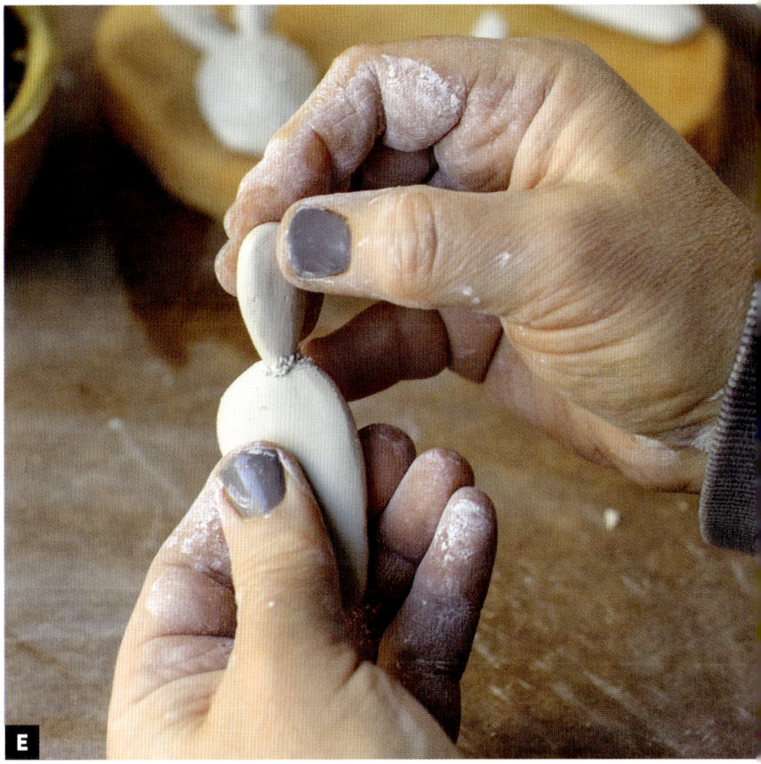

Shape the cactus pieces with a surform and a serrated rib and then smooth the surface with a soft red rib or even a little water on your finger. **[C] [D]**

Now the fun part, putting it together. Be patient and put it together in stages. Attach the foundational (largest) segment to the next piece. You can work from a drawing or start holding up the pieces to see where you think they should attach. Remember that gravity exists and you need to work with it! Pick your placement of the next segment attachment. Score and prep both sides of the attachment points. Pick out small groupings to put together and let the attachments rest and firm up. **[E]**

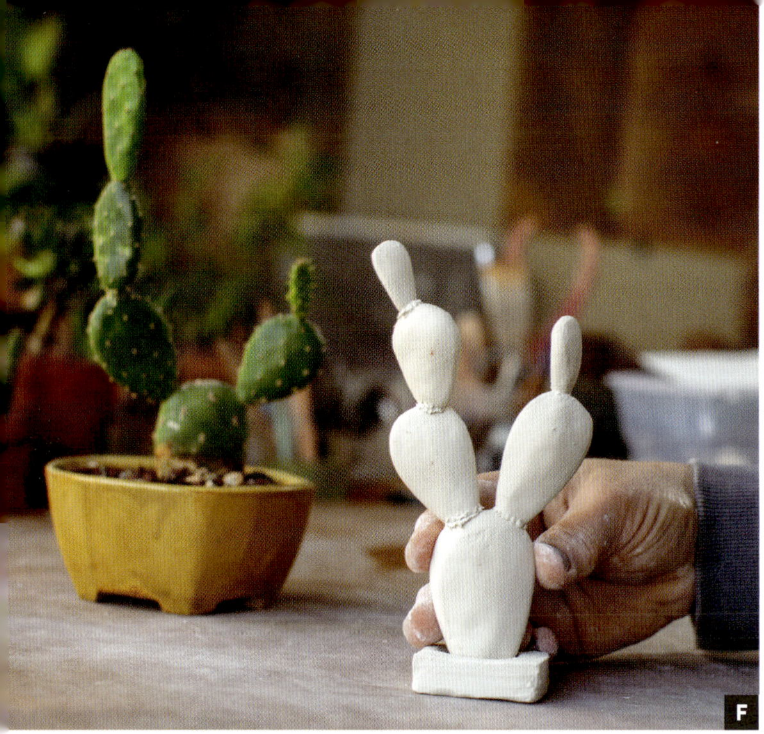

F

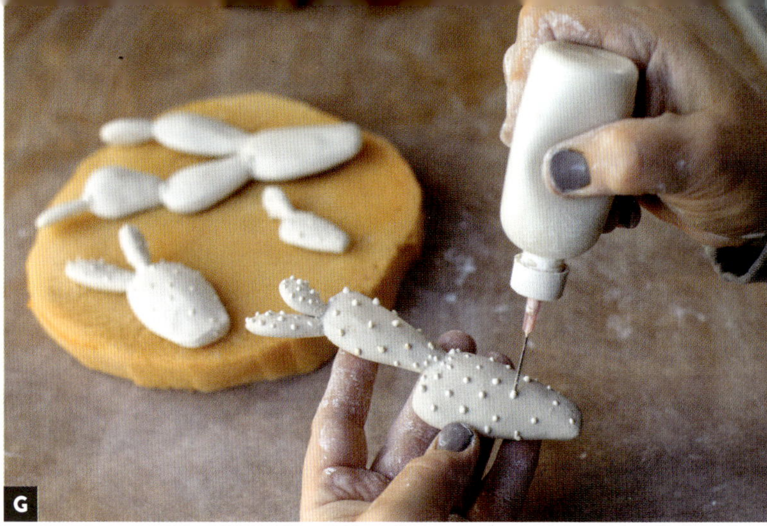

G

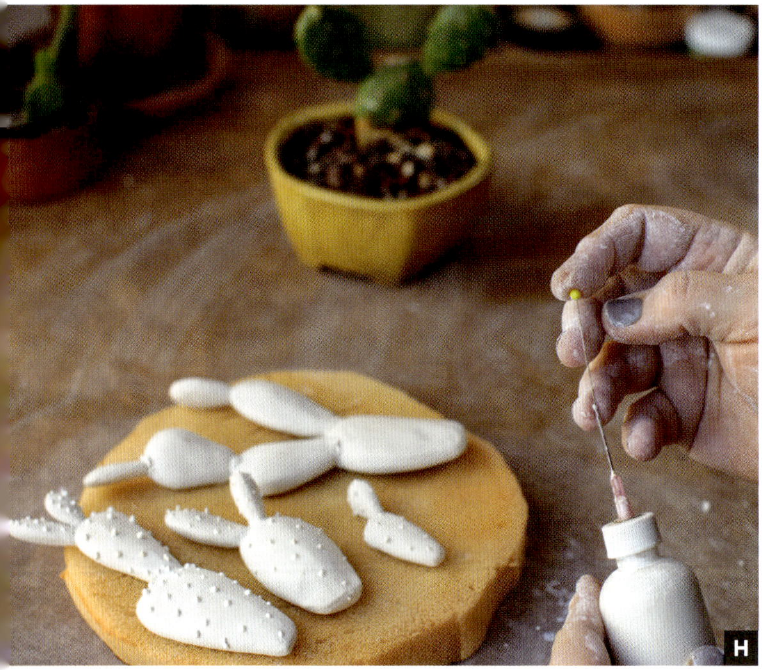

H

Then attach the groupings to the larger piece. Be sure and support the already attached segments. The attachment points are fragile and should be given time to set before cleaning and refining. Rest the objects horizontally on a piece of foam to let them come together. Once the sculpture is complete, drape plastic over it to allow the entire piece to come to the same temperature again, and then do your last refinements. **[F]**

Use the reference images **[G]** to create the details on the surface of the cactus where the spines protrude from. Use a slip trailer or a fine tip brush and slip made of the same clay to make the marks. This method will require time to let the slip dry before you can manipulate the pieces. One side at a time. **[H]**

NOTE *To make slip using your clay, use the shaving or dried parts that have been taken away during this process and put them in a small, Tupperware-style container. Add a bit of water to reconstitute the clay into a soft slurry. If you don't have a lot of shavings, take a bit of your clay from the bag and put it in the container and add some water and mix until it is liquid enough to use with a slip trailer.*

Tips for Success

× × × × ×

This object should be fired horizontally, with the base fired at the same time but unattached. Also, as this piece is not going to be glazed (it can be once fired), that means it can be fired to its completed temperature and not bisqued first. This is one of the perks of working with just the clay surface as your end goal.

When the piece comes out of the kiln, attach it to the base disc so you can display it with ease. Use any epoxy-type material to attach the clay pieces.

This object is fragile. I broke several of them in the making stage as well as the post-firing assembly stage. I am more of a bull-in-the-china-shop kind of person. I found if I slowed down and made sure to have soft surfaces to work on, I had much better luck. I really employed my patience and allowed lots of time for the objects to set up before I assembled the whole larger piece. My suggestion is to make multiples and work your way up to the larger forms. This is still one of my favorite projects in this book, despite it testing my limits! Don't let yourself be discouraged if you have some failures. Instead, take some deep breaths and try again.

SLIP TRAILER: *The name is somewhat self-explanatory, but it is a tool used primarily in applying slip decoration. Slips can be made in many different colors and are usually applied to leather hard work before the bisque firing.*

CREATURES

One of the best things about working in clay is how diverse your expression can be. While making art you can be a mirror or a filter. As a mirror, it is possible to create objects that are 100 percent realistic or representational. As a filter, you see an object and it passes through you and becomes part you and part subject. You determine what values and characteristics are important. Both types of expression are interesting and challenging goals. It is for you to decide which avenue works for you.

For this project we are dipping our toes in the beginning stages of abstraction. Playing in the abstraction realm is more about cultivating ideas and departing from strict representational art. What can make it hard to work more abstractly is a lack of trust in our own ideas and interpretation. We can get caught up in what others may think and how they may judge us. In addition to working on your abstraction/filtering skills, I encourage you to work on being kind and generous with yourself. No negative self-talk, no, "I can't do this," or, "I'm not creative enough to make something up." We are playing in clay; find the joy and laughter this assignment can bring. (I know I am on the right path if something I make makes me laugh out loud.)

Set an intention to take a playful approach for this project. I want you to investigate an animal/creature that interests you. It's always a good idea to work from images. Draw them yourself or find pictures online or in books—even pictures of your own animals can be a great place to start. Heaven knows they are a constant source of inspiration and hilarity for me! Another next-level approach is to invent your own animals. Write a backstory to an imaginary creature. Imaginary animals are a wonderful way to give your inner voice license to play. Start by making a list of the physical attributes of the creature, as well as how you see its personality and spirit manifest through qualities such as playful, mischievous, lonely, social . . . you get the idea. Those human qualities we understand can be filtered to the creature we are actualizing in clay. This is not only an interpretation of an animal, but also the qualities and values *you* are drawn to.

While you can make your creature any size, keep in mind that working much smaller or larger than what you see here can present additional challenges. Once you have a handle on the concept and the skill set, you will be ready to adjust your methods to the challenges. I chose a fox for my demonstration. My creature is on all fours, but again, once you have the concept, you may always divert from the specifics and find your own way.

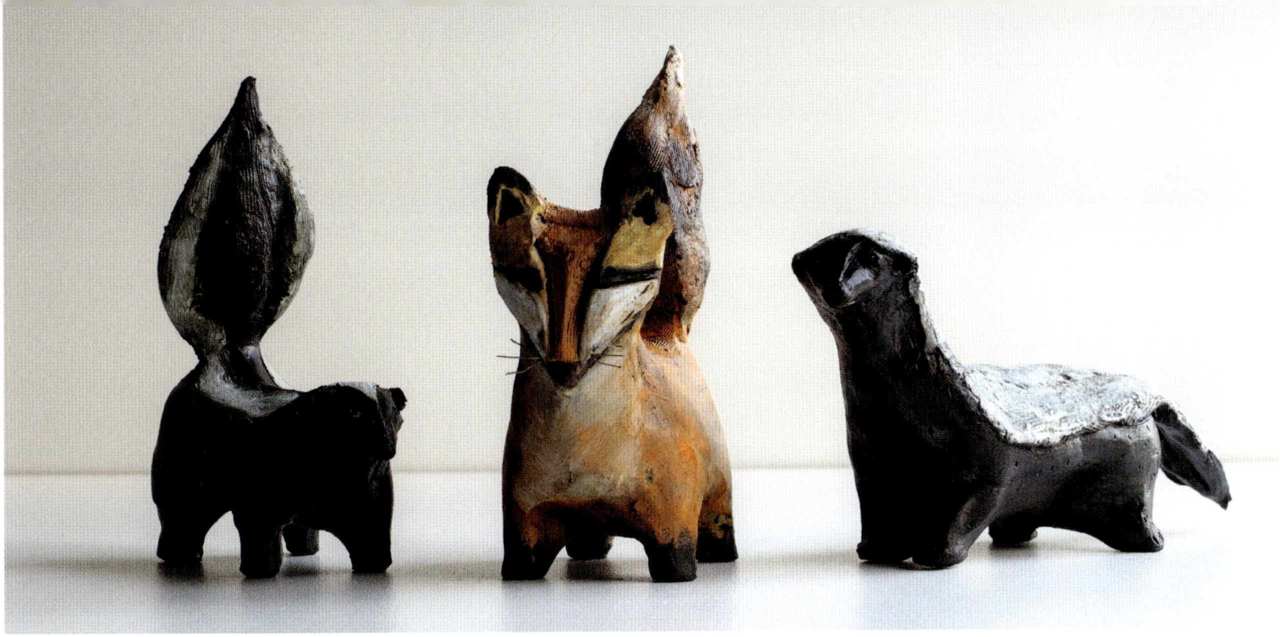

CONE 5, exposed clay and commercial underglaze glazes (two separate applications at bisque temperatures)

TOOLS AND MATERIALS

Basic Tool Kit (page 37)
Sketchbook
Kanthal wire
Pliers
Wire snips

Roll out a ¼" (.63 cm)- to ½" (1.3 cm)-thick slab. Make it large enough that you can cut out a rectangle 8" (20.3 cm) tall x 6" (15.2 cm) wide. (When rolling out a fresh slab of clay, use about 1½" [3.8 cm] of clay from the end of your clay bag; this should give you the right size of finished slab to complete most projects.)

Bevel both the *short* edges, so they will overlap. Score and wet one side. Using both hands, stand the slab up gently and bring together and attach the beveled/scored edges, making a wide tube shape. **[A]** Clean up and compress the seam, inside and out.

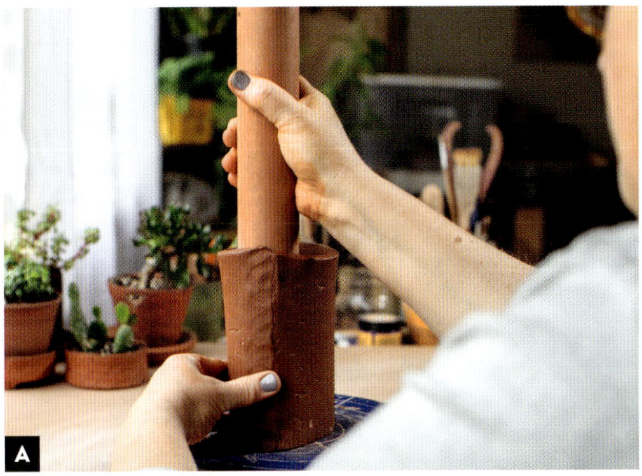

A

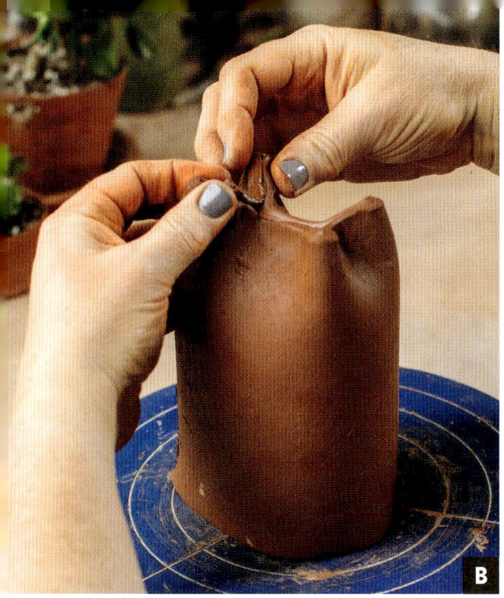

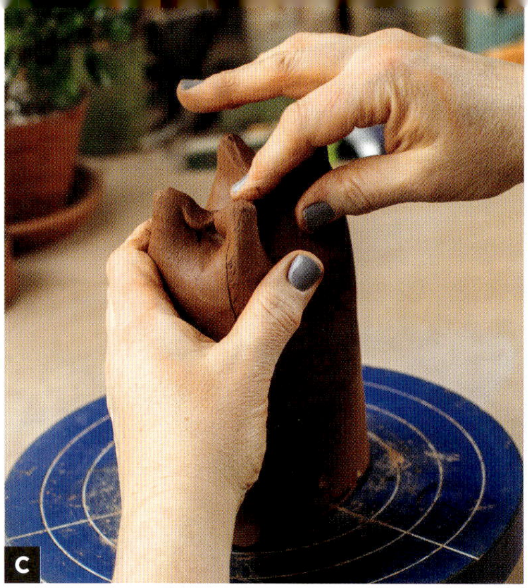

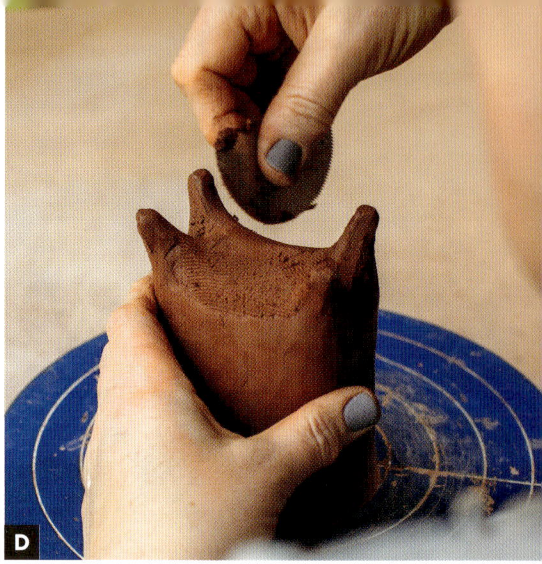

Square up the tube into more of a rectangle. The seam should be in the middle of one of the shorter walls. Start to squish the four corners into legs and bring the center together. Score and overlap the center seam. Continue using both the forefinger and thumb on both hands to work the corners slowly into the shape of a stout leg. When the corners get close to closing in, use a little water or slip to create a seal, if needed. **[B] [C] [D]**

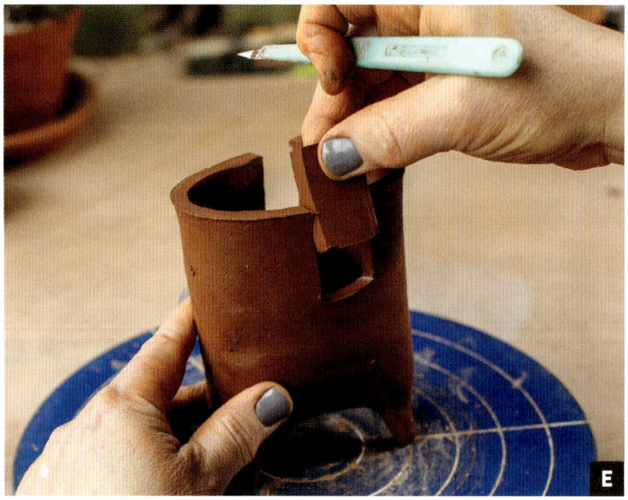

Once the feet are formed, turn the object right side up in your hand and, using a wood tool, rib, or the end of a rolling pin, compress and clean up the inside seams. Make sure to support the outside seam with your hand.

Set the piece down gently on a flat work surface. Measuring from the front (which will be the head), mark 1.5" (3.8 cm) and then leave a horizontal gap of 2" (5 cm) and make the same mark again. Do this for the other side as well. The marks should line up. In this tab section, measure down 1.5" (3.8 cm) and make a line between the two vertical marks. Repeat for the other side.

Using a scalpel, start at the low point of the intersecting lines and cut straight up on the marks. Cut across the horizontal line, pull the tab of clay out, and put it back in your clay bag. **[E]**

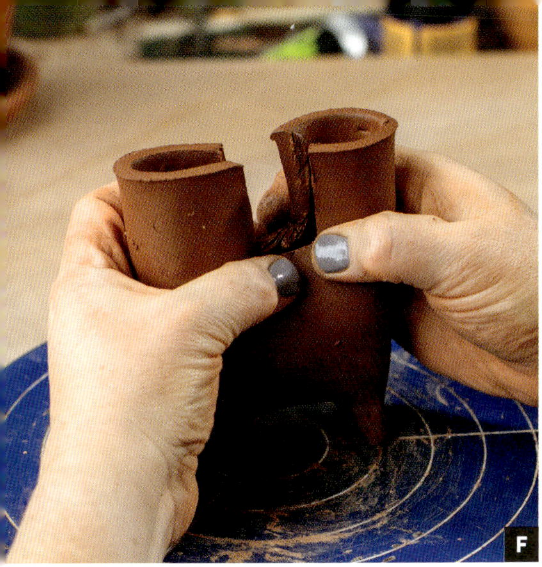

F

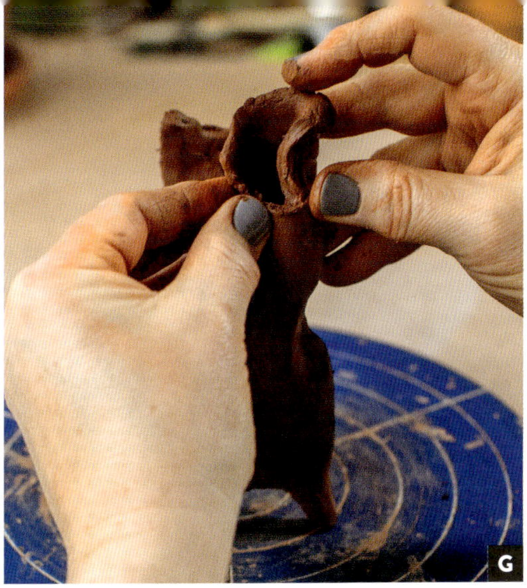

G

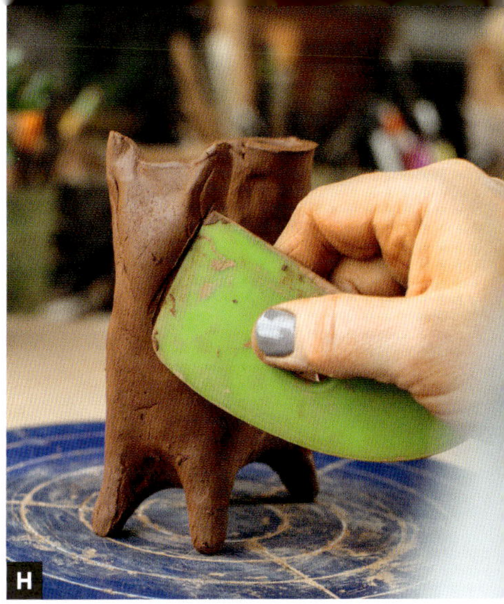

H

Slip and score the edges, if needed, and bring together the tail section, back, and head of the creature. Make sure your seams are well-connected and then use a tool or your finger to shape the tail and head. You may need to add a small slab to the tail to give it extra height. **[F] [G]**

Use a wooden knife or rib to start roughing out the haunches, feet, belly, and tail. Refer to your photos. If your form doesn't have much volume or you want more than is present, use a scalpel to cut a hole in the very center of the underbelly section, big enough to slip a narrow tool or your finger inside without damaging how the form will sit on a tabletop. (You will need a hole in the form anyway, so don't worry about making one now to help yourself.) **[H]**

Once the shape is generally formed, define and refine the details of the animal. Differentiate limbs, fur texture, and facial features. Now is also the time to add any additional clay elements. Be sure to slip and score and let the attachments rest to become closer to the same temperature.

This project is wonderful for practicing greenware surface treatment: try different mark-making tools at different stages of dryness to get an idea of what kind of mark making is needed. Be sure to let the form rest when needed and keep it wrapped up if you plan to work in stages.

Make sure you poke a hole to release trapped air. It's smart to look for an overhang or natural crevice in the surface to use your needle tool or scalpel to make your puncture. I used my needle tool to puncture the little *X* on the backside of my little fox. **[I]**

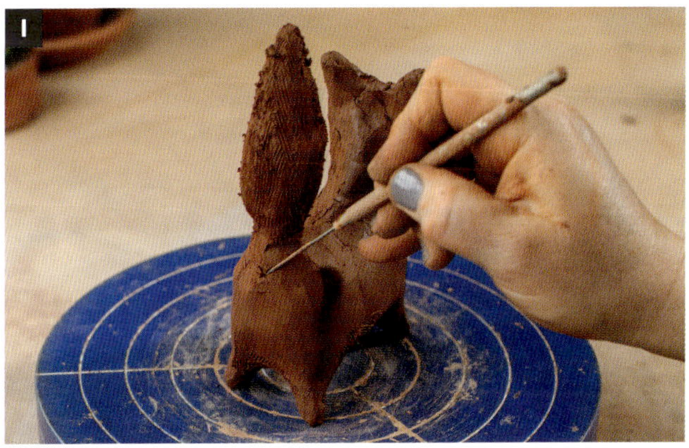

I

WALL TILES/HANGINGS

Wall tiles may seem simple to make, but what's interesting to me about creating wall pieces is taking a traditionally 3D material and making a more two-dimensional form to work on. We are essentially creating our own canvas. That opens up our options for shapes. It is possible to group shapes together to create a mosaic of shapes and story. It is up to you to add the content and decoration to your tiles!

Although the shapes and approaches shown here are very straightforward, I want to introduce to you the idea of reverse-engineering your ideas/projects. For a wall hanging, the key feature is to hang on a wall. You'll need to consider the scale, depth, and weight of the tile and the possible decoration ideas (which might transpose into each of the criteria listed). Then you should start construction of the tile to fit your perceived needs. As we all know, sometimes things don't go according to plan; it is good to have options and a willingness to alter course if something unforeseen happens during your making.

I demonstrate two approaches: one is very straightforward, with a catch that is visible and part of the overall appearance; in the second, the catch is part of the design but hidden from view, with added dimension that also needs decoration consideration and could be hung in a variety of ways.

TOOLS AND MATERIALS

Basic Tool Kit (page 37)
Kanthal wire
Pliers
Wire snips
Tiny drill bits (see page 80)

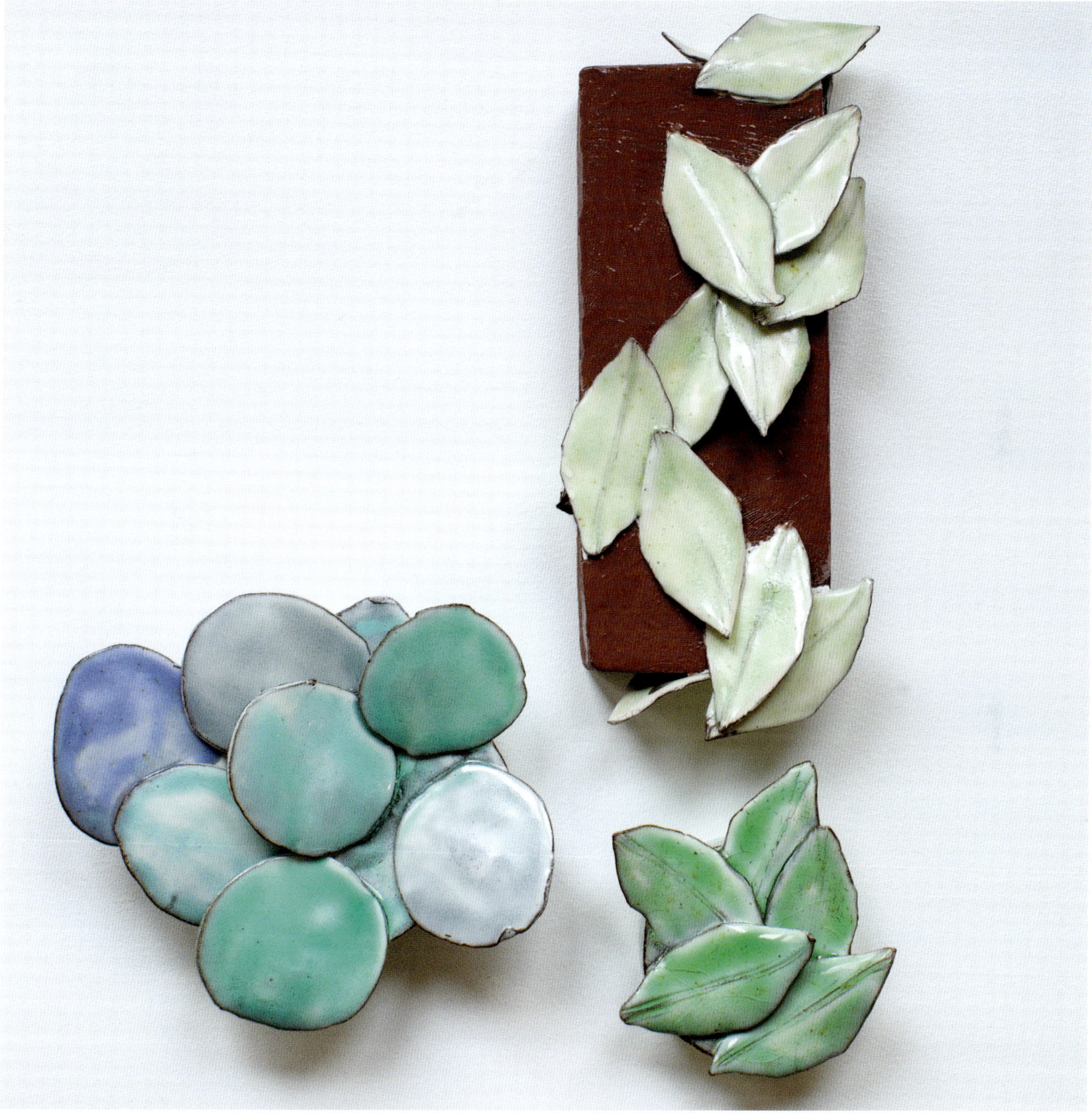

CONE 5 RED CLAY, white slip, celadon style commercial glaze

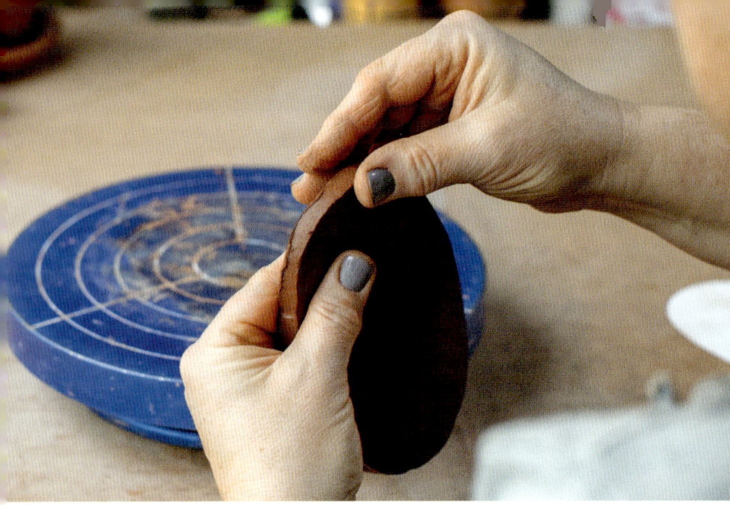

A

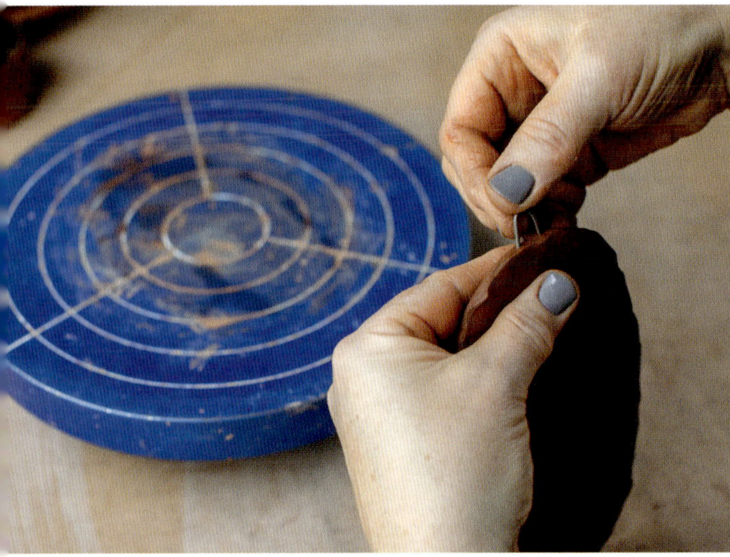

B

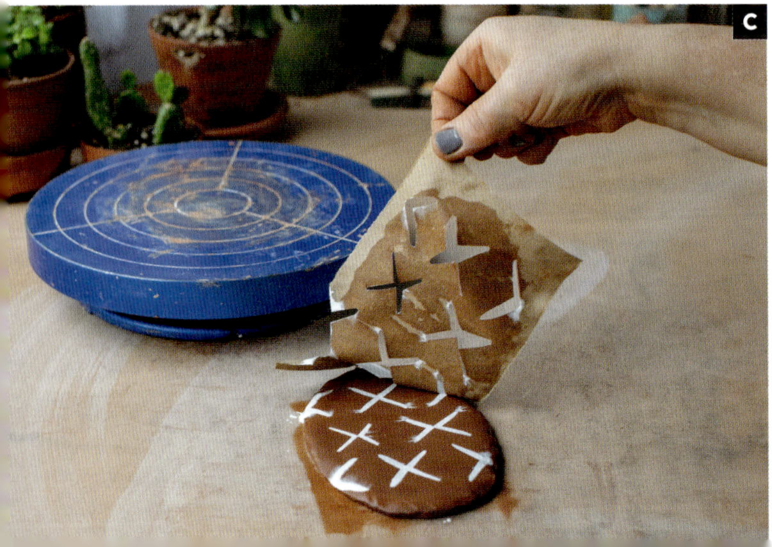

C

Wall Tile 1

Roll out a ½" (1.3 cm)-thick slab a bit bigger than your desired shape.

Cut out your shape (pictured is a 4" x 6" [10 x 15.2 cm] rectangle). Move it to a flat, clean bat or ware board. Compress with a rib and clean up the edges. **[A]**

Cut a ¾" to 1" (1.9 to 2.5 cm) section of Kanthal wire, and then bend it evenly with your pliers. Leave it slightly flared open.

If your tile is soft clay, gently push the wire about ¼" to ½" (.63 to 1.3 cm) deep, leaving the bent ½" (1.3 cm) loop extending from the top. **[B]** If your clay is more leather hard, use a drill bit about the same thickness as your wire to drill two starter holes on the top edge of your tile about ½" (1.3 cm) apart from each other. This will help alleviate cracking issues.

Clean up the edges and loop area.

Let the clay rest between two boards to a leather-hard state and then decorate to your heart's content. The demonstration piece pictured is decorated using colored slips layered with paper stencils. **[C]**

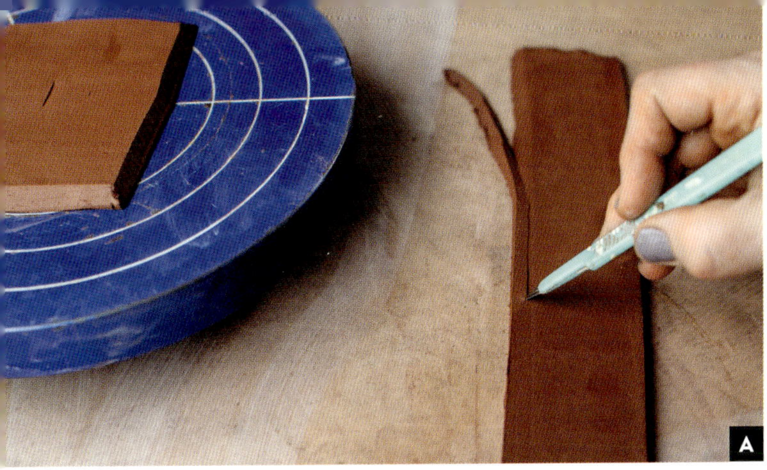

A

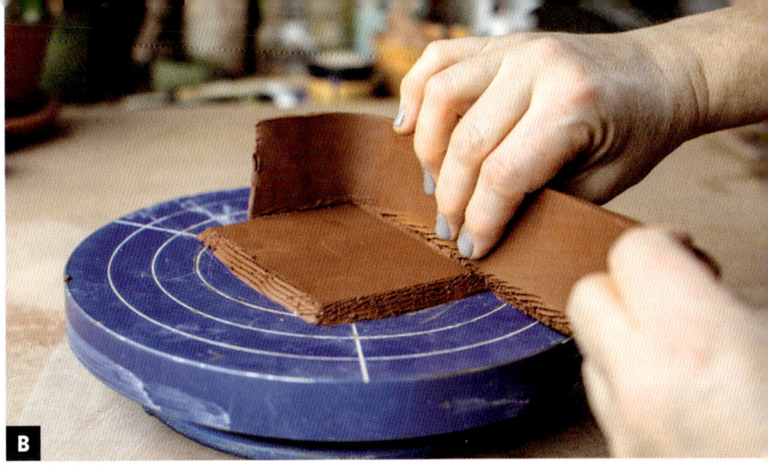

B

Wall Tile 2

Roll out a ½" (1.3 cm) thick slab: a roughly 12" x 12" (30.5 x 30.5 cm) square should be large enough. Cut a 4" x 4" (10.2 x 10.2 cm) tile, and two strips that are 1½" (3.8 cm) wide and the length of your prepped slab.

Move the 4" x 4" (10.2 x 10.2 cm) tile to a working surface, such as a bat or ware board. Bevel and score around the top outside edge of the square. **[A]**

Using the 1½" (3.8 cm)-wide strip, bevel, score, and slip the bottom edge and begin to attach it to the footprint of the tile. Start some place mid-wall, as connecting the seam here is easier and will be stronger than in a corner. One strip may get you around the entire shape; if not, use the second strip, making sure to bevel, score, and slip the connection points. **[B] [C]**

Using a right-angled rib, clean up the interior and exterior attachment areas. **[D]**

NOTE *Now is when you can take a little coil of clay to backfill any areas that seem problematic. This is optional and you can skip it if you feel like the attachments are strong. If you are just starting out, use your best judgement: try both methods and see what works for you.*

C

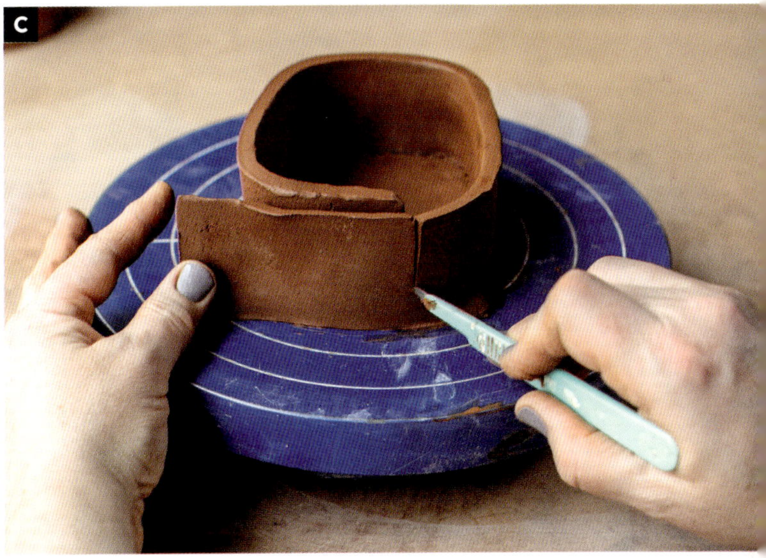

D

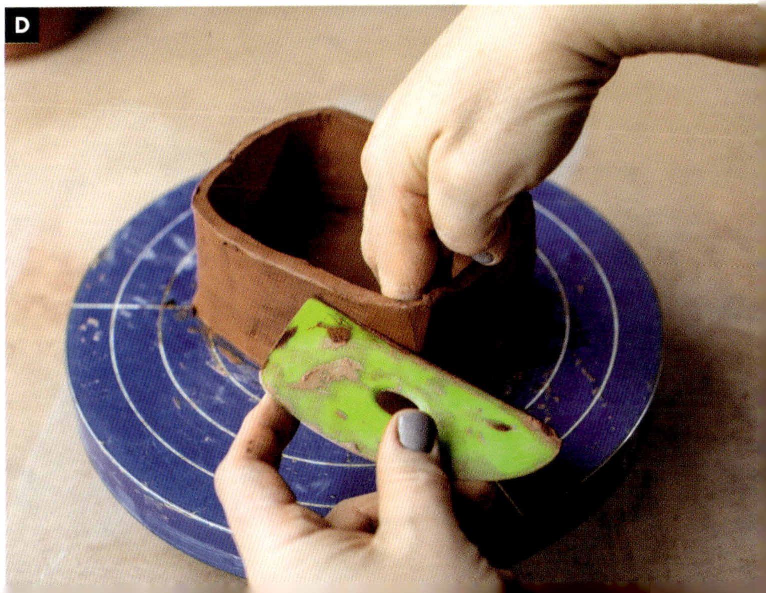

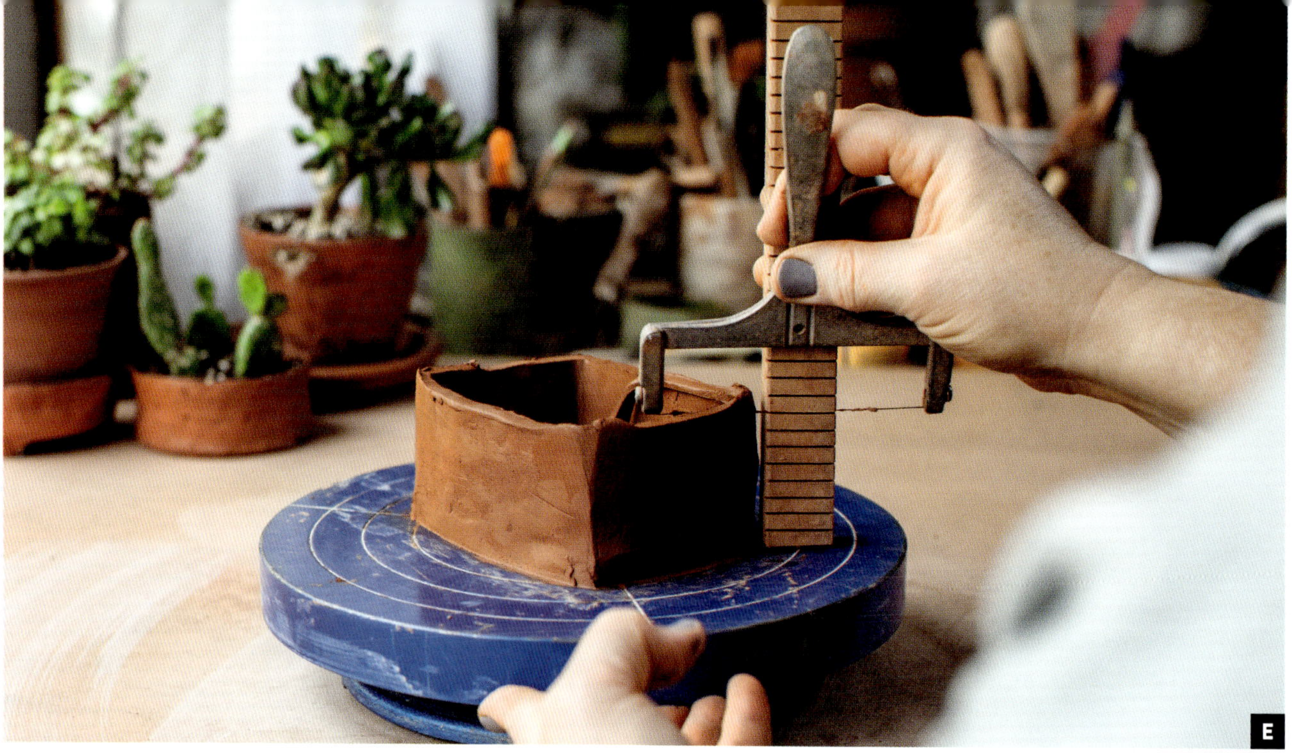

E

Make sure your walls are vertical and not swollen out anywhere, and that all your seams are compressed, and you can't see any dark shadows in the corners or at the connection points. Let the form set up.

When the form is a soft leather hard, use a surform or cut-off tool to even off any discrepancy in height. **[E]**

Let the form equalize and meld together before moving it off your working surface.

Finishing Options

What follows are three different options for finishing this wall hanging. Choose one and execute before moving on to decoration.

OPTION 1

Trace the square of the form you just made onto the remaining slab. Cut out the square. The 4" (10.2 cm) tile section should be leather hard on both sides. Avoid letting the slab droop into the form. (This could cause warping and cracking.) Score the edges of the wall and square, wet one side, and attach. Clean up the edges using a right-angled rib. Use a ruler to measure and mark 1" (2.5 cm) down from the top edge and 2" (5 cm) from the side—this should be the center. Mark first, and then cut a 1" x ½" (2.5 x 1.3 cm) slit out of the center. Slightly bevel the interior top edge. Use a green scrubby or drywall paper to soften the edge. **[NOT PICTURED]**

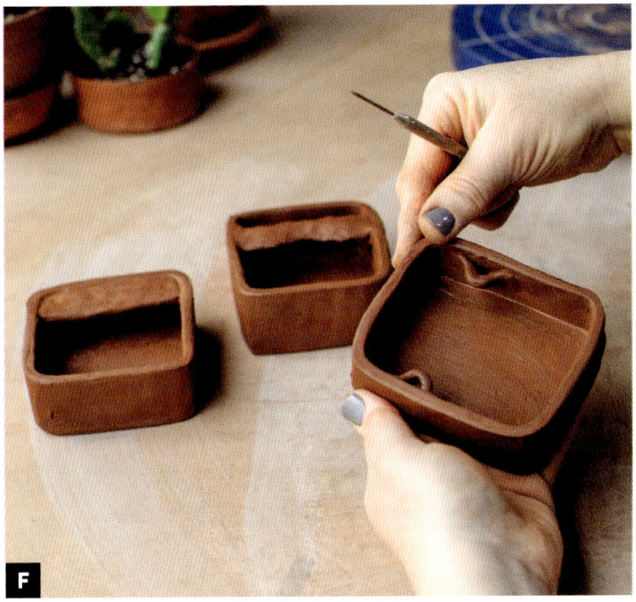

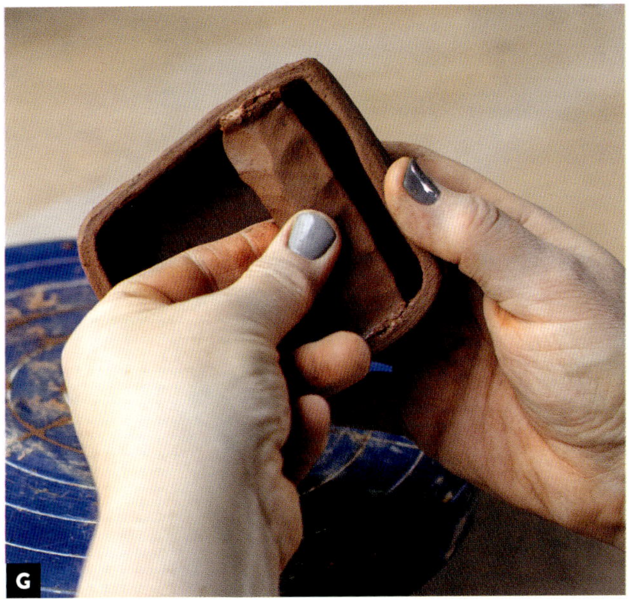

OPTION 2

Make a thin 2.5" (6.3 cm)-long coil. Cut into two equal sections. Drape the coils evenly over the handle end of a needle tool. Gently flatten the outside edges of each coil, leaving the loop form. Let them rest while you deal with the box. On the interior of the box wall tile, measure down 1" (2.5 cm) from the top edge on both sides of the form. Score both sides of the flattened loop, hold up to your mark on the box interior, and score so they line up, loop facing toward the center and just below the edge of the wall. Attach and repeat for the other side. Get as close to the same placement as you can. Clean up. After the form is fired, you can add picture hanging wire to hang the tile. **[F]**

OPTION 3

Make a medium-sized 2" (5 cm)-long coil in the shape of a triangle. Depending on which direction you want the tile to hang, score the sides, top, or possibly a corner. Score the coil accordingly and attach. When attaching the coil, line up toward the outside edge, but take care not to over shadow on the far edge of the tile. Gently give inward direction to the pinched coil. Use a rib to clean up and make sure the coil is flush with the wall. Use a green scrubby or drywall paper to soften the edge of the coil. **[G]**

CLOUDS

What are your thoughts about clouds? My mind springs to childhood daydreams. Remember lying on your back trying to find shapes in the drifting masses overhead?

This project is a way to begin playing with our narrative abilities. You'll figure out how to create a shape of which the viewer knows the intended content. Art is communication at its heart, in that elusive series of concept and idea to execution to eventual showing, and then hopefully comprehension by the viewer. We must start at the beginning: let's daydream about what a cloud looks like . . . and what better way than by looking at clouds? What comes to your mind's eye? How different is it from what you witness when you stare up at the sky? Do you see clouds as the flat, two-dimensional imaginings of a child's drawing? Don't toss that idea away because you think it isn't sophisticated enough. There is something beautiful in children's renderings of clouds: they are kind of like drawing a line around what we imagine to be there. Now the challenge for today: How do we take ephemeral fluff and flesh it out into the 3D world?

In this project we will do so by making hollow forms. What's fun about making cloud pinch pots is that we are creating an enclosed hollow space that will trap air, which will help us form a cloud-like shape around the air. Truly, this process could be applied to any kind of small 3D object: the sky is the limit (pun intended!) Also, note that this would be a good project to pair with the Mobiles on page 94.

TOOLS AND MATERIALS

Basic Tool Kit (page 37)

Kanthal wire

Pliers

Wire snips

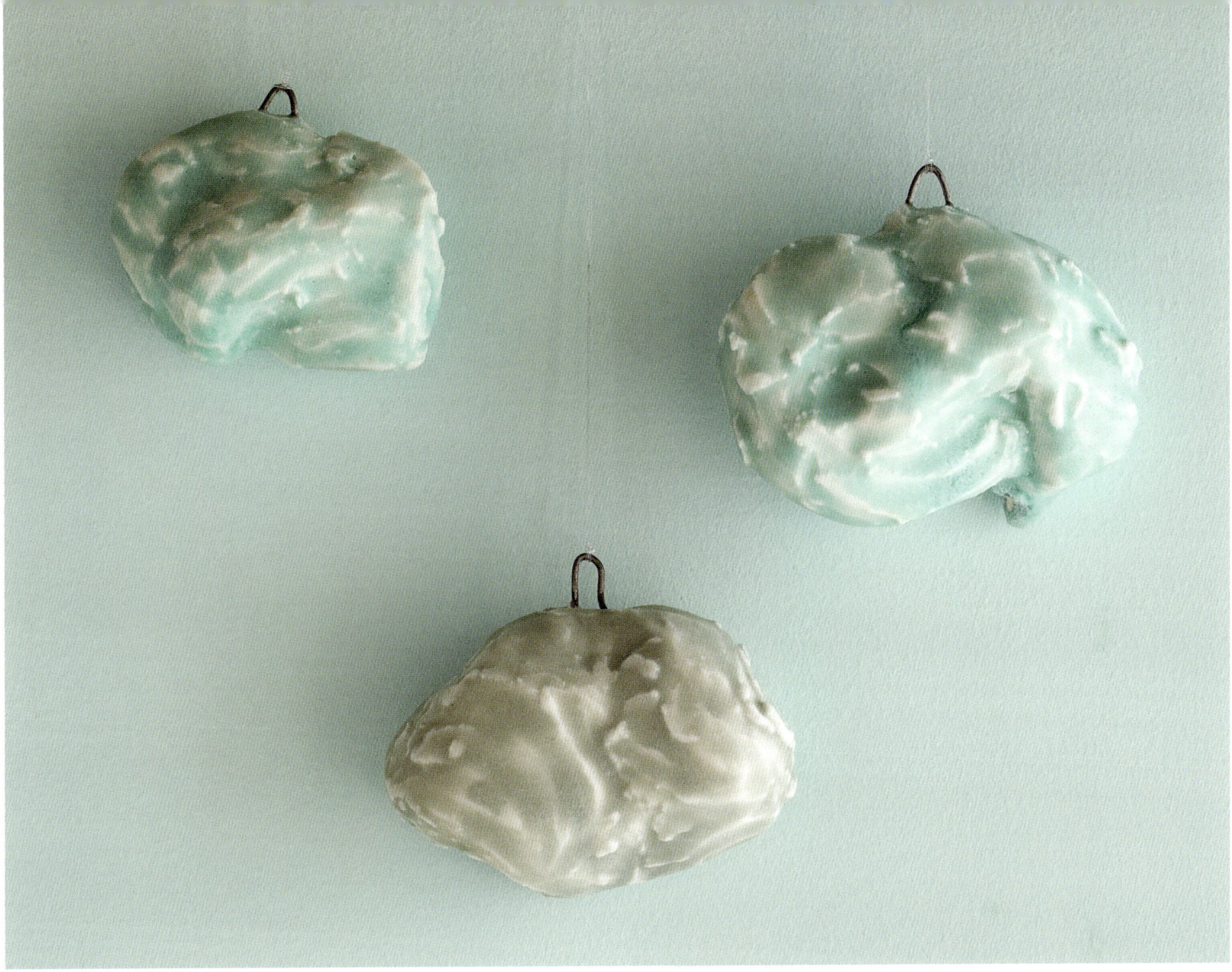

CONE 5 PORCELAIN, celadon style commercial glaze

Cut about 1 lb. (.45 kg) of clay from your bag. Visually aim for a large handful, about the size of a large orange. Separate into two roughly equal sections.

Cup one of the sections in your left hand and place the thumb of your right hand in the center of the piece and begin to "pinch" or, more accurately, compress, the clay. Work in a circular motion from the center out to the edge. **[A]**

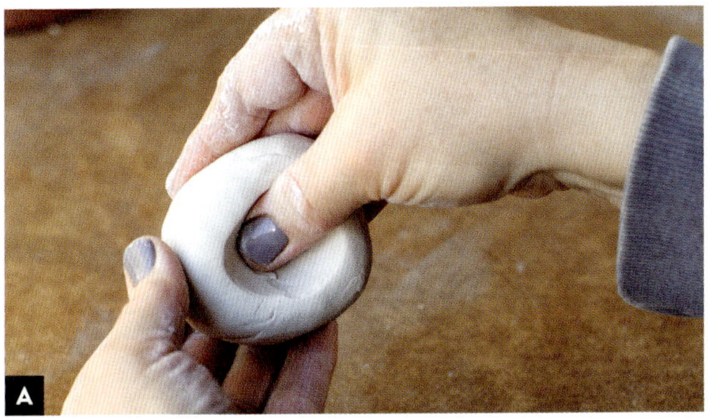
A

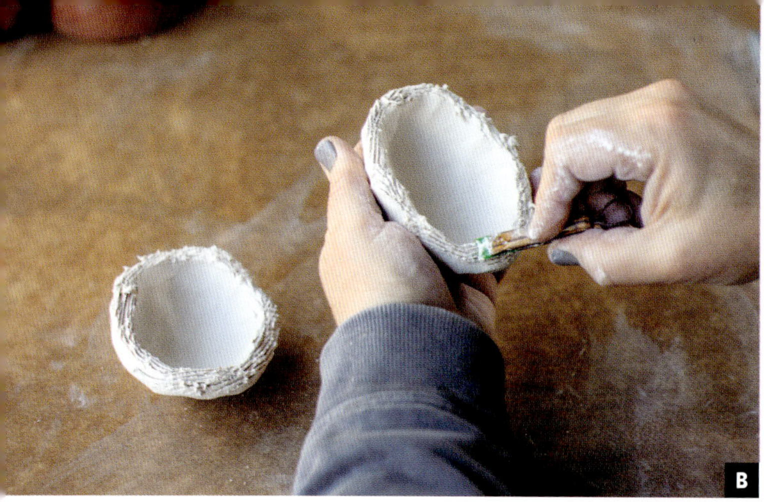

B

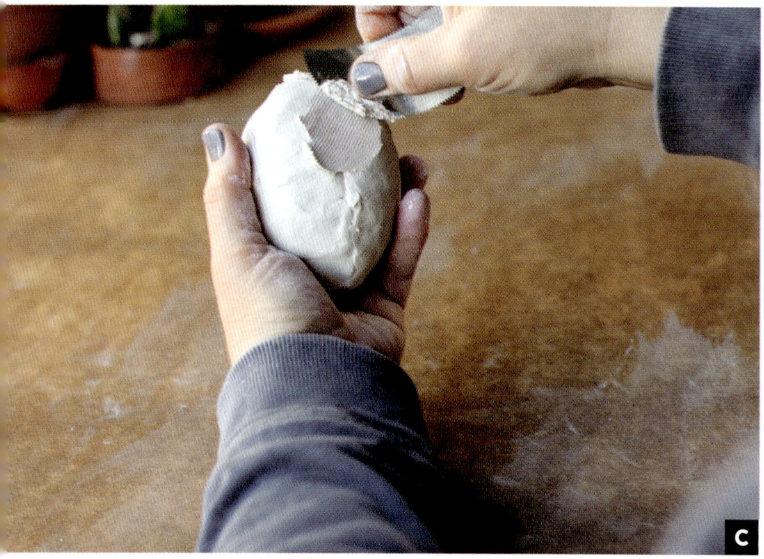

C

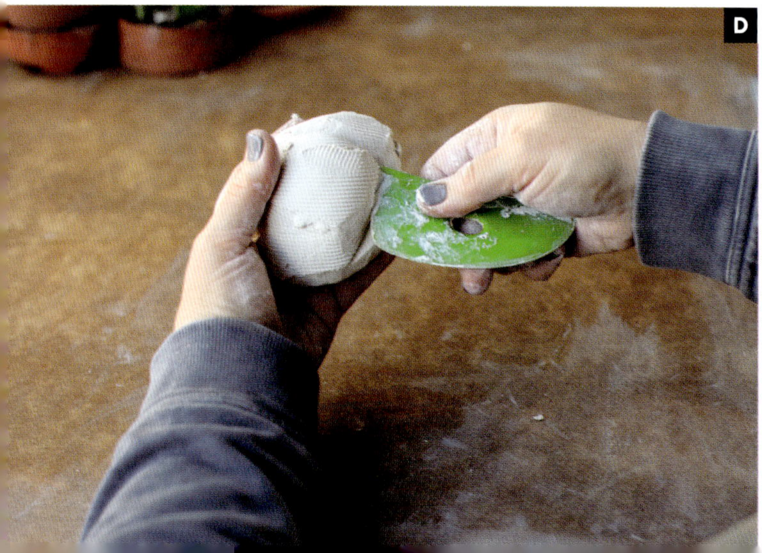

D

Work until the piece has grown in size, roughly ½" (1.3 cm) thick from the center to the edge, aiming for a wide bowl shape. Repeat for the other section. Aim for each piece to be similar in outer edge circumference; this will make attaching them easier.

Attach the two halves. Score the outside edges, wet one side, and attach. It may take a bit of finagling to get them together. Be patient and try to get as much of the wall edge to attach to the other as you can. **[B]**

Clean up the seam. I like using a serrated rib to work the edge together. This will take practice, and you will get better at it over time. **[C]** Let this ball rest for about five minutes, just so that seam is 100 percent together.

Now that the form has rested for a bit, it should still be very soft and workable. Using a wooden knife or a rib, begin shaping your cloud. Go slowly and be careful not to press so hard you bust the seam or cut into the object. The trapped air will give you a bit of pushback that should allow you to maintain the volume of the form. **[D]**

You may need to pause and let the form firm up from time to time in the shaping. Have a soft piece of foam or a towel handy to let it rest. If you rest it on a flat, hard surface, you will find you have a flat spot on your cloud. Make a few forms while you wait, so you can practice and vary scale and thinness to flex your pinching muscles.

When you have a general shape of a form you are happy with, use a serrated rib and begin texturing the cloud; the goal is not to take clay away but to give the surface some movement and directionality. Fluff! **[E]**

Once your shaping is complete, it is imperative that you make a hole someplace inconspicuous on the form. With no hole, the trapped air in this object is enough to make it hazardous to fire in a kiln. It is much easier and safer to make a hole before you put it on the shelf to dry. It is too easy to forget this step! **[F]**

NOTE *Air, when heated, expands. If clay is trapping that air, the object could explode in the kiln, making a huge mess and destroying your object.*

As a somewhat thicker form with damp air on the inside, this project may take some time to dry out.

NOTE *You may want to think about how you are going to display the object. If you're using it for a mobile project, or maybe an ornament, you may want to add a hanging catch with Kanthal wire, or possibly just a drilled hole at the top so you can add something post-firing. This will also solve your trapped-air problem.* **[G]**

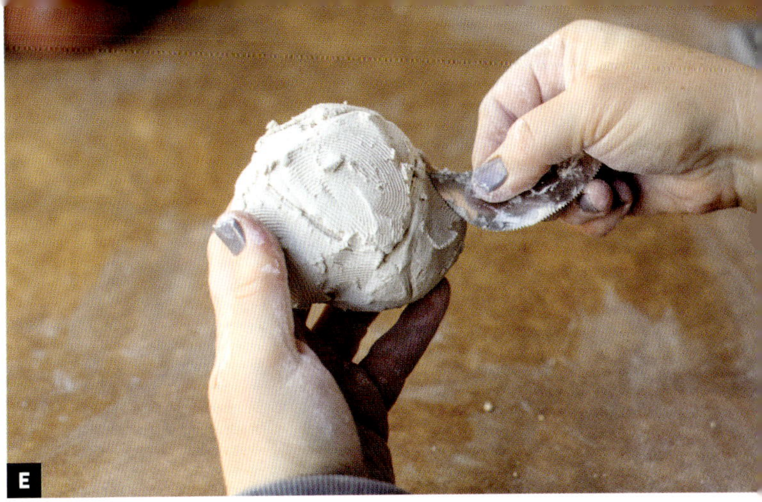

E

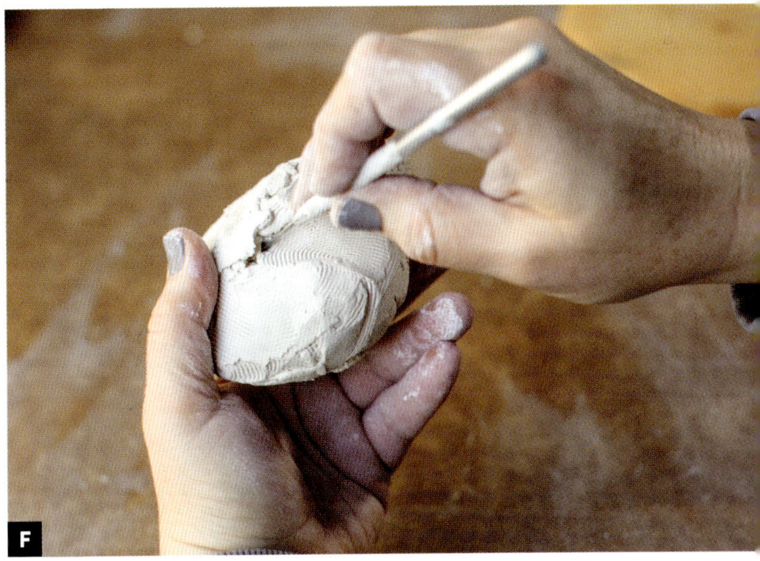

F

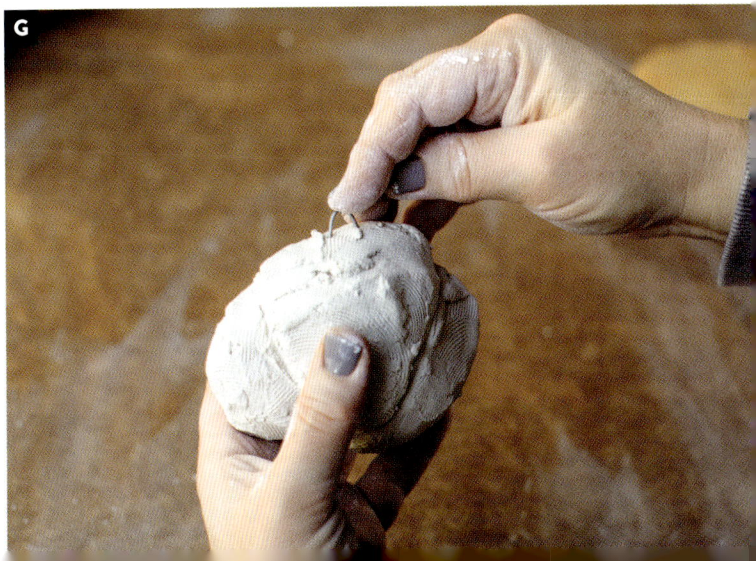

G

SOAP DISH

One of the questions I often ask my students is whether they live with handmade objects. Do they use their own pottery? Sometimes in the beginning, we make a variety of things and give them away, as we are in love with making and just want to keep making. This means, in some ways, we are blind to negative outcomes.

For example, one of my first gifted objects, which survives to this day, is a soap dish built like a clawfoot bathtub. Cute, right? Well, it would be cute and more functional if I had thought to put a drainage hole in it! Luckily it has mostly been used to hold hairbands, from what I'm told.

Anyway, when we observe our space and the functional items in it, handmade or not, we can develop an understanding about why things are made the way they are. When we use things we make, we learn how to make them function better. What a maker is always trying to do is find balance between aesthetic choices (how things look) and the functionality of the object. This is something I still struggle with, especially when developing new forms. There is a give-and-take with some objects, and we learn over time and practice and use where we have wiggle room to make objects interesting and beautiful as well as useful.

This project is my take on what a soap dish should be. It is funky and bizarre, but fun and practical in a weird way. Its design is based on how I use bar soap and my need for a nail brush to get all the clay off my hands. (This is always where you should begin a new functional-object investigation: how do you engage with it?) We will be incorporating high-fire Kanthal wire to keep the soap from resting in the water that may drip below! Curious? Let's get started!

TOOLS AND MATERIALS

Basic Tool Kit (page 37)

Kanthal wire

Pliers

Wire snips

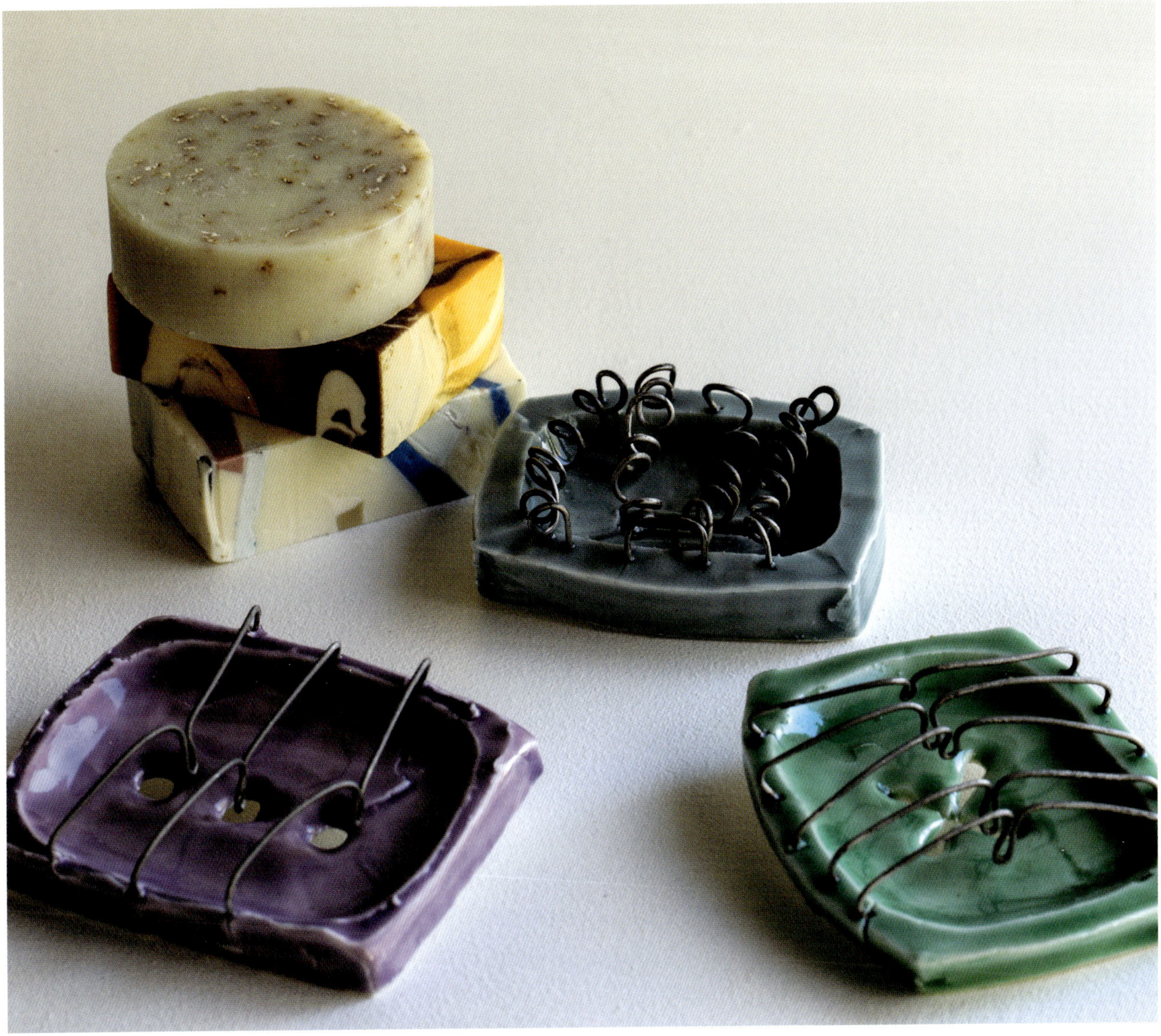

CONE 5, porcelain clay, celadon style commercial glaze

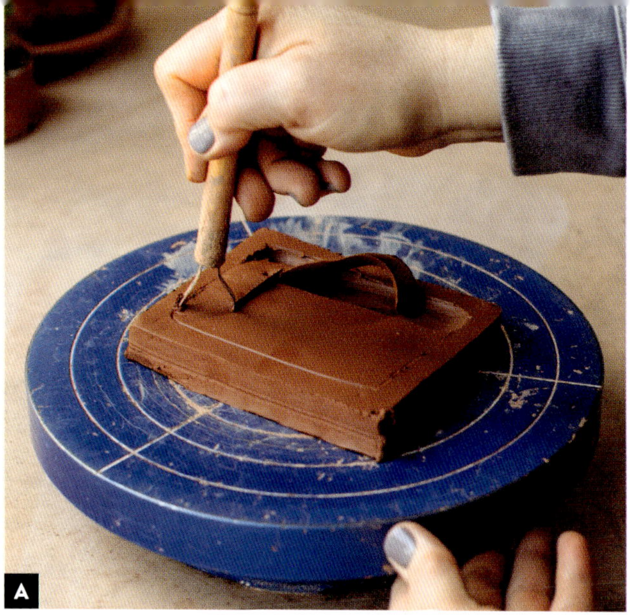

A

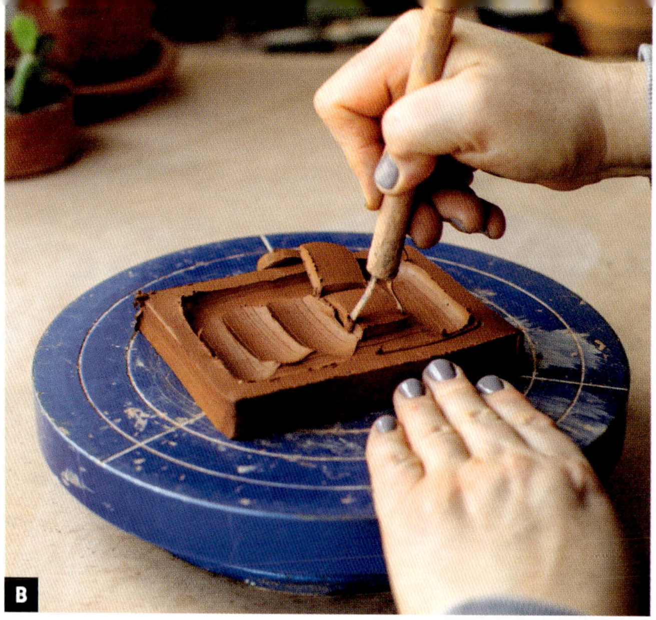

B

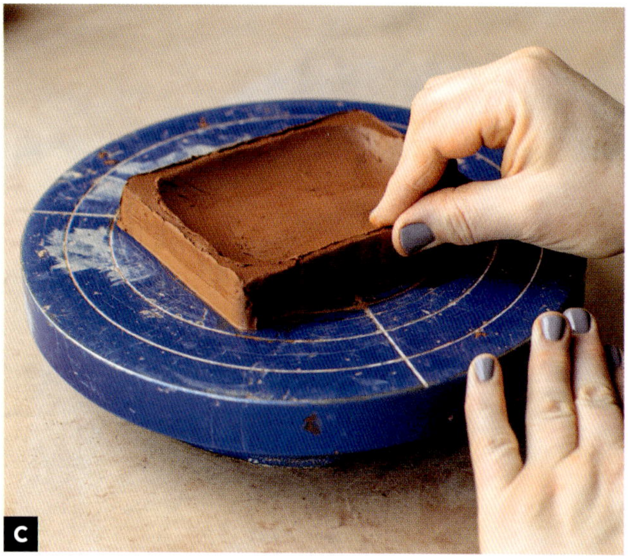

C

Using a ruler, measure out a shape 4" (10 cm) long and 3" (7.6 cm) wide on a piece of paper, and cut it out with scissors. Congratulations—you just made a template! It is that easy. This is the template for the soap dish.

Roll out a small thick slab, about ¾" (1.9 cm) to 1" (2.5 cm) thick and a bit bigger than the shape of your footprint/template. Use your template as a guide to cut out the shape. (Use a fettling knife or a needle tool for the thicker clay.) Try to keep the edges crisp. Once you're done, let the slab dry on a flat surface, firming up until it's soft leather hard.

Using a needle tool, make a line about ½" (1.3 cm) from the edge all around the top. This will be your guide when using a trim tool to cut into and dig out a shallow dish. **[A]** This part can be a bit tricky; start someplace mid-wall and gently dig in about ⅛" (.32 cm) to ¼" (.63 cm) deep and make a shallow "dish." After you are done carving out the dish, use a metal rib to clean up the interior. Work until you have a nice shallow dish and make sure you clean up and soften the edges. Let it firm up again to a soft leather hard. **[B] [C]**

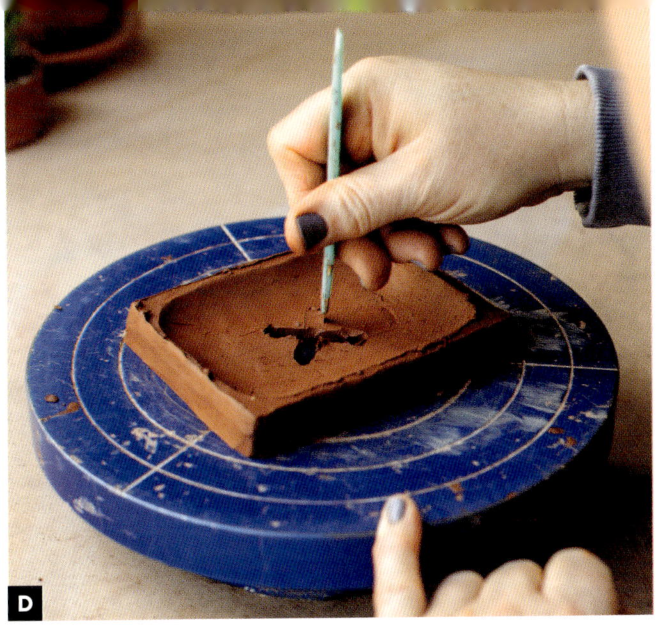

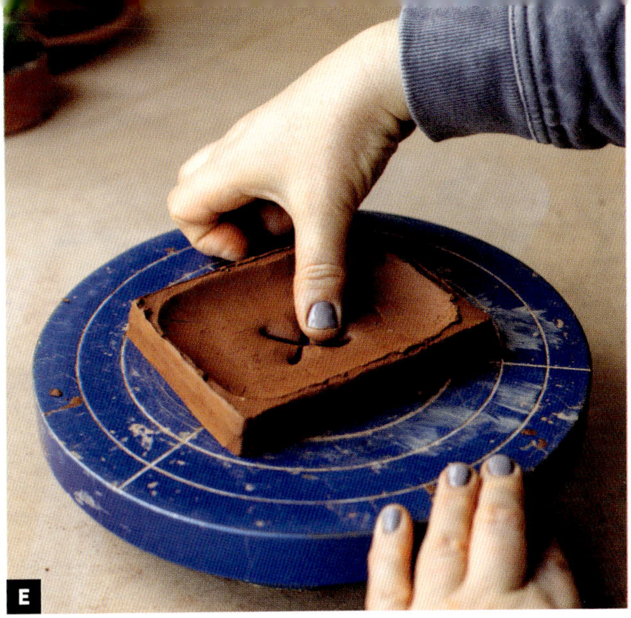

Let's make some holes for drainage. Using the blunt end of a wood knife, make an *X* in the center of the dish. Use a scalpel to cut around the edge of the *X* shape. Remove the cutout and gently squish the *X* shape to soften the edges. This is a quick method and can be done without waiting for the clay to get super firm. **[D] [E]**

VARIATION You are welcome to cut out any shape you like. I also play with using drill bits to make holes. Your form should be close to medium leather hard. Use a ruler to create grid a pattern and use a medium-sized drill bit to create holes at the intersection of the grid. You can attach the drill bits to an actual drill or use your fingers to twist the drill bit into the clay. To create successful, clean drill holes, I have a few tips. You want your clay a perfect (medium) leather hard. If it's too dry, you run the risk of cracking the clay and punching through to the backside, with no way to clean that up. If it's too wet, you will get gummy and mushy clay around the holes, and the result is a poorly defined drain. Let your form firm up, and try different stages of dryness. (Make a slab to practice on if this confuses you.) For any burrs that happen, let the clay dry a little and then can use a dry paintbrush to clean up the holes.

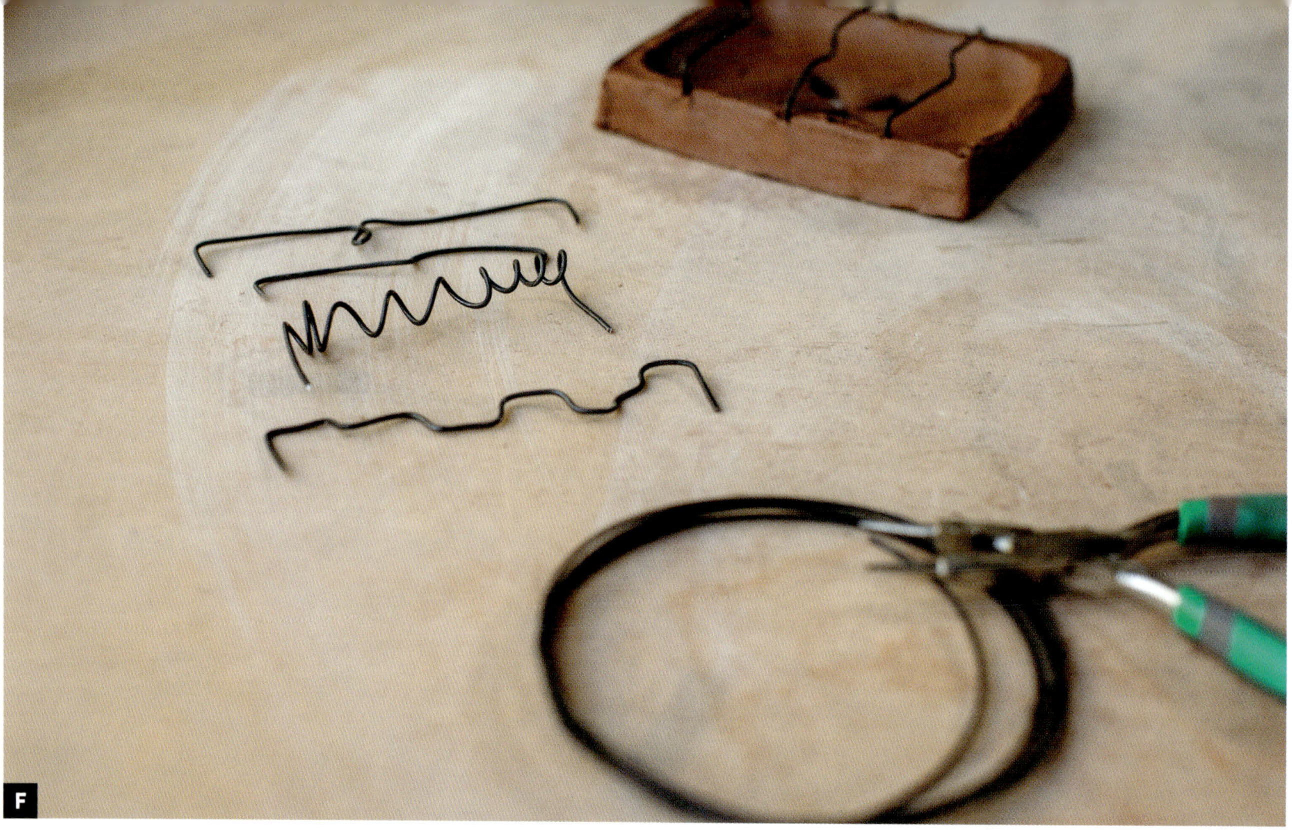

F

This is where this soap dish gets a little funky. Get out the Kanthal wire and your wire snips and a pair of needle-nose pliers (helpful for shaping, depending on wire gauge), and have some fun! **[F]** In the image above, there are a variety of patterns and ideas for shapes easy to achieve with your wire and pliers. I suggest testing new materials so you understand how they will react with your clay and glaze and firing method. (For this soap dish, the form is glazed and the wire is not.) Cut some wire and try bending it. (I used bailing wire to practice making a variety of shapes before I moved onto the Kanthal wire, as it's inexpensive and usually found at the local hardware store.) As with anything, it takes some practice to create consistent bends and shapes. Remember that your ends will go about ¼" (.63 cm) to ½" (1.3 cm) into the clay, so make sure you leave your ends a bit longer to have some ease of assembly.

TIPS ON USING THIS HIGH-FIRE WIRE. It survives the firing well, but it can become a bit brittle, and maybe a bit flaky. Spanning long distances is not recommended. (A heavier gauge will hold up better; in the beginning, try to keep it under a 3" [7.6 cm] span.) Your clay will shrink around the wire as it dries and fires, so small cracks can occur, as well as possible breakage. Don't panic—there are always risks when combining materials, but the more you practice and understand what occurs, the more you will be able to compensate and have successful outcomes.

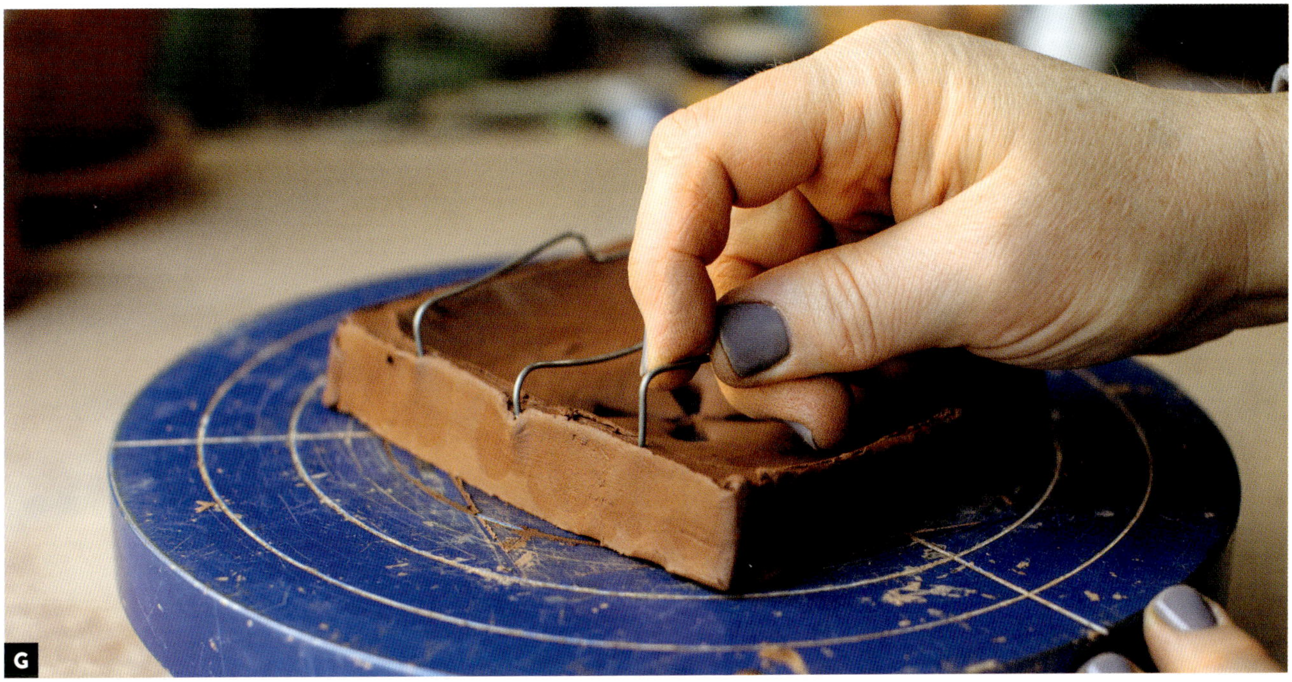

Cut out pieces of wire and shape, using the shapes to grid out where you want your wire props. Just press down gently to get an indention where the holes need to go. **[G]** Count and make enough shapes to finish your form. Make sure they are all close to the same size, width, and height.

NOTE *For this project, I decided to use wire as my rest perch, where I intend to rest a nail brush and a small bar of soap. My goal with the wires is that as the soap shrinks through use, it will be able to sit easily on the bed of props.*

Using a tiny drill bit, create a series of small holes where the wires will slide into. Or, if your clay is soft enough, gently press the wires into the appropriate holes. If your holes are a little bigger than the wire, I recommend dipping your wire into some thick slip, which will fill in any gaps in the assembly. If your drill holes feel tight, be careful and press in gently. There is more chance of cracking, as the holes will get tighter around the wires. (Clay shrinks, but wire does not.) If it feels like too tight a squeeze, gauge up your drill bit, re-drill the holes, and insert a bit of slip. The wetter the clay, the easier it is to insert the wire, but the clay shrinks more. If the clay is leather hard, it has already shrunk a bit. Drilling the holes will help ease any cracking.

Clean up any sharp corners of the form, and use a soft, damp brush to clean up any stray slip or burrs.

MOBILES

To be honest, I had visions of making Calder-style mobiles when I came up with this project. Grand mobiles that take up a whole room . . . I was thinking big! Then I realized I was getting carried away with myself, especially because I had never attempted a mobile before! What I realized when I got into this project idea is that clay is a very different material than wood or metal. No matter how I approach teaching this project, every person's interpretation will be vastly different. (Which is awesome, and I can't wait to see what you all come up with!)

In some ways, this is another interpretation of the cloud project, and a practice in just how different clay can respond to our touch. This project can be done with any shape you want. I toyed with the idea of getting some dinosaur cookie cutters and playing with my nephews, for example. This project is very approachable and straightforward in the making. Have fun—this project would be perfect to set up with the kids in your life or with your "stitch and bitch" group!

Keep in mind, assembly is required. Arranging the pieces into a cohesive and balanced mobile will take some patient trial and error. But that will happen later, so don't stress.

TOOLS AND MATERIALS

Basic Tool Kit (page 37)

Kanthal wire

Pliers

Wire snips

NOTE Post-firing you will also need a fishing line and bailing wire to construct the hanging elements.

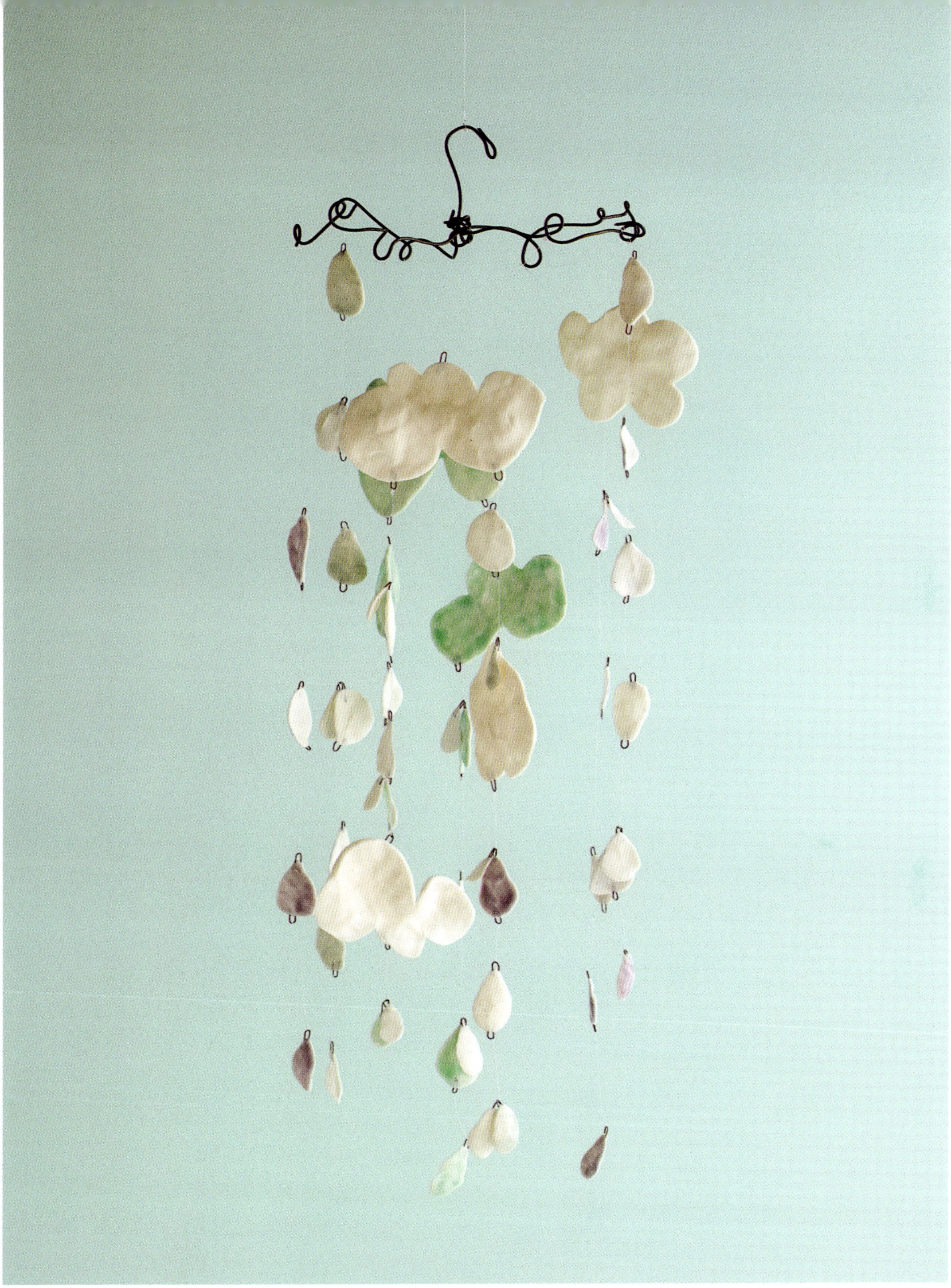

CONE 5, exposed porcelain clay and celadon style commercial glaze

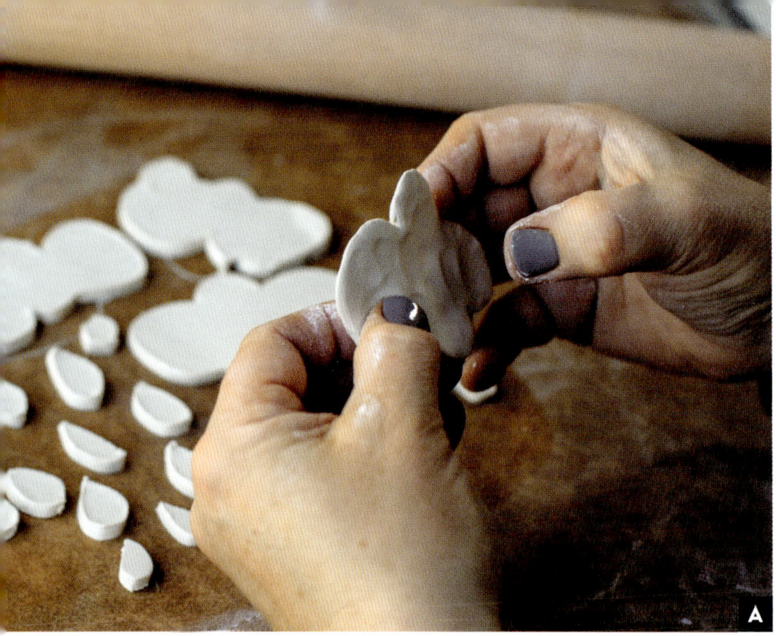

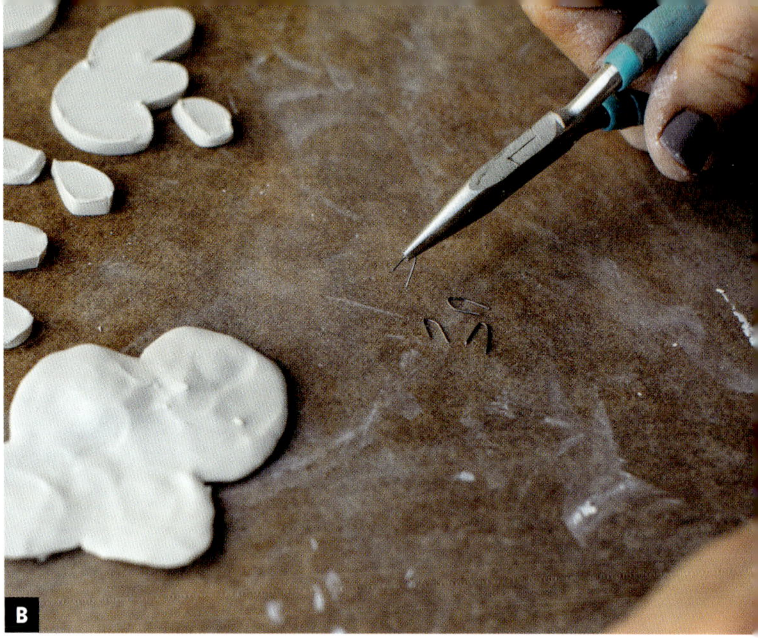

Roll out a 1' (30.5 cm) square slab, roughly 3⁄8" (.98 cm) thick. The thinner you can work with, the better. (Keeping the overall weight low can be important.) Also keep in mind you want to be able to handle and manipulate the clay and still get a small Kanthal wire hook inserted.

Using a scalpel, cut out your shapes. I chose freehand cutouts of clouds and raindrops for this project. Make the cutouts a bit smaller than you think is the prefect size. You will be pinching and manipulating, so the shape will grow a bit.

Remove the excess clay and put it back in your bag. Begin to pinch and shape the pieces. Work from the center out. I chose a translucent porcelain for this project, so the thinner the clay, the more translucent it gets. But any clay will work. Focus on creating soft, billowy textures and forms for the clouds and raindrops. This process takes longer than you think . . . slow down and enjoy the texture and feel of the clay. Refine your hand skills. **[A]**

Once all your shapes are done, cover them with plastic, keeping them as soft as you can until you insert the wire. For the wire hangers, use pliers and a thin-gauge Kanthal wire to make lots of small *U* shapes. Mine are roughly 1⁄2" to 3⁄4" (1.3 to 1.9 cm) long, bent in the center. The process goes quicker if you cut out a bunch and have them at the ready. **[B]**

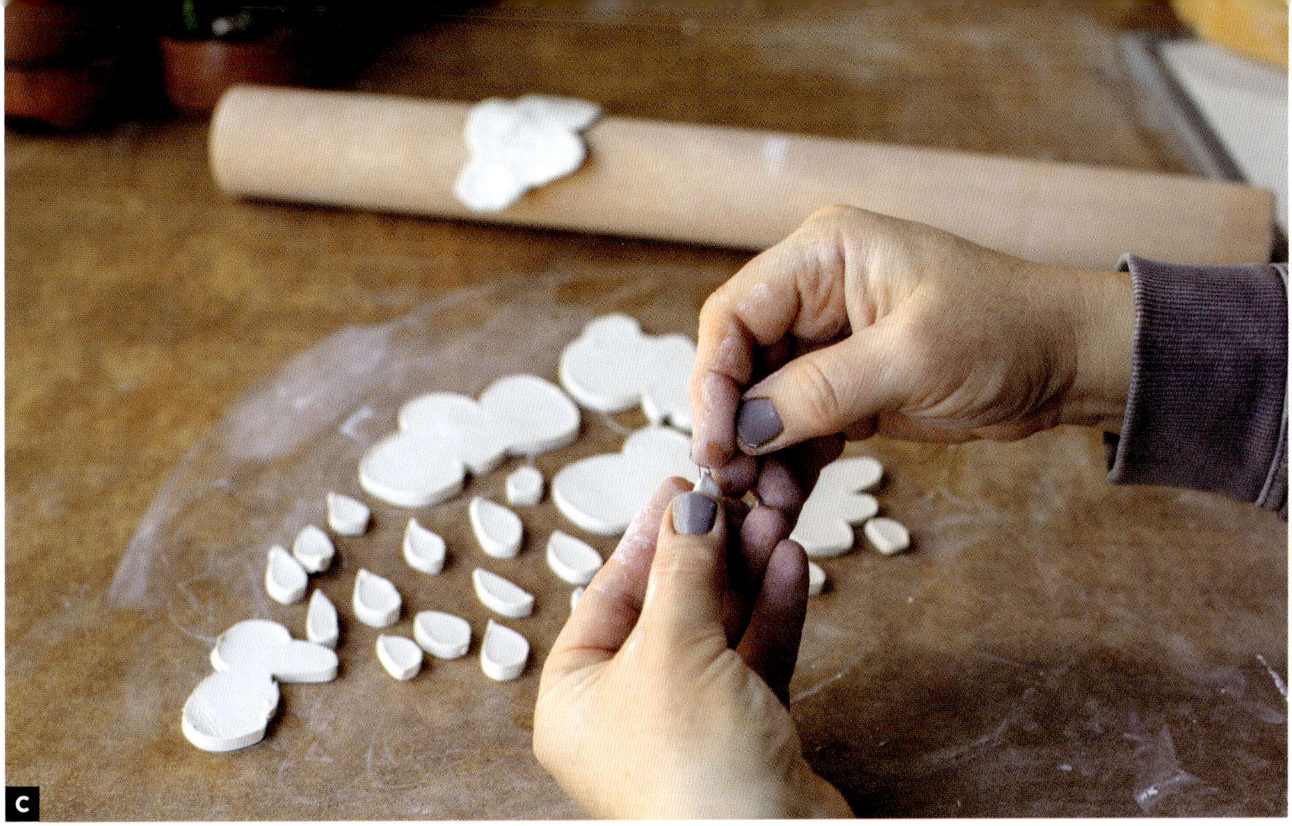
C

Insert the wire. Do this when the clay is still very soft. I suggest laying out the pieces according to how you envision the mobile going together, and then inserting the wires. Play around, make extras, and give yourself some possible alternative choices. **[C]**

NOTE *If you can't find Kanthal wire or find this part too challenging, add wire or some kind of hanging device after the firing. There are lots of choices at your local hardware or craft store, such as epoxy or hot glue. Experiment with materials and find what works for you.*

In my example, I glazed some pieces and left others raw to play round with hints of color. You do what you think is best! Once you have the pieces out of the kiln, experiment with assembly. I used bailing wire (found at the hardware store) and a fine fishing line to assemble the mobile.

NOTE *Again, play around with materials that you find work for you and to which you have access. Remember, if you don't like how it turns out, take it apart and reassemble. Nothing is finished until you decide it is. Enjoy!*

CANDELABRA

This project came to me in a dream. (Are you dreaming about clay projects yet?) This dream probably happened because I had candelabras on the brain from researching and daydreaming about this project and conjuring up my internal stories related to candles. To me this idea is all about play, ceremony, and self-care. When do you light candles in your home? Candles are lit in my home when I slow down and become quiet and reflective, making the space around me a relaxing place to spend time, or when I am entertaining company and sharing a meal. For me, this project is about connecting beauty and ceremony within a playful and practical (don't want to burn the house down) interpretation. Although there are all the practical needs of a candlestick holder to be met, I am making something that I want to hold space in the landscape of someone's home.

Here are several things to ponder if you decide to venture from the script: First, a candle holder should be stable and not at all prone to tipping over (again, avoid making a fire hazard!). This is true whether it's a single candlestick holder or an elaborate, multi-candle sculpture. Second, know the height and width of the candle for which you are designing. There's not much worse than a beautiful holder that doesn't properly fit the candles you want to use with it. Last, in addition to affixing the candles to the form, there should be a receptacle for dripping wax; you don't want to ruin any furniture. Once you figure out those elements, this project can branch off to any number of interpretations.

TOOLS AND MATERIALS

Basic Tool Kit (page 37)

Ruler

Template (page 162)

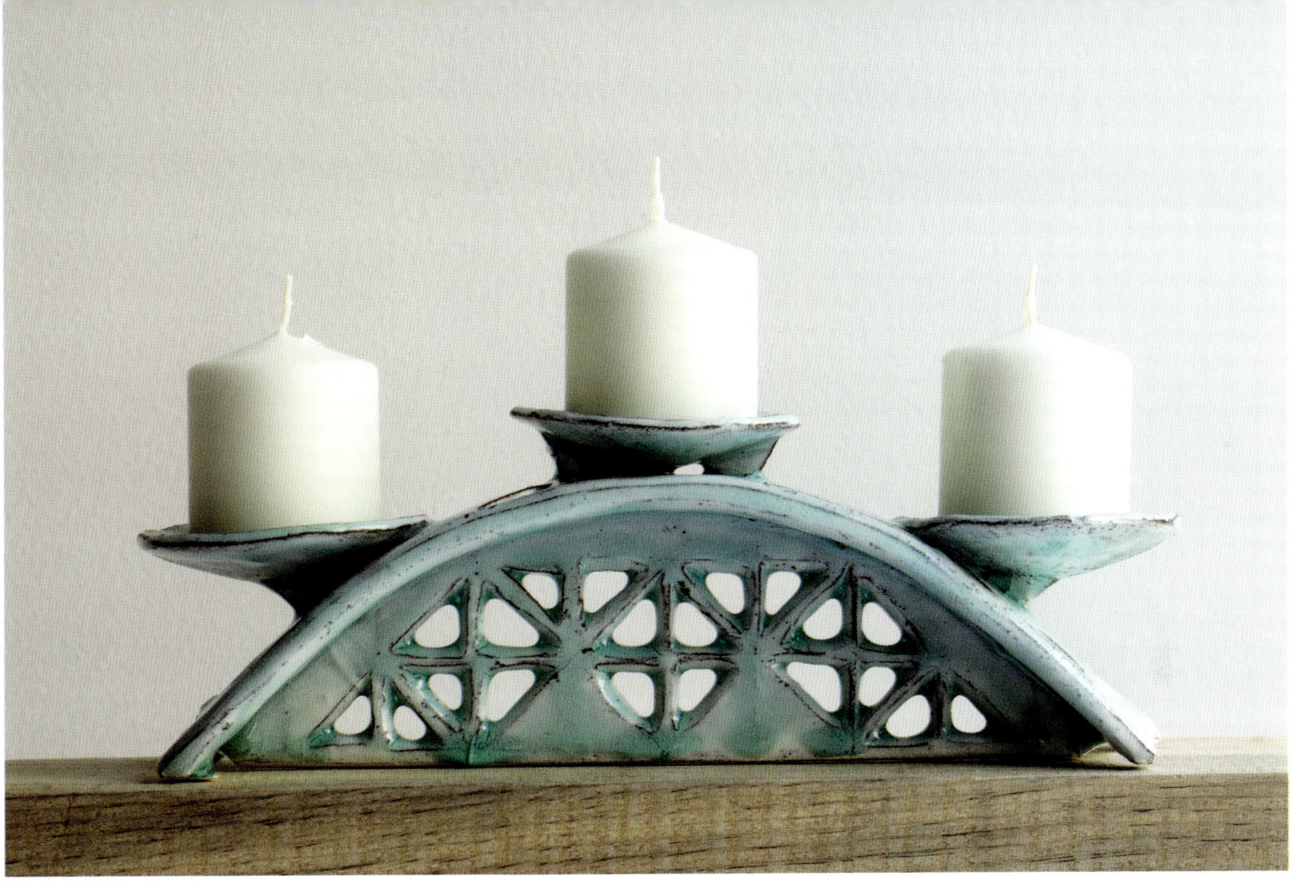

CONE 5, red clay, white slip, commercial glaze

Roll out a 6" (15.2 cm)-square slab about ¼" to ½" (.63 to 1.3 cm) thick. Using the template for the candle cup (page 162), cut out three of the shapes. This template can be scaled up or down depending on your preferred candle size. Bevel and score along the pie-shaped cutout. Repeat for all the cups, then set aside. **[A]**

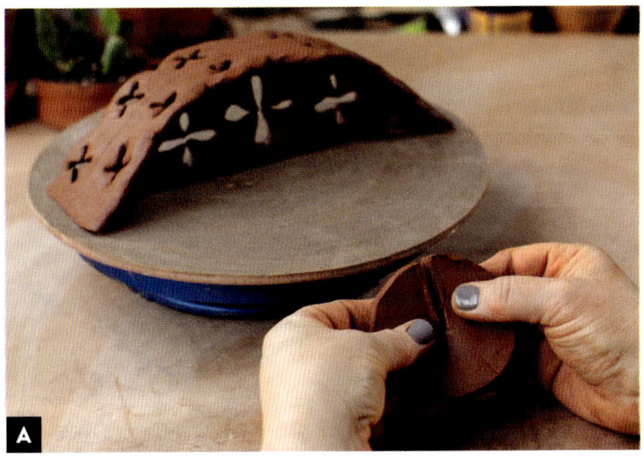

A

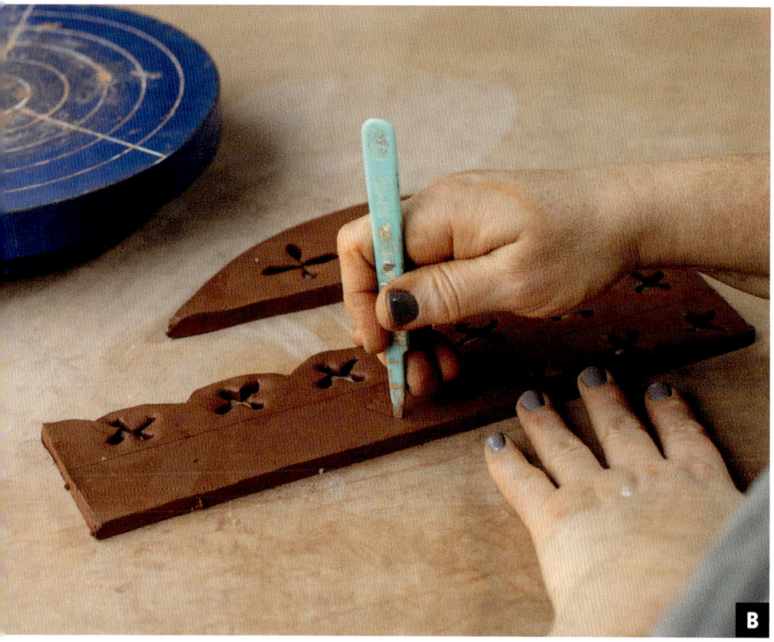

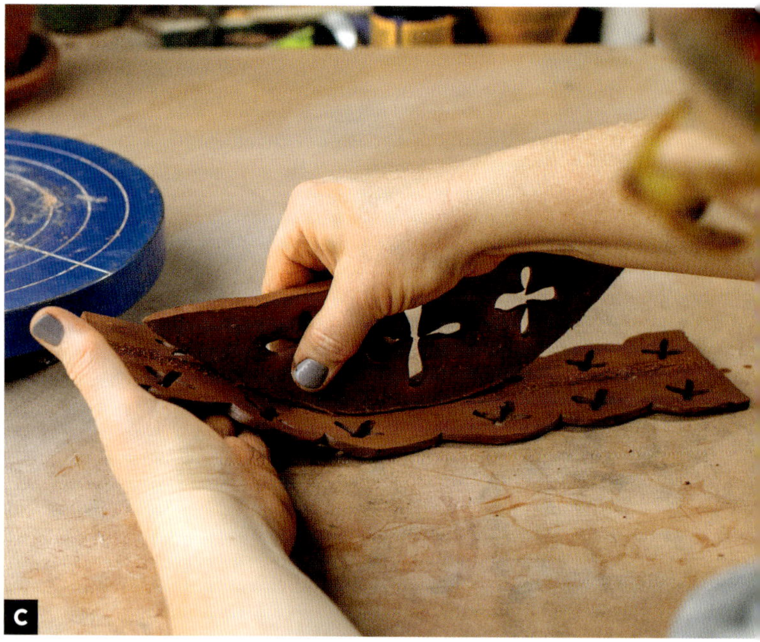

While you are waiting for the candle cups to firm up to a soft leather hard, prepare another slab, closer to ½" (1.3 cm) thick. From this piece, you will cut the half-circle template (10" [25.4 cm] long by 3" [7.6 cm] wide) and a rectangle 12.5" (31.7 cm) long by 3" (7.6 cm) wide. These will need to firm up to a soft leather hard. You can design a cutout pattern or apply texture to the pieces at this stage. (Save some of your scraps for a few steps from now by wrapping them in plastic.) **[B]**

Refine and clean up the candle cups, address the edges, and "finish" the cups. I do this with a surform around the outside and a serrated rib to give some texture to the inside and outside of the cups, and then gently compress the edge. Set aside under plastic.

Assemble the base. With a needle tool and a ruler, mark a center line down the rectangular slab and score a ½" (1.3 cm) swath down the length. On the half-circle piece, score the curved top edge. With the rectangular piece flat on the table, center the half-circle piece on top, matching the scored sections. Press down firmly, but don't distort the shape. Once it is secure, bring up the sides of the rectangle to meet the shape at the score marks. **[C]**

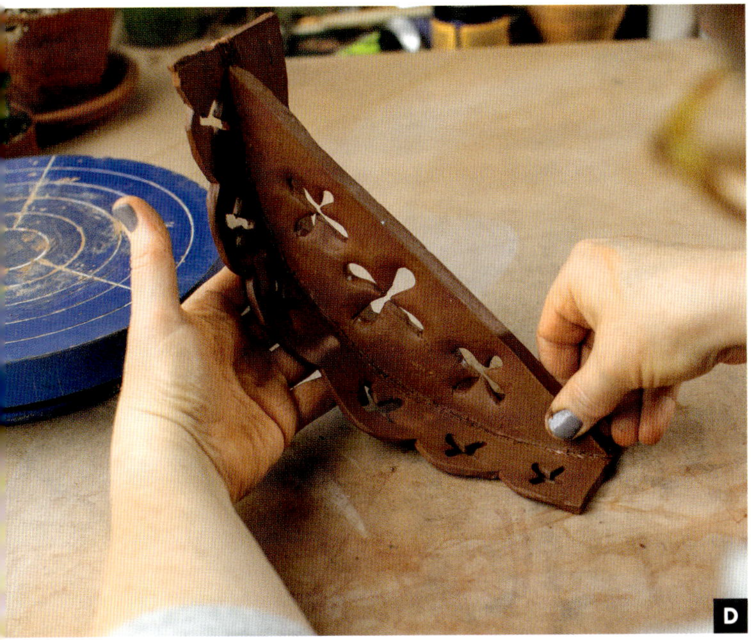

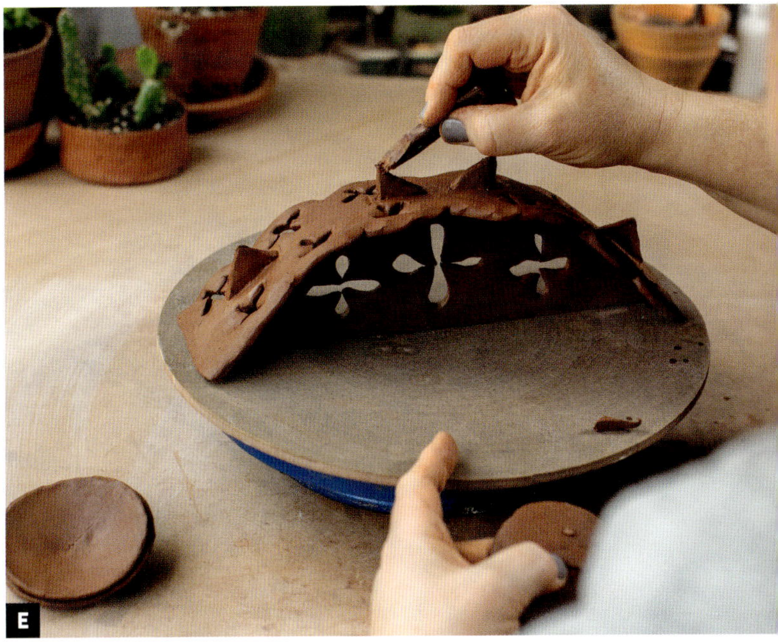

There should be a bit of overhang at the ends. Using a scalpel or a surform, cut the ends down to match or cut them just a little extra off the center brace. **[D]**

Flip the object right side up. Check how it sits; you may need to address some of the supports with a surform to make sure the form doesn't wobble. Another solution is to give the form feet at the ends and surform down the center brace a bit.

Attach the candle cups. Using some leftover bits of your leather-hard slabs, cut out two rectangles ½" (1.3 cm) tall by ¾" (1.9 cm) wide. Cut those in half on the diagonal. These are the braces to attach your candle cups. Find the center on your base and set the small triangles, long side down, about an inch (2.5 cm) apart from each other along the center line, with the tall corner of the triangle toward the outside. Center your candle cup and step back and take a look: make adjustments to make sure your cup sits level. Score and attach the triangles to the base. Then score and attach the cup to the triangle supports. **[E]**

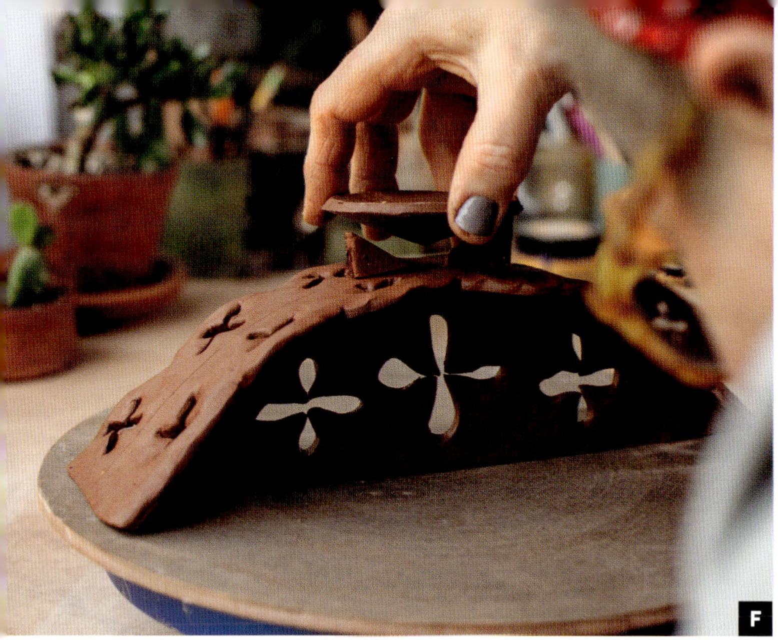

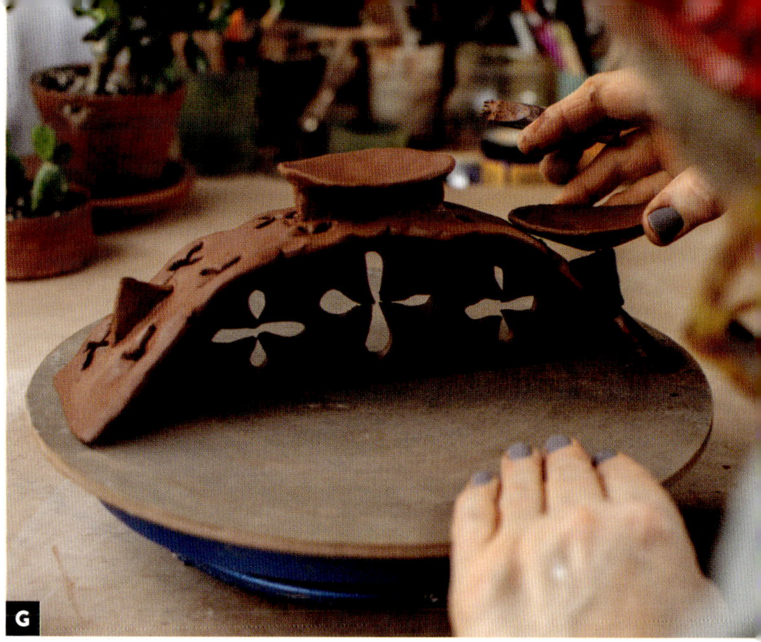

Remember that the side cups will hang off the base a bit (refer to finished candelabra image on page 99), so your remaining triangles will act as a perch. Place the triangles long side down, with the tall side toward the outside, about 1½" (3.8 cm) up from the tabletop. Place your candle cup on the perch and make sure your cups don't overlap with the center cup. They can be close, but you want them to be apart from each other. Adjust if needed, and then score and attach the triangle first and then the cup. Part of the side cups will attach to the base as well as the attached triangle. Repeat for the other side. **[F] [G]**

Clean up all your attachments, make sure the form is still stable, and then let dry slowly under plastic.

MAKE A SHRINK SLAB (OF THE SAME WORKING CLAY). Make a slab ¼" (.63 cm) thick, 3" (7.6 cm) wide, and 10" to 11" (25.4 to 27.9 cm) long. Big enough for the candelabra to sit on and not hang over. Let the two pieces dry together and then fire the candelabra and the shrink slab together for the bisque and the final firing. (Do not glaze the bottom footprint of the candelabra.) This will help prevent any shrinkage cracks during the firing process. As the clay fires, it shrinks and drags across the kiln shelf, which can put stress on longer, heavier forms—a shrink (or waster slab) can save your piece. Discard the shrink slab after the final glaze firing.

GALLERY

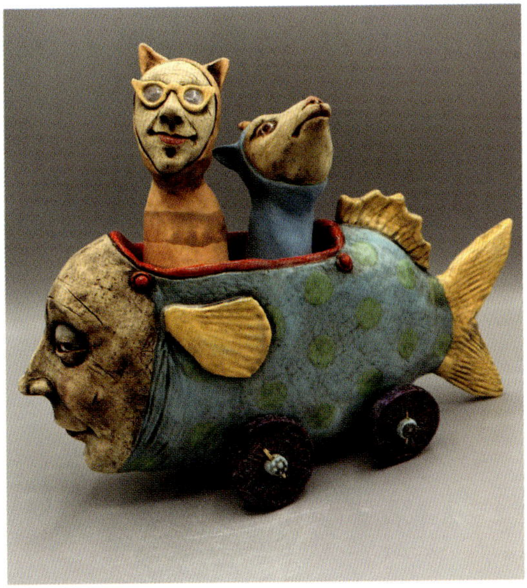

Jeanine Pennell, *Blue Fish Car*, slab and pinched.
Photo Courtesy of the Artist

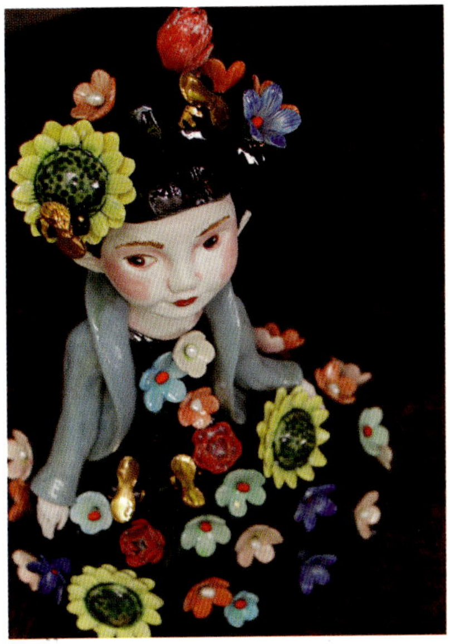

Clairy Laurence, *Serendipity*, pinch built.
Photo Courtesy of the Artist

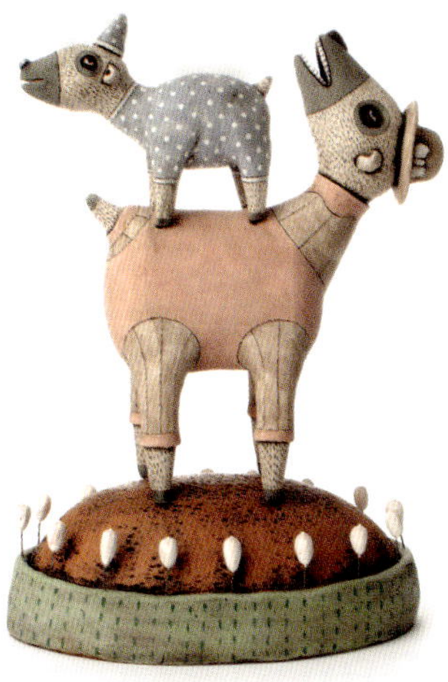

Rickie Barnett, *Mother May I?*, slab and pinch.
Photo Courtesy of the Artist

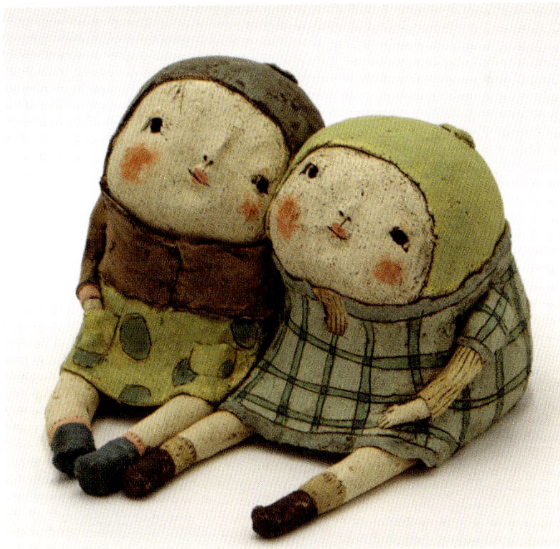

Anne-Sophie Gilloen, *une belle aventure*, coil built.
Photo Courtesy of the Artist

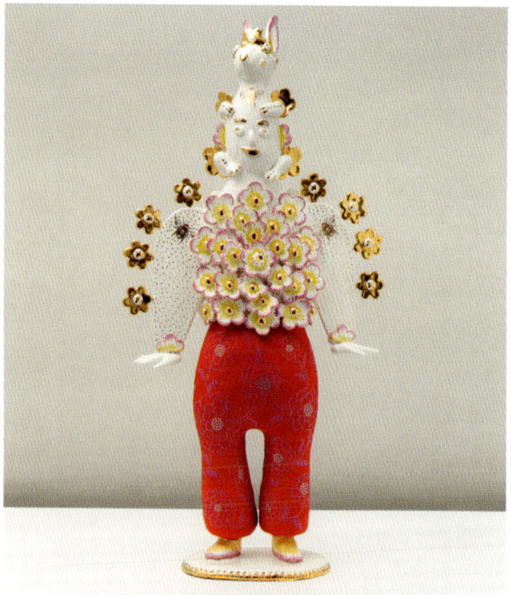

Vipoo Srivilasa, *My Sunshine Doesn't Come from the Sky*, pinch and coil. *Photo Courtesy of the Artist*

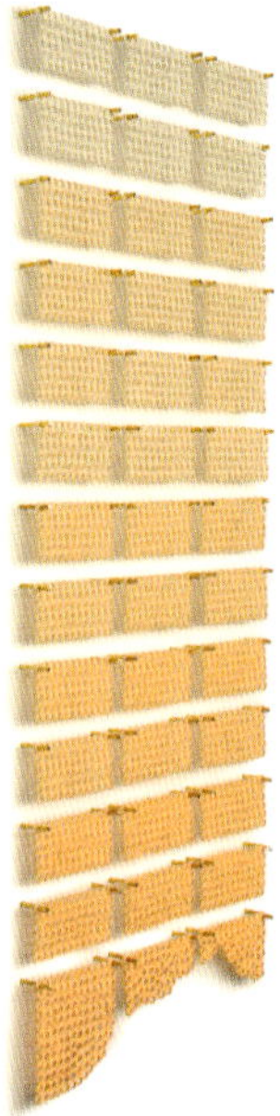

Amanda Salov, *Mount Constance*, pinch and assemblage. *Photo Courtesy of the Artist*

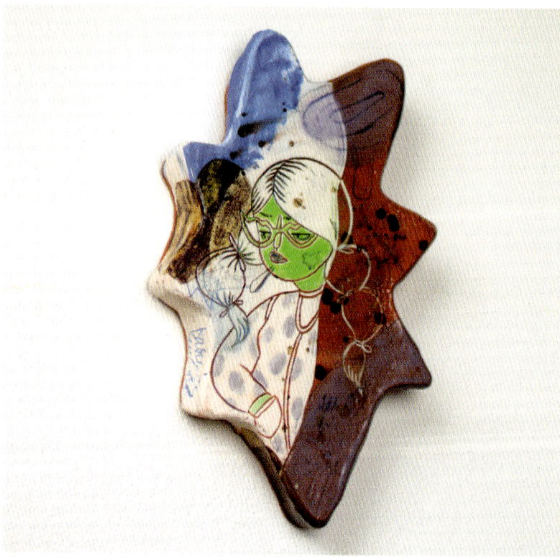

Kristy Moreno, *Wall Tile*, slab built. *Photo Courtesy of the Artist*

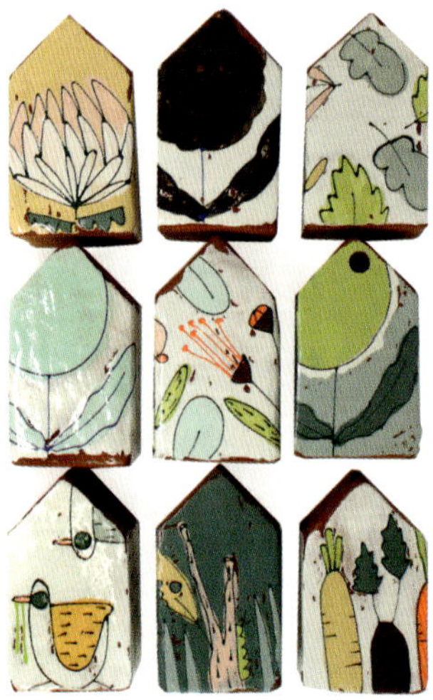

Catie Miller, *Houses*, slab built. *Photo Courtesy of the Artist*

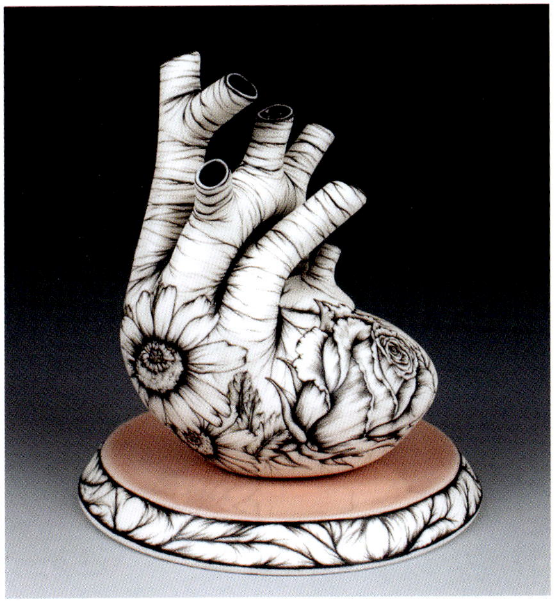

Mallory Wetherell, *Burst*, hand-built porcelain, hollowed out forms. *Photo Courtesy of the Artist*

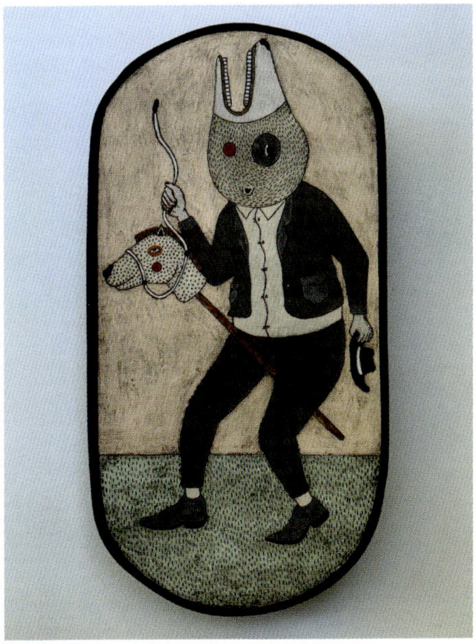

Rickie Barnett, *We're All Fools*, slab-built wall tile. *Photo Courtesy of the Artist*

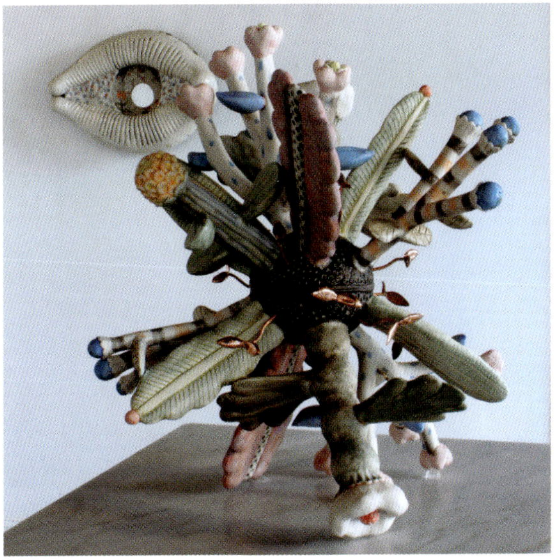

Momoko Usami, *Diversity Seed*, pinch and coil. *Photo Courtesy of the Artist*

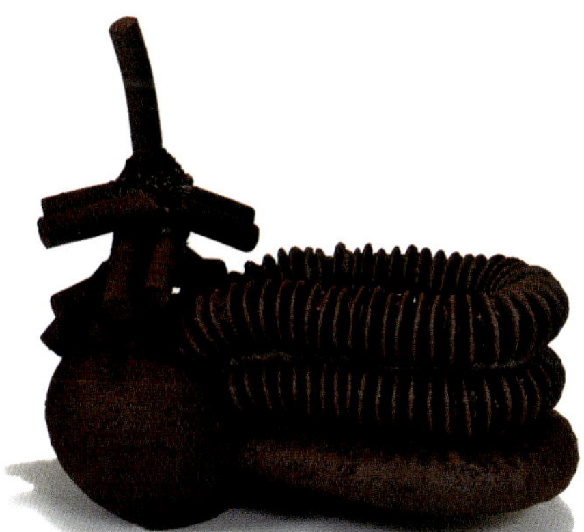

Colby Charpentier, *Disc Vessel*, assembled from coiled and pinched parts. *Photo Courtesy of the Artist*

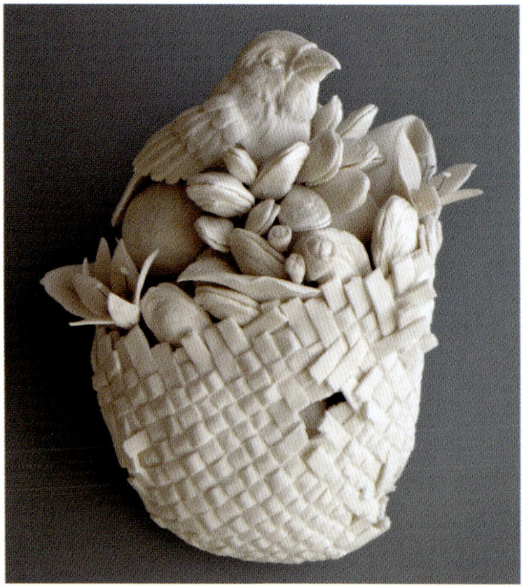

Malia Landis, *Apapane with Citrus Nest*, hand-built porcelain.
Photo Courtesy of the Artist

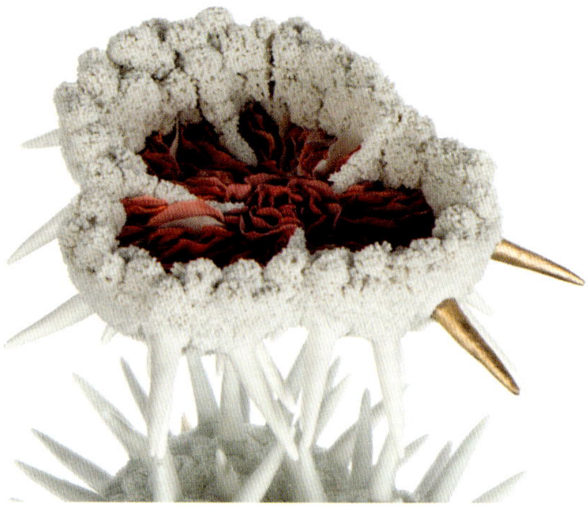

Erum Aamir, *Pollinis III*, rolled, pinch, coil.
Photo Courtesy of the Artist

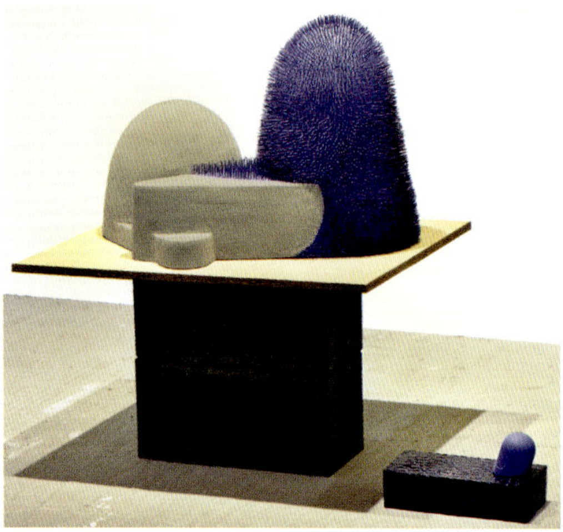

Iva Haas, *Yugoslavia*, slab and pinched.
Photo Courtesy of the Artist

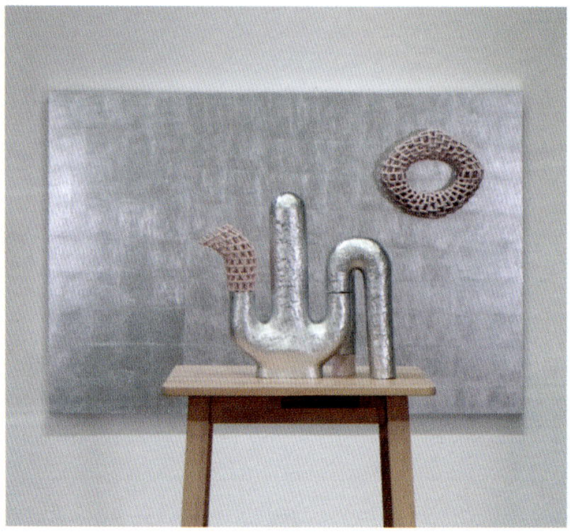

Iren Tete, *Phosphene Memory*, coil, slab, and pinch.
Photo Courtesy of the Artist

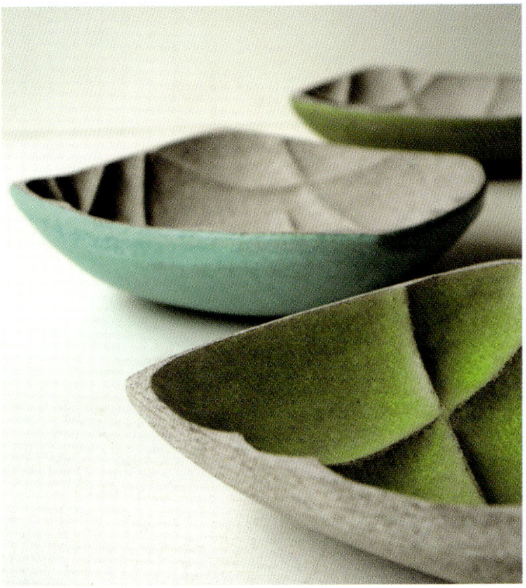

Michele Bianco, *Fracture Bowls*, slab built, hand carved.
Photo Courtesy of the Artist

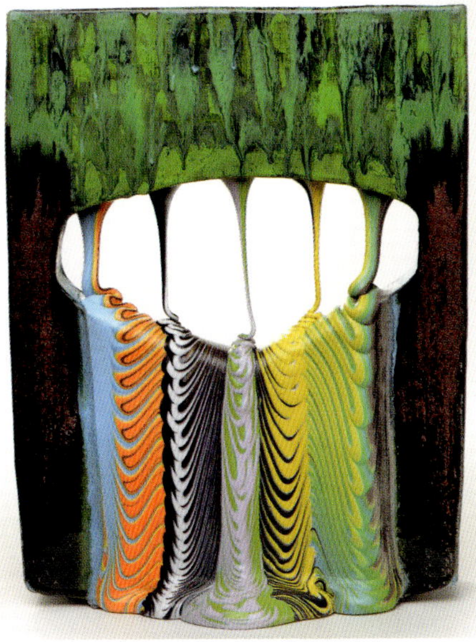

Lauren Mabry, *Glazescape (Green Shade).*
Photo Courtesy of the Artist

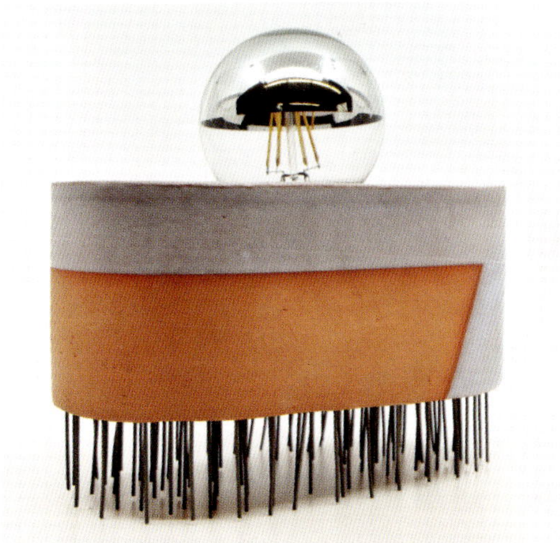

Iva Haas, *Lavender Lamp*, slab built.
Photo Courtesy of the Artist

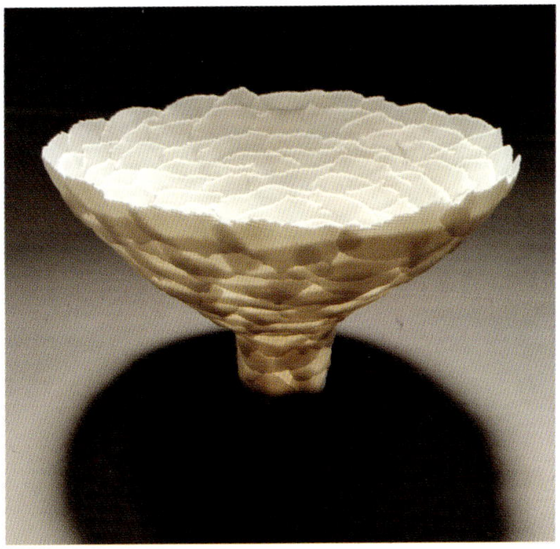

Leah Kaplan, *Piecework Dome*, layered slab assembly.
Photo Courtesy of the Artist

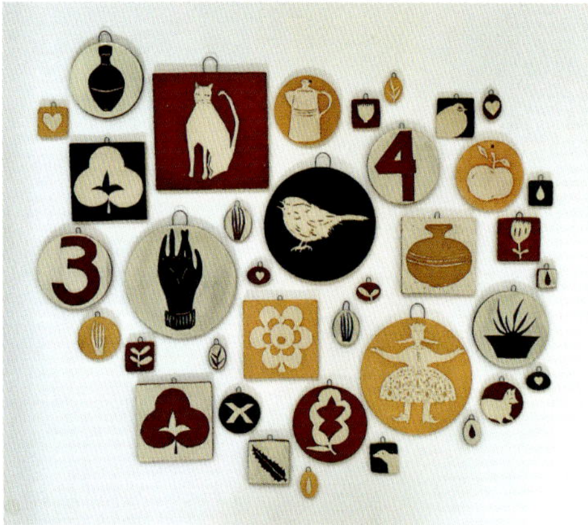

Diana Fayt, *A Day In The Life*, Stoneware clay, slip, glaze, nichrome wire. *Photo Courtesy of the Artist*

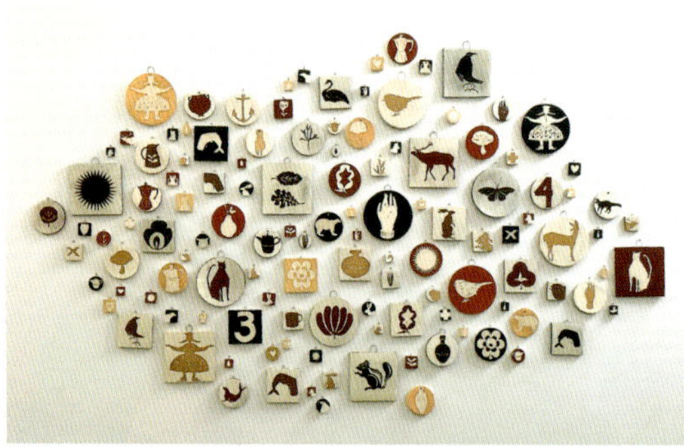

Diana Fayt, *Wishing Wall,* Stoneware clay, slip, glaze, nichrome wire. *Photo Courtesy of the Artist*

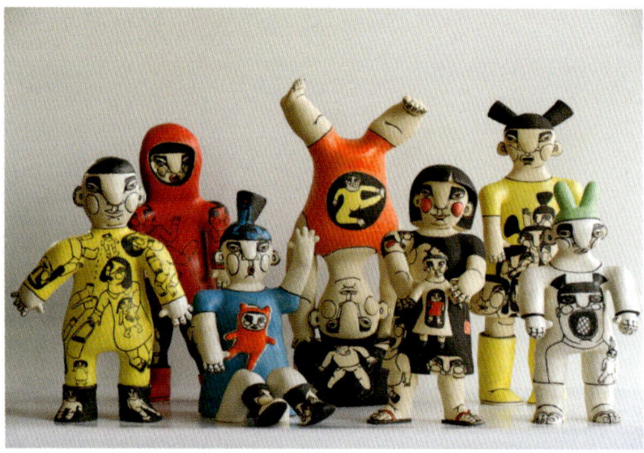

Janina Myronova, *Taiwanese Children*, Chamotte clay, underglaze, high firing glaze. Hand forming and painting. *Photo Courtesy of Ma Kang Li*

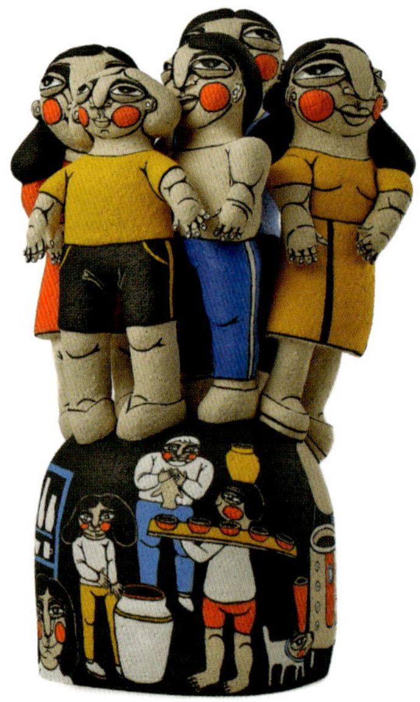

Janina Myronova, *Ceramic Family*, Chamotte clay, underglaze. Hand forming and painting. *Photo Courtesy of Dzikie Studio*

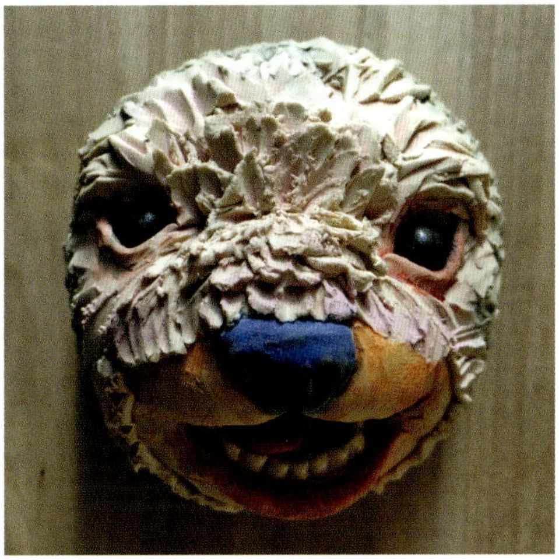

Magda Gluszek, *Blue Nosed Sloth.*
Photo Courtesy of the Artist

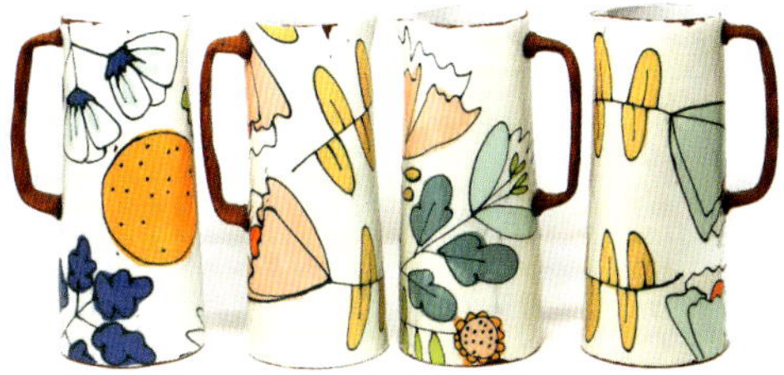

Catie Miller, *Pitchers*, slab built.
Photo Courtesy of the Artist

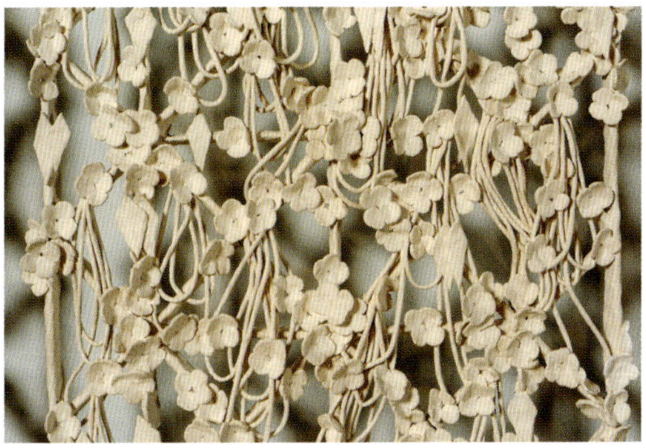

Joanna Poag, *Installation Detail*, pinch, coil, assemblage.
Photo Courtesy of the Artist

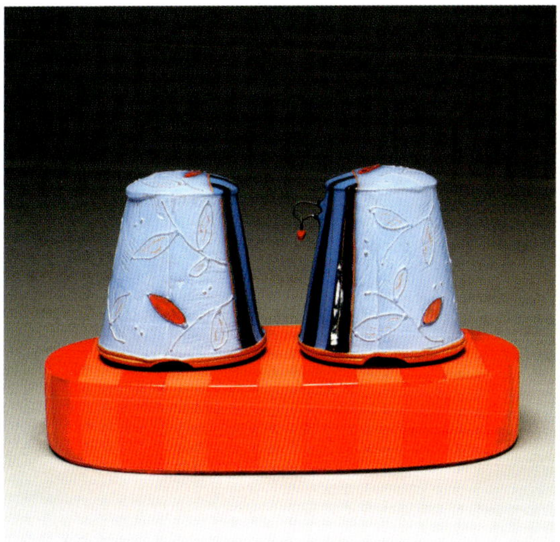

Liz Zlot Summerfield, *Salt and Pepper*, slab built.
Photo Courtesy of the Artist

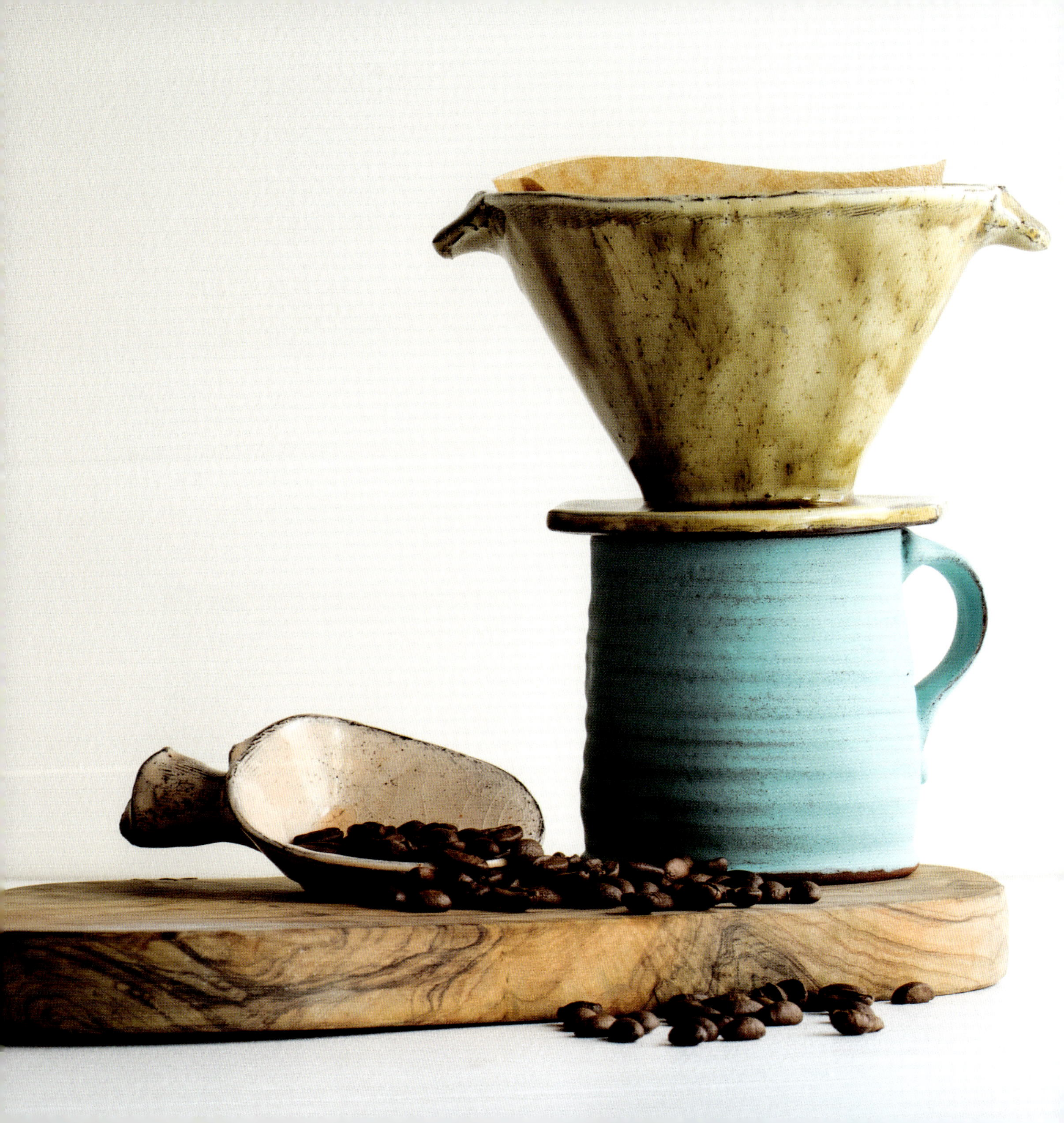

section

3

FUNCTIONAL PROJECTS

Making functional objects is how I fell in love with clay. They set me on the path to finding my way to becoming an artist and maker. There was just something about how making something as simple as a cup or a bowl connected me to other people... it profoundly impacted me. I wanted to make beautiful, useful things that would have a life and purpose beyond my own limited definitions. Often my investigation into functional objects is about an effort to slow folks down and find a quieter pace to life to help build memories and find special moments. To stop and smell the roses, to use a well-worn phrase.

When most folks think of functional ceramics, they think of wheel-thrown pottery. Pottery is not limited to the round wheel-thrown objects we are familiar with, such as bowls and cups. I moved into the world of hand building functional wares because I no longer wanted the limitation of making round things on the wheel. I started with coil building and discovered that slowing down my process left an opening for my creative brain to daydream. I think of hand building and wheel throwing as tools to achieve specific ends. With throwing, I go to the wheel with specific objects in mind, usually well-defined and with a clear objective. I can crank out those forms quickly and efficiently (after years of practice). With hand building, so many ideas come from just working. I can be coil building a pitcher or slab building a box, and maybe because of the slow, methodical process, my brain makes small but continuous decisions about form and functionality, offering up ideas and other avenues to explore. I have to keep a notebook handy to jot those ideas down for exploration at another time. This practice of hand building allows that creative problem-solving part of the brain to exercise. Much needed time to percolate and come up with new ideas and solutions for the assignments we give ourselves.

This section is full of a variety of functional objects, some of which I had never made prior to writing this book. This was the assignment I gave myself. An essential part of a creative practice is challenging oneself, jumping into new territory not knowing the outcome. Remember it's about the journey, not the destination. (I try to practice what I preach.) As you work on the functional projects in this section—pinching, coiling, slab building, and carving away—notice whether your brain gives you some ideas with which to work. Grab that notebook and jot them down, do a little sketch, and keep them handy to try sometime soon. You have it in you to create amazing, creative, and playful functional objects with the skills you are learning.

SCOOPS

In my own studio practice, I tried early on to make spoons with very little success. I couldn't see the point in my hyper-focused attention being on the functionality of objects. Being a somewhat clumsy person, I found it difficult to make spoons. Then, using the ones that survived, I broke them. So I dropped the investigation.

As I have gained more experience in clay, I have learned that you never say never! In my case, what drew me in was the scoop. In my ceramics collection, I have a beautiful black jar by Lorna Meaden with a cool (and useful) scoop that hangs from the side. I use it to dole out kitten treats every night to my cats—who are not shy to remind me if I forget! This form inspired me to begin my new exploration. I drew inspiration both from that scoop and from a utilitarian metal scoop that I picked up to scoop and measure flour for making sourdough bread.

If you struggle with sketching to explore 3D forms, I encourage you to grab some paper, tape, and scissors and make some paper scoops. It is a simple way to explore with both scale and form quickly. Think not only of scoop shapes but also other variables, such as the angles for the handle. You'll soon learn a lot about the functionality of a scoop, as well as the scale that transpose the task at hand. There are two templates on page 163 that give you a place to start. I designed these shapes through this same method. These templates can be scaled up or down and modified to your desires. After you make a few scoops, you will get an idea about the thickness, size, and shape you are interested in exploring.

TOOLS AND MATERIALS

Basic Tool Kit (page 37)
Serrated ribs
Paper
Tape
Scissors
Templates (page 162)

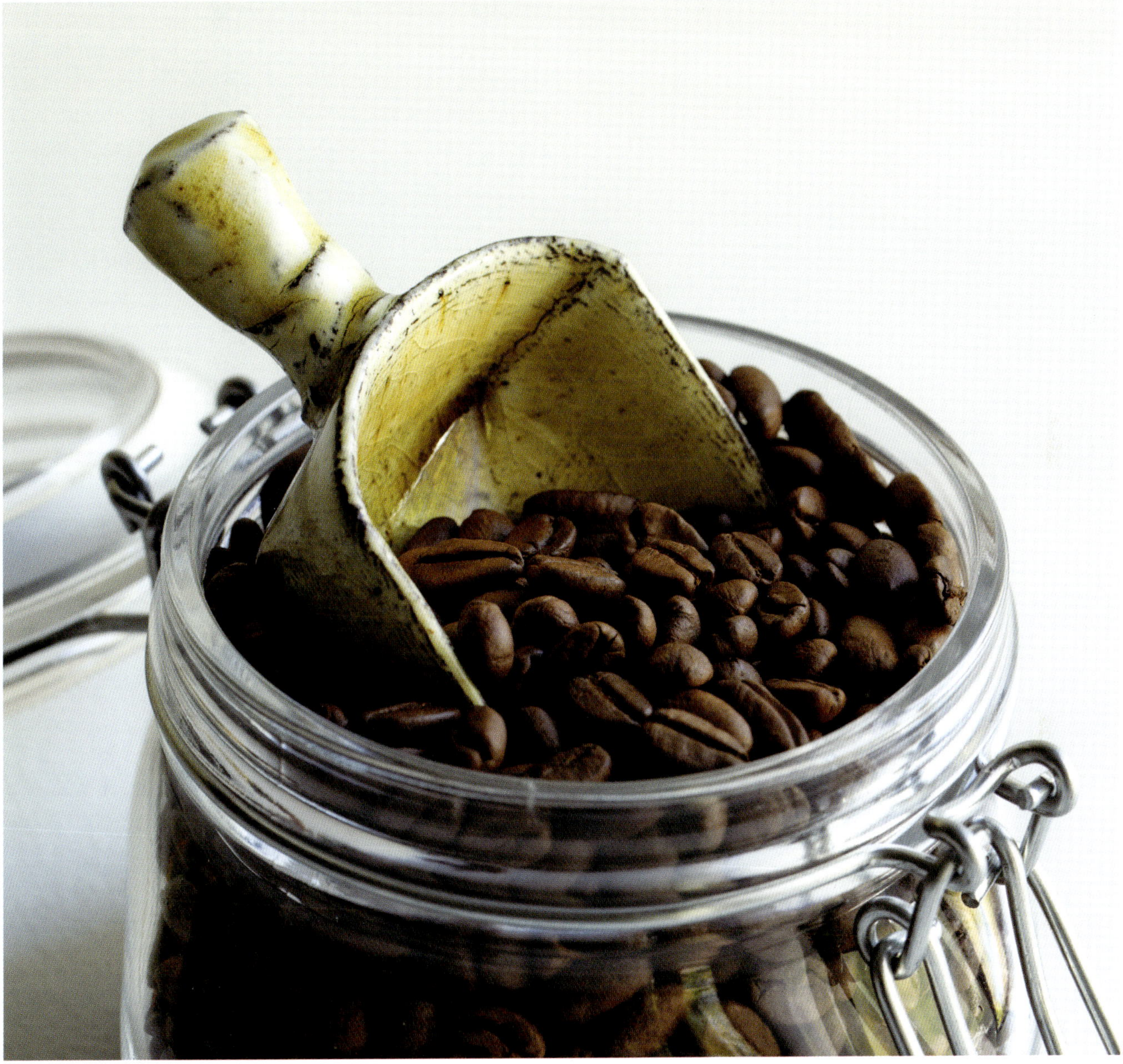

CONE 5, red clay, white slip, celadon style commercial glaze

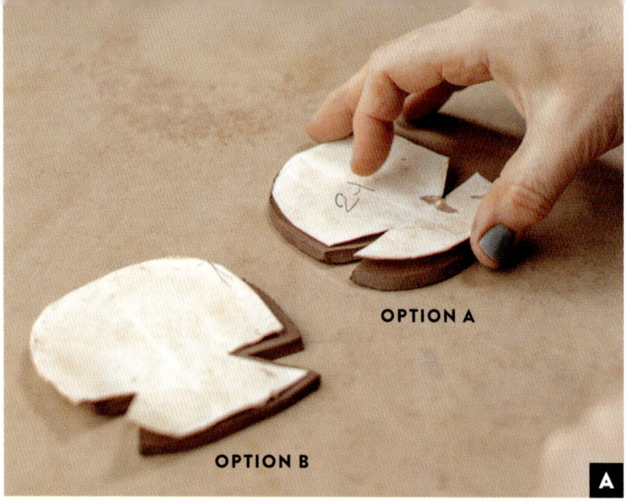

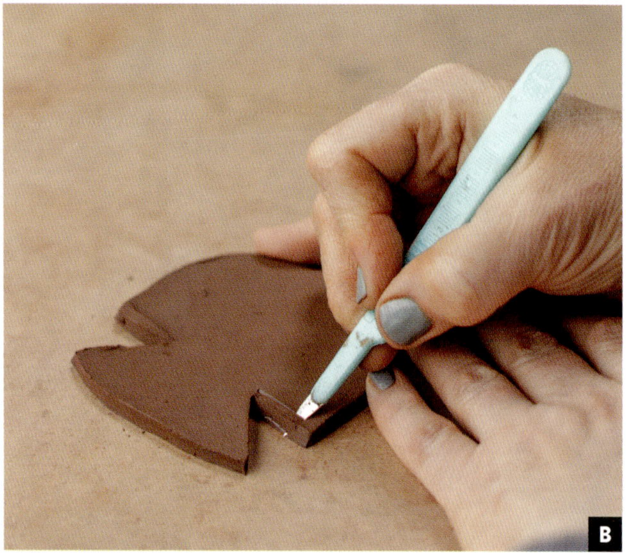

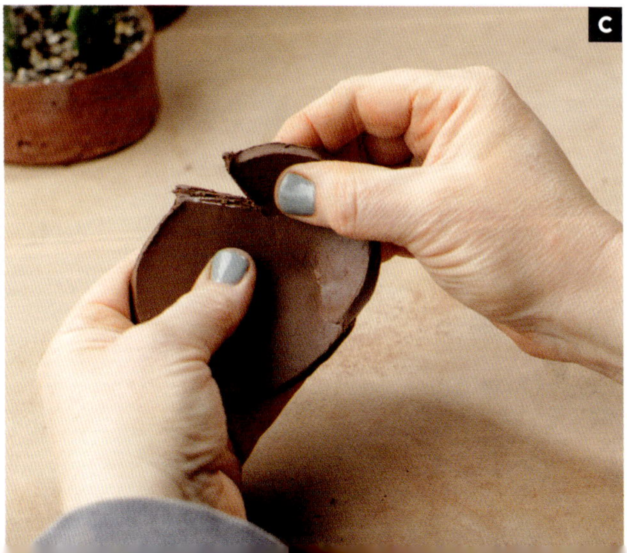

Roll out a slab just under ¼" (.63 cm) thick and large enough to cut multiples of your scoop template shapes. This form requires some intense handling while making, so choose a clay you are comfortable with. This form may also be subject to some amount of warping if overly thin.

Using a needle tool, cut out as many of the shapes as you can fit. Put the excess clay back in your bag. It is always a good idea to make in a series. Your third attempt is always better than your first, I promise! **[A]**

TIP *Don't let the paper template sit on wet clay; peel it off your cutouts as soon as you are finished. This will extend the life of your template.*

It is important to this particular form to have a flat, clean cutout of the template shape to start with. If it got a little mangled when pulling the shape off the cutting board, just lay it flat, rib gently, and use the template again to recut the shape. The ribbing and recutting reenforce the form so it "remembers" and hopefully warps very little.

Now to make a scoop! There are two options. I recommend option A to get started, and then option B once you have an understanding of the assembly process. Bevel the pie-shaped cutouts with a scalpel to increase the surface area of this connection. Score each side, wet one side, and pull the edges to slightly overlap and attach the seam. Pulling the edges together will cause the form to curve into a scoop shape. **[C] [D]**

Compress the connections with a rib and clean up your seams. Make sure any seam in the area inside the scoop is very neat and tidy, with no gaps that might trap food or be sharp to the touch. Gently set aside on a piece of foam or a bat in a fashion that will help retain the shape you just formed—open bowl side down. **[D]** Let it set up to a medium leather hard. Assemble the rest of the shapes. By the time you get to your last, check on the first one you made. If it's ready, move on to the next step.

It's time to refine and shape the scoop. Use a surform to shape the outside edge of the scoop and be especially careful at the seam attachment. If present, take away any excess overlap on the seam (option B). **[E]**

Cup the form in your hand and grab your serrated rib. Gently start scraping the inside of the scoop. This will thin out the form and give some texture and definition to the scoop. Be mindful of the seams; they are the most fragile section. Texture as much as you want. I used several different gauges of serrated ribs, working first with the larger tooth and then moving to the smaller-toothed ribs. Creating texture is 100 percent an aesthetic choice once you have taken care of the technical construction and shape of the scoop. **[F]**

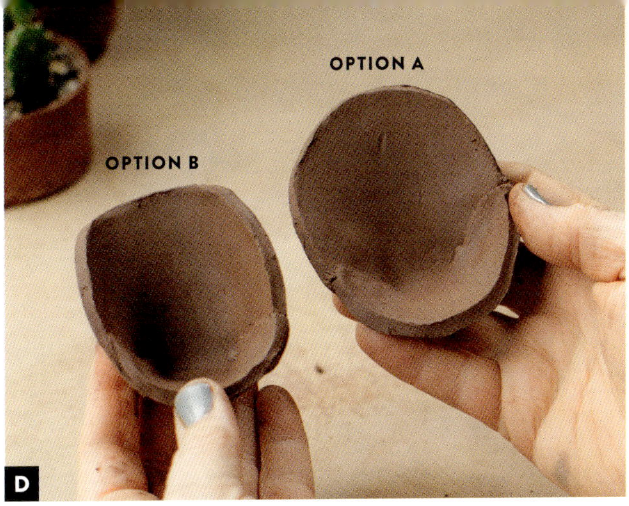

D

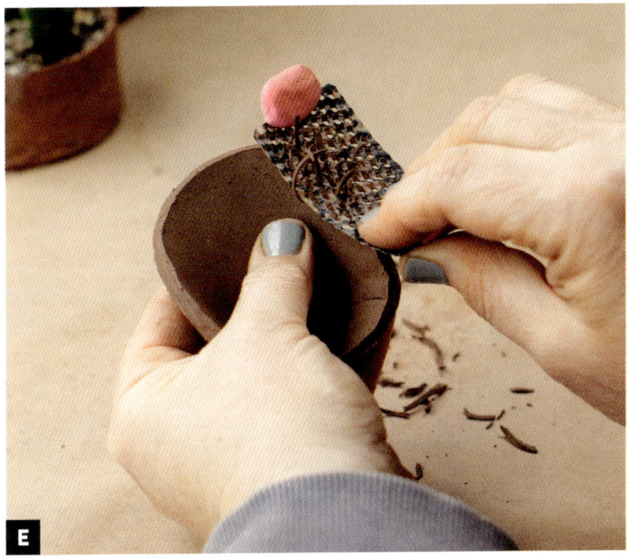

E

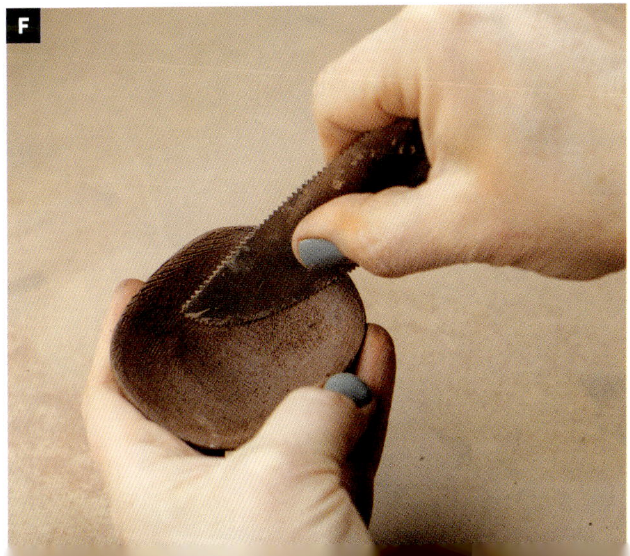

F

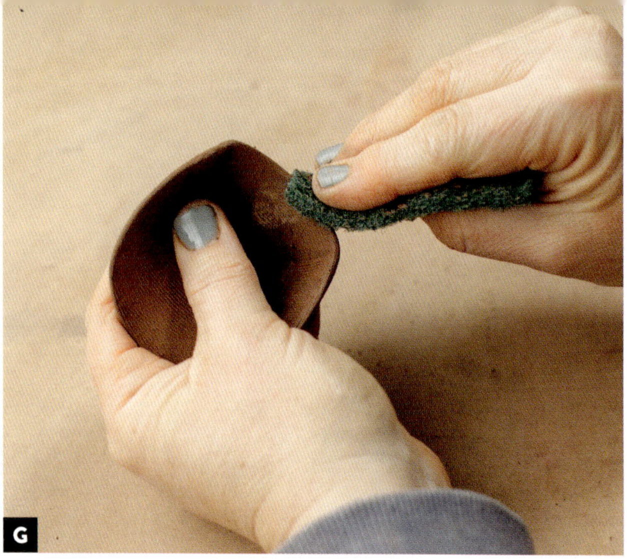

G

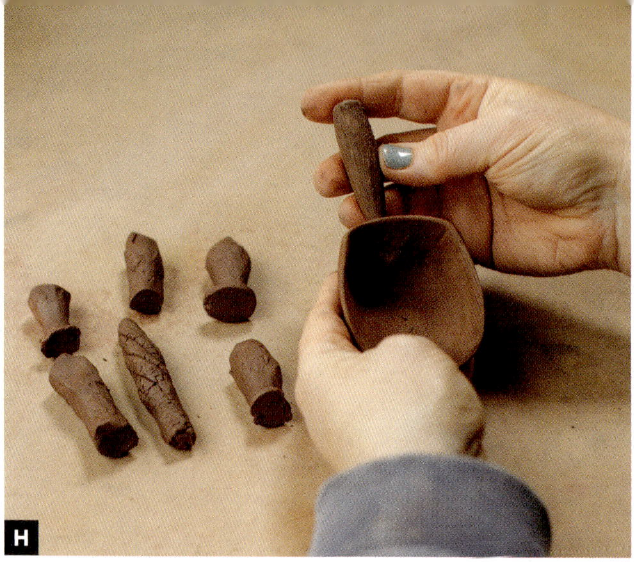

H

Begin the edge work. Depending on your hand skills, you may be more comfortable using tools, versus your fingers, for the edgework.

Pinched edge: Using your fingers and thumb, gently compress the edge of the scoop, working your way slowly around the entire form. You may need to do several slow passes to get a uniform appearance.

Tooled edge: Using the serrated rib, gently scrape the edge until you have created a bevel on the edge of the scoop. Do not make the edge into a sharp point, this can make it prone to chipping. On the back side of the scoop, take off the sharper edges of slab. I really like a small piece of dry-wall sandpaper or a green scrubby for this job. Gently work your way around the edge, rounding and smoothing the lip of the scoop. The goal is to take away any hard/sharp lines and leave a refined, tapered edge. **[G]**

Now hopefully you followed my advice and have a few scoop bodies made. Keep the scoops in a damp box or under plastic while you work on the handles. Don't let them dry out.

There are two handle options. Both involve sculpting using a reductive process, one with soft clay and the other carved and shaped from leather-hard clay. Both result in a solidly built form. For either option, make a couple of handles for each scoop you assemble. That way, if you mess one up, you have a backup. Try the different techniques and a variety of styles (e.g., tight vs. loose). You might surprise yourself with what you are drawn to. **[H]**

Slow throwing: Using a banding wheel, take a golf ball-sized chunk of soft clay and center it on the wheel head. (The size can vary depending on your scoop size.) Using your fingers and hand, gently work the clay into a shape a little bigger than the handle size you want. Spin the banding wheel slowly and use a small metal rib to take away clay to reveal your handle. Give it more shape and definition as you work your way around. (This will take some practice and probably several attempts. Keep it simple at first; you can get more elaborate as your skill grows.) Using a cutoff wire, take the handle off the banding wheel and set it aside to set up, aiming for a similar temperature as the scoop.

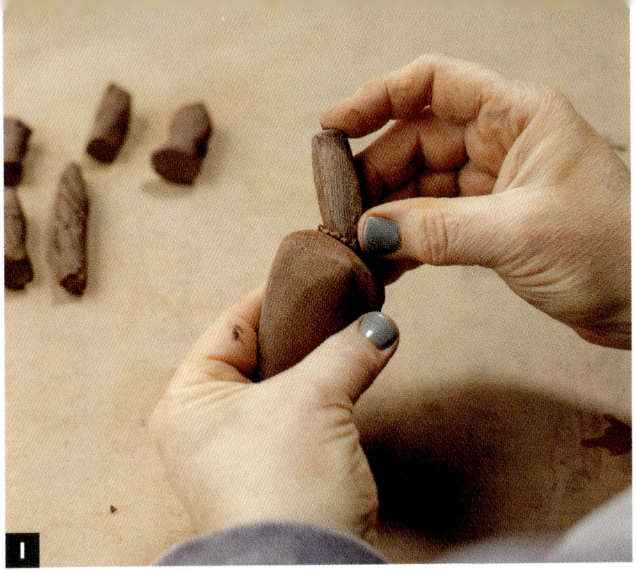

I

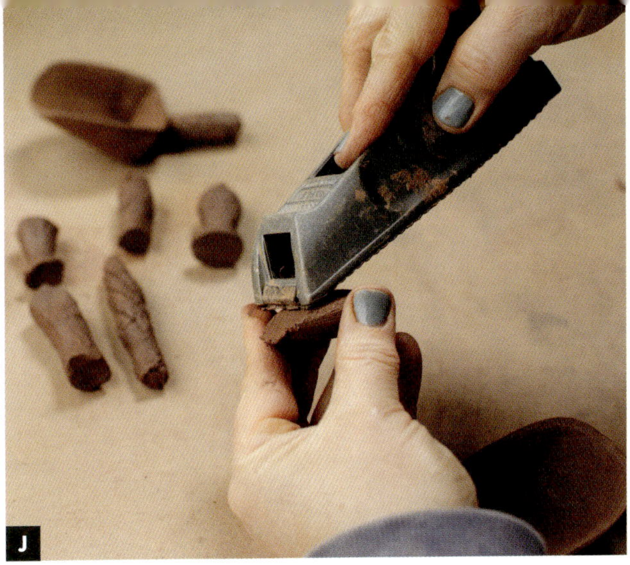

J

Leather-hard carving: This method requires a bit more patience but may be more to your liking, as it's less reactive than the soft, wet clay. Take approximately the amount of clay you think you may need for your handle in relation to your scoop, plus a little extra. Remember, you may be cutting a little away to make the right angle to attach to your scoop.

Rough out a few different shapes. Make several with different variations (volumes and shapes). Let them firm up to a medium leather hard.

Use your surform to refine the shape. The goal is to have a symmetrical form that is comfortable to handle and has a bit of extra length on one end to attach to the scoop.

Keep refining until you are happy with the shape. Once the shaping is done, use a combination of drywall sandpaper, a green scrubby, or a red rib to smooth out the surface.

Attach the handle. Take both your scoop and handle options out. Match a couple that you like and hold them up together. Pick the combos you like best, keeping the rest under plastic. While holding up your pieces, look for the angle at which they should be attached. **[I]** This is up to you and what you think is comfortable and functional. Make a preliminary cut with your fettling knife or use your surform to create the angle at the end of the handle that will be attached to the scoop. This may take a couple of cuts, so be a little cautious. (You do have backups if you make a mistake.) **[J]**

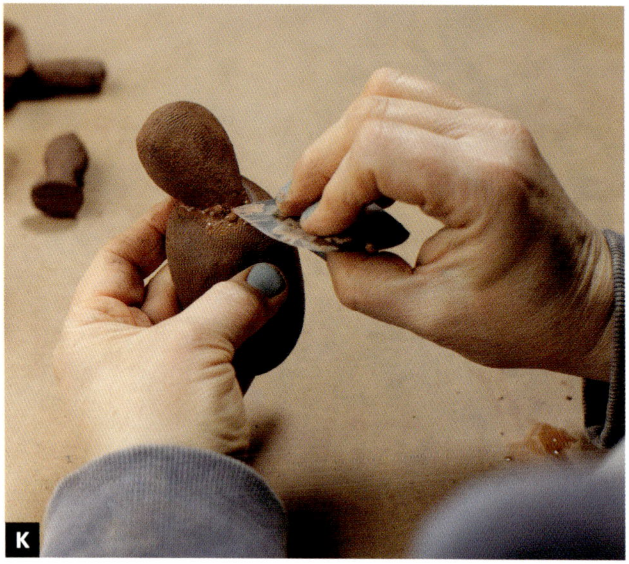

Once you have made your adjustments and have the angle right for the attachment, center the handle on the scoop and trace around the handle onto the scoop if necessary. (You can always eyeball it, if you prefer). Score both areas, wet one side, and attach. **[K]**

Clean up the attachment and make any final adjustments. Gently drape with plastic so the scoops dry slowly and evenly. Voila! You have yourself some scoops.

Tips on Firing Scoops

Any part of the scoop that touches the shelf will need to be unglazed. If you want to glaze the whole form, look for a firing stilt, a three-pronged stilt (compatible with your targeted firing range), on which your scoop can be balanced and fired. The little marks left by the stilts can be sanded/ground away with a Dremel tool.

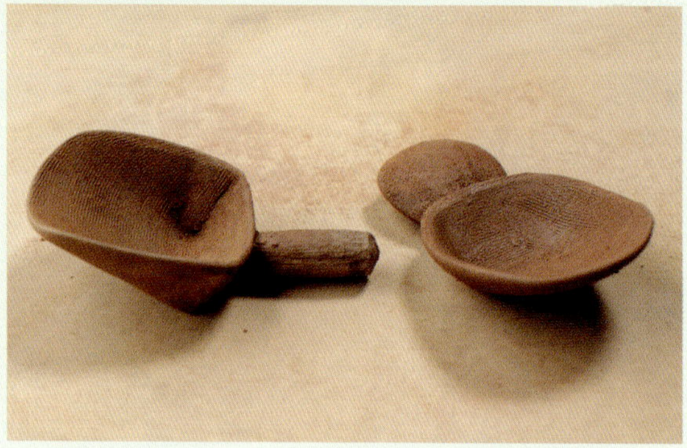

CITRUS REAMER

A good citrus reamer is an indispensable kitchen tool. From making cocktails to citrusy desserts to salad dressings, my ceramic reamers are some of my most unexpected kitchen treasures. When developing this object, you want to remember there are several types of citrus fruits out there, and they vary in size and shape. Think grapefruit versus lime. As with all functional objects, try to get as detailed as possible in your research. Use your kitchen habits to inform the type of reamer you make. Also, use your hand size and your strength to help inform the handle shape. Be as specific in your thought process as you can and start there. You can always refine and make changes once you have your foundational object.

Keep in mind this form will require some patience and gentle manipulation. It is built in two pieces and carved and shaped from leather-hard bits of clay. This project can be made with any clay. Just be mindful of the fact that this will be worked solid and carved, so clays that are sandy or groggy might be problematic when carving. Glazing these objects can be tricky as you will need to set them on firing stilts or leave some space unglazed so they can sit on the kiln shelf.

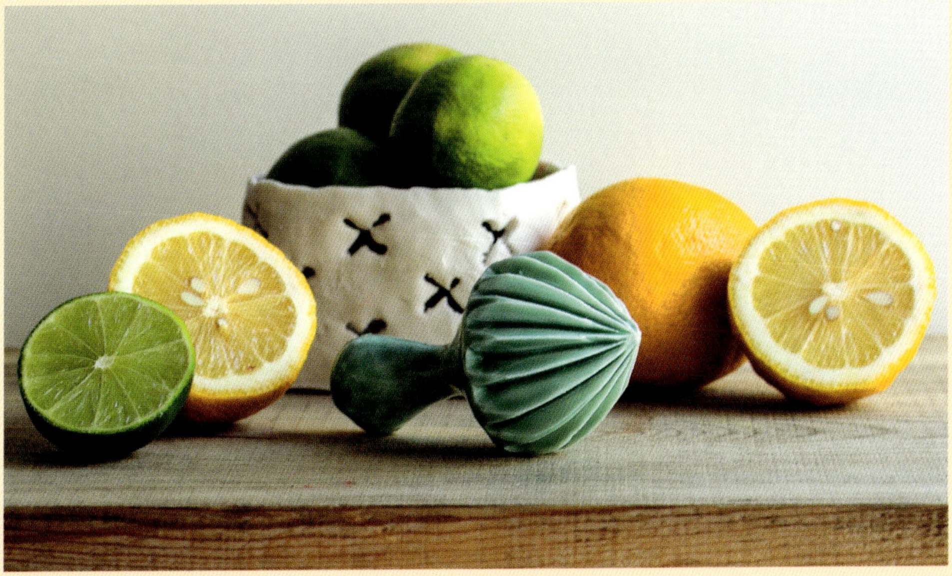

CONE 5, commercial glaze

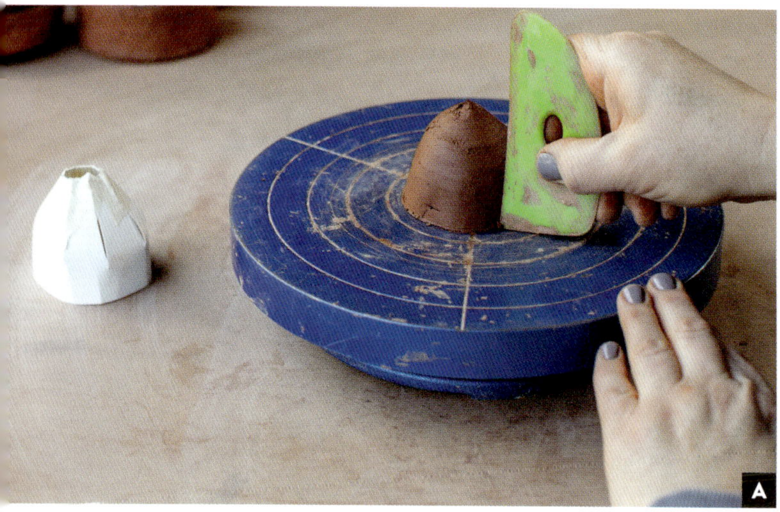

A

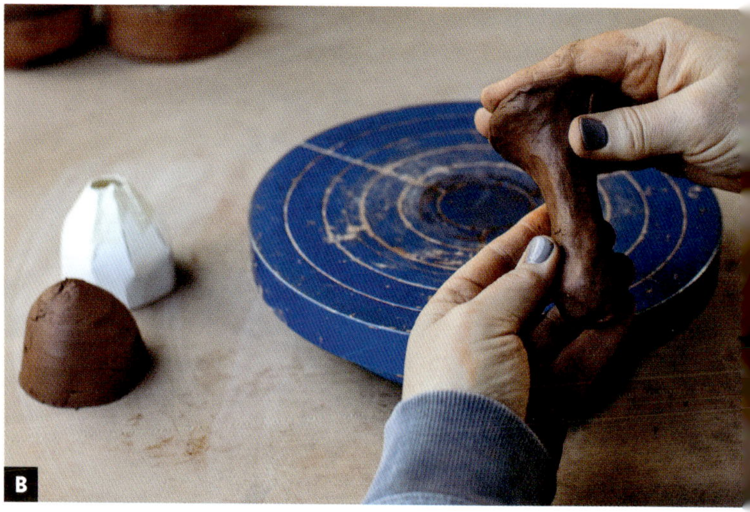

B

TOOLS AND MATERIALS

Basic Tool Kit (page 37)

Template (page 163)

Circle template measurement tool

Use the template of reamer head shapes (page 163) and tape them together according to the pattern. These will give you an idea of the shapes you will rough out in clay. You are welcome to scale the size up or down.

Using your preferred clay, rough out the reamer head shapes. Make several (you will mess up a few!) and let these firm up to a solid leather hard. You want the form to be as symmetrical as possible; once it is set up, you will be refining and carving it. Make sure you have plenty of clay to work with, and if you have difficulty making a symmetrical form using just your hands, use your banding wheel and a rib to help. **[A]**

Design and rough out the handle shape. I didn't include any pattern for this, as this shape is open to interpretation. You may want to sketch out a few ideas to get started. Remember, this is meant to fit your hand and provide enough handle to sufficiently get into your citrus. It should match at the connection of the base of the reamer head, creating a strong connection point. There will be lots of torque on the connection—make sure it won't snap off. The object should be both utilitarian and visually pleasing. Let these set up until leather hard. **[B]**

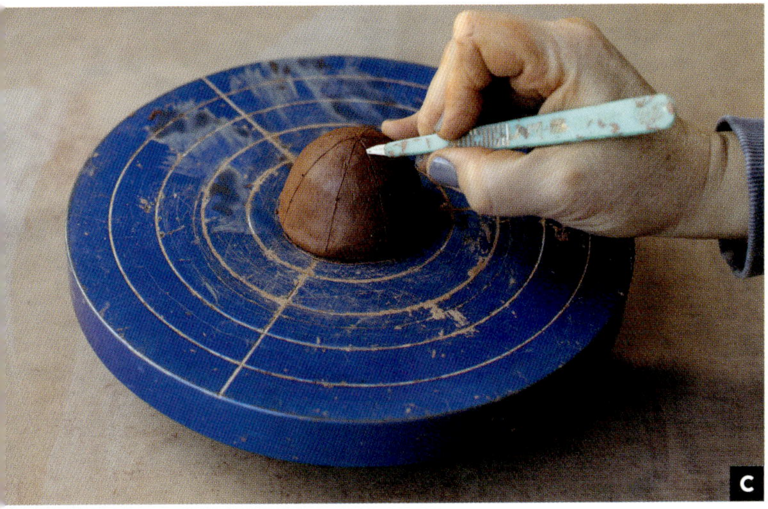

C

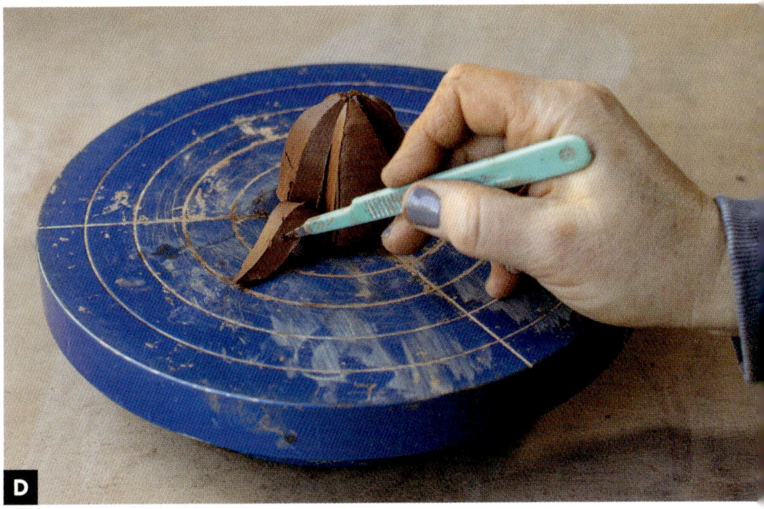

D

Next, shape the reamer and handle. Use your surform to start making the shapes symmetrical (the handles may be asymmetrical). If the clay starts to feel tacky and gums up the surform, stop and let the clay firm up some more. You want a really clean pass with the surform, like you are grating a hard cheese; the clay should easily fall away.

Place the reamer head in the center of your circle guide. (There is an example in the tools section on page 36. It's very simple to make one of your own; these are very handy if you are going to play around with the number of ridges.) Make a small mark to denote the center (peak) of your shape. With a ruler and a needle tool, make lines to the peak in the center of the form. These lines will be the high points of your ridges. This example has six ridges. This is a curved shape—try your best to keep the line straight while adjusting for depth. **[C]**

Cut the ridges. (This is where your extra tools may come in handy.) Using a scalpel or utility knife, bevel cut to the center of the ridges, changing the depth as you move from the top down. Go slowly and steadily, working in one direction, and then the other to help with consistency. **[D]**

Let these sit and harden up. You have exposed some clay that is a bit softer, and it will be easier to refine once it is a consistent hardness. Using a wooden knife, compress the valleys.

Once they are set up and easier to handle, use your fingers or tools to gently clean up, refine the shape, and compress the reamer head. Place in a damp box or under plastic.

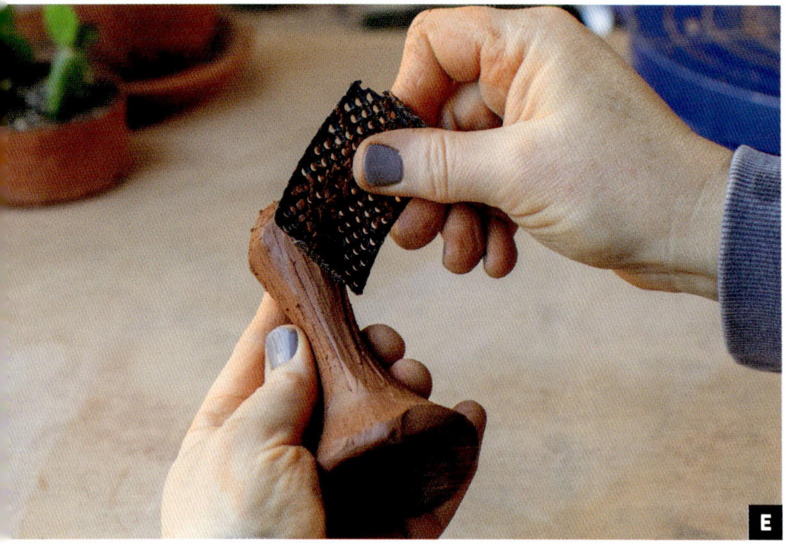

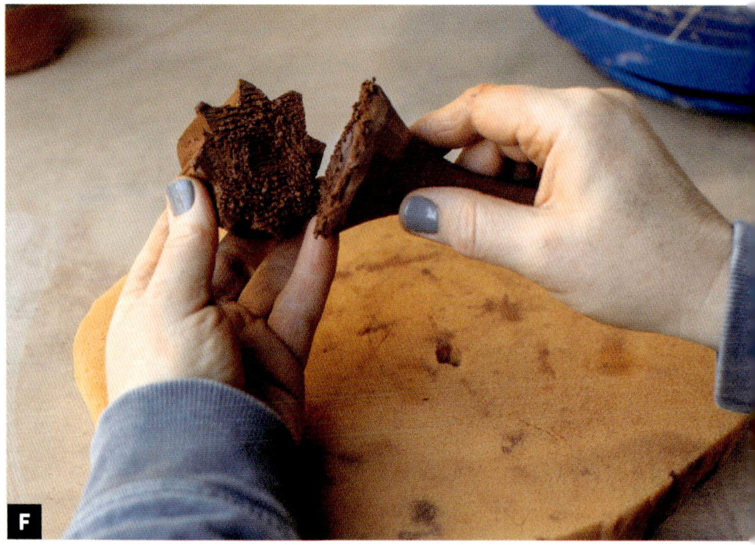

Shape the handle. Remember, you generally want the shape to fit in your hand and have a flared base that will be scored and attached to the reamer head. Use a surform to refine the general shape. Don't worry about the marks left from the process; we will deal with them in the next step. Once you have gotten closer to your finished shape, you may need to move to a serrated rib to start a shallower reductive refinement/shaping process. **[E]** This process can be a little hypnotic, and one can easily take away too much clay. Be mindful of your shape goal and keep checking in with your sketches or the image of the finished reamer image to stay on target.

Once you have finished refining your shape, it's time to smooth out any surfaces that seem too rough. Starting with a metal rib held at an angle yields more compression than scraping. Start smoothing. After you have gone over the form a few times, use a soft red rib to really get a smooth surface. This process will help compress the small particles of clay back into the form. Sometimes during shaping, we expose a lot of rough, groggy, or sandy particles in the clay, and compressing with the rib ensures a smoother finish, which is a nicer surface to handle, and the glaze will go over it more smoothly.

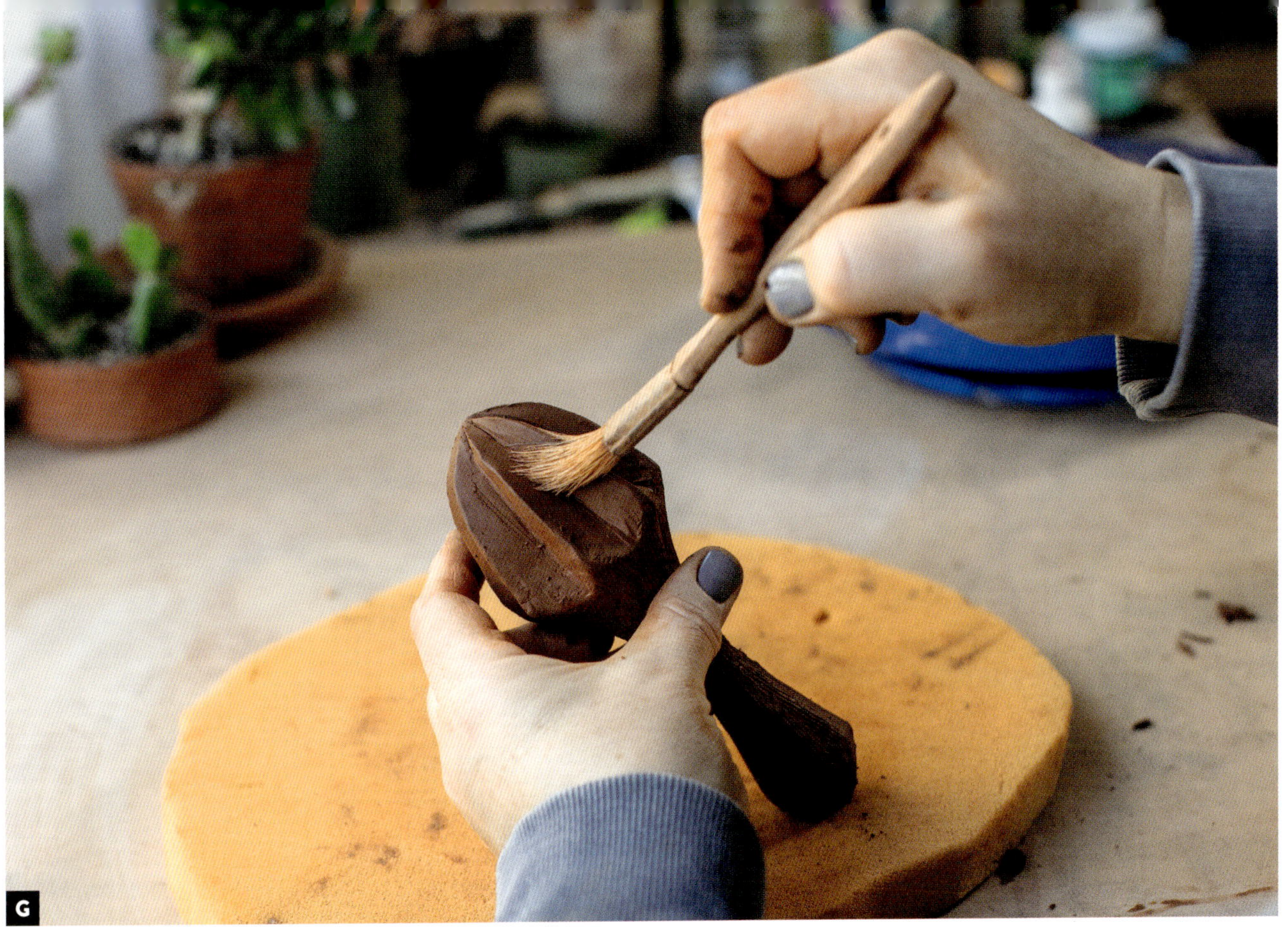

G

Before you attach the two pieces, double-check that the reamer base and handle match in size where they will be attached. Address any fit issues now by adding or taking away clay. (It is easiest to adjust the handle side.) Score each of the attachment points. **[F]** This form will benefit from some slip on one side, which will help equalize the attachment of the two leather-hard pieces. Clean up the attachment zone as needed and set up a space for it to dry. I recommend a soft foam surface to avoid flattening out any of your points. Done! **[G]**

BUTTER BOX

When making functional objects, it is important to design from your experience and use. They are sure to be better for most people if you rely on your experience, and if not, well, you're never going to please everyone! For me, living in Southern California, if we left the butter out on the counter to keep it nice and soft, it would turn into a puddle. So when I thought about a useful and functional butter dish, it was an object that could move from the counter or table to the fridge easily. No huge bottom dish or tall knob on the cover for me. Those features would totally make a butter dish impractical for the way that I use that object. I realized what I wanted was a box close to the shape of a stick of butter. Simple enough, right? Believe it or not I went through several variations of this little form, due to some unexpected previously unobserved human behaviors.

These are what I consider a couple of universal truths about lidded vessels (especially ones meant to hold butter): First, no matter how well you indicate how a lid should fit, people will always—and I mean always—put it on wrong. It's better to focus on making a well-fitting lid and whatever kind of key (an identifying mark to indicate how a lid should line up) you like. This is leading the horse to water, and that is all you can do! Second, always put the flange (what holds the lid in place) on the bottom, as, for some reason, folks don't look when applying the lid . . . and if that flange is on the lid, it gets mashed into the butter!

Basically, what I'm getting at here is that this form looks straightforward but has a lot of consideration behind it, as well as quite a few steps to make it. I guarantee, with a bit of practice, all the elements will come together so you too can create a lovely little box. What is great about this design is you can make any style of cap lidded box once you have figured it out. It's all about the flange. Where you add it is what makes the object either a butter box or just a regular old box. You can also do whatever symmetrical shape you want. This project is demonstrated as a rectangular shape, but you can do a square or circle just as easily.

TOOLS AND MATERIALS

Basic Tool Kit (page 37)

Paddle

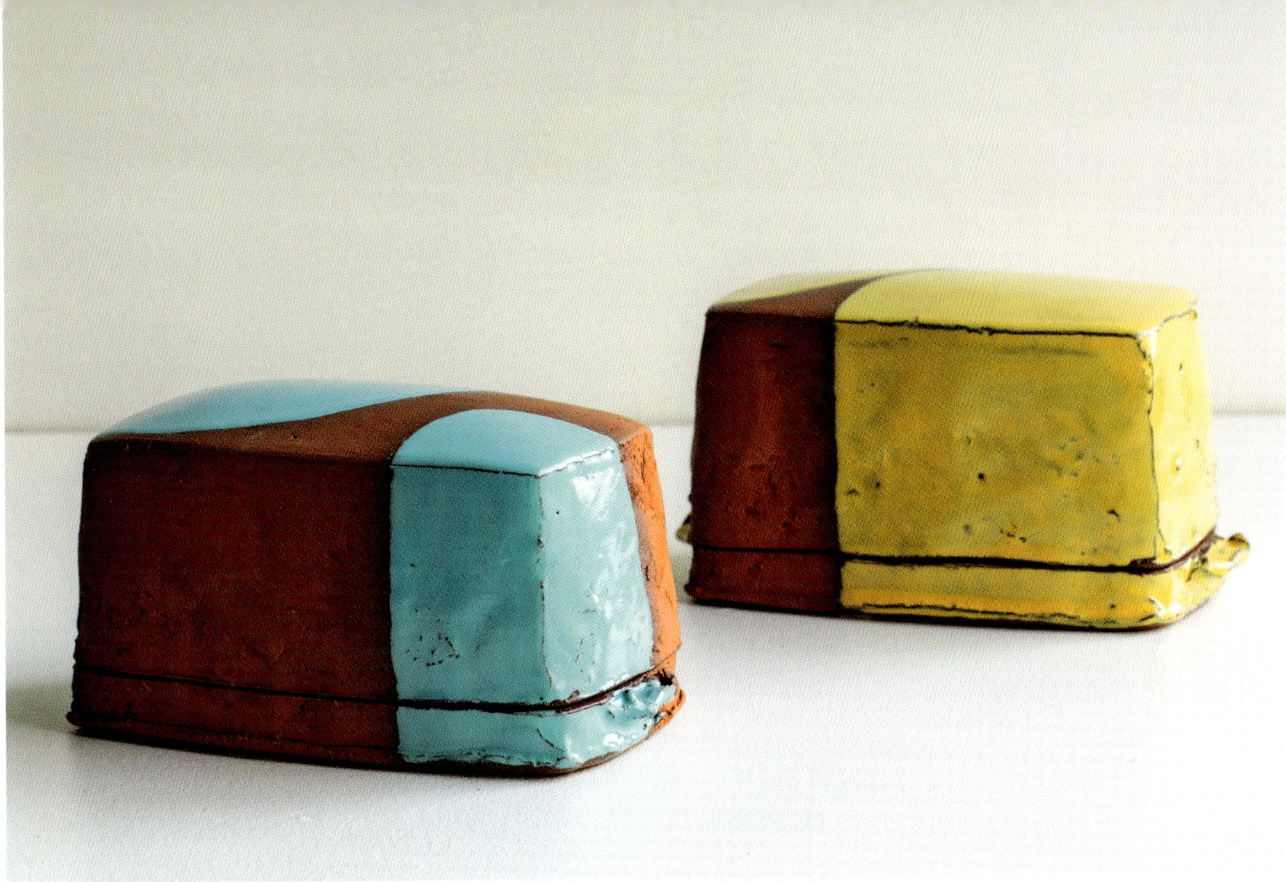

CONE 3, exposed clay and commercial glaze

Roll out a ¼" (.63)- thick slab for your footprint. Using a ruler, cut out your footprint. I am using the measurements of 3.5" (8.9 cm) wide and 5.5" (14 cm) long.

NOTE *You might be wondering why I don't have a template for this project. I don't want you to be limited to the templates at the back of the book! They are just a starting point for your ideas. We can sometimes lean on those templates for longer than they suit our ideas. Making your own templates and determining your own footprints is a step into making an object your own interpretation. It is as simple as getting out your ruler, paper, pencil, and scissors to get started. Plus, maybe your butter won't fit in my ideal measurements!*

Taper your footprint. Anytime I make something with corners, square or rectangular, I taper the outside of the footprint. This helps the form seem squarer and more architectural looking once built. I found if I built on true square shapes, the form always seemed bulgy and clumsy looking. To taper your footprint, find the center on the long side. On the short sides, mark ¼" (.63 cm) up from each edge. Line the ruler up at the center to your marks on the side, and cut off the extra. Do that for all four corners. Repeat the process for the short sides as well. In all you will make eight cuts to the shape. (If you like this project, make yourself a template with your perfect measurements plus the taper to save time in the future.)

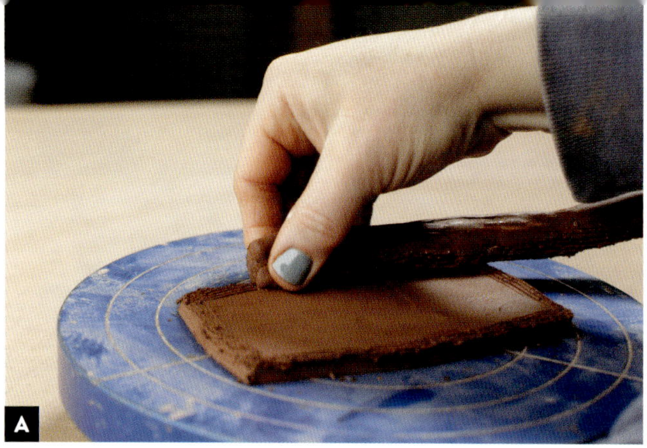

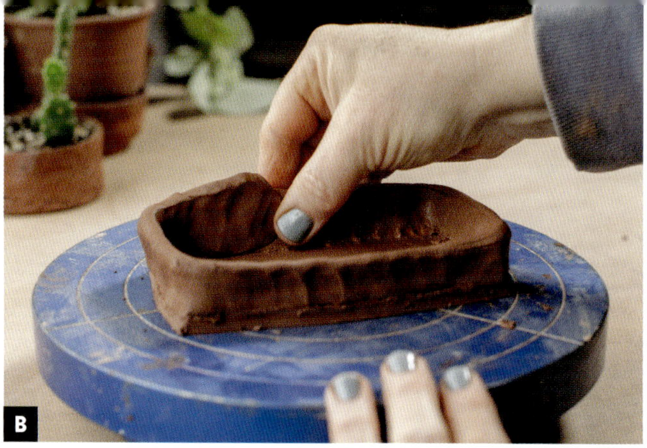

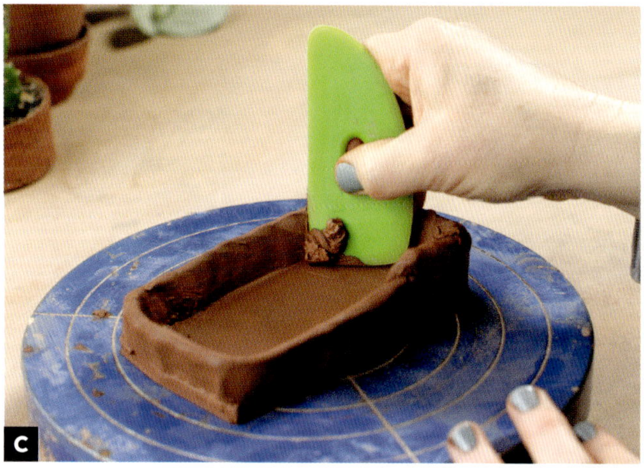

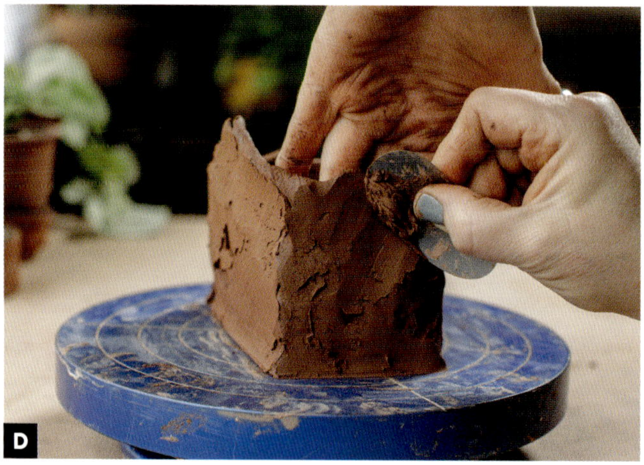

Score the top edge of your footprint and your coil. Pick someplace mid-wall to begin attaching the coil and work the coil all the way around the form, breaking off the excess when you come to your starting point. Make sure not to overshoot your footprint. Your footprint is your foundation and should be used to keep your form as square as possible. **[A] [B]**

NOTE *Our inclination is to start in the corner of a squared form, but your corners will be harder to compress and result in weaker wall strength if you begin and end a coil there.*

Using a right-angled rib, clean up the connection and wall thickness, and define your corners, inside and out. **[C]**

Continue with your next coil and then move on to ribbing and definition. Taper the walls slightly toward the center. **[D]**

If you have trouble with your form flaring out, use the darting method (see page 48) to get the form under control. Remember, one coil at a time, rib for thickness, attach, and define, inside and out, and then move on to the next coil. This takes roughly three passes around the pot inside and out. **[E]** For detailed instruction on coil building, see the Foundational Skills section (page 45).

Cut the form off evenly at 3.5" (34.3 cm) tall. Let it set up until it becomes a soft leather hard. **[F]**

Roll out a fresh slab. The thickness should be similar to your wall thickness and the same shape and size of your footprint with an extra ½" to 1" (1.3 to 2.5 cm) around the entire slab. It's easier if the slab is a soft leather hard for this next step.

Using your object as a drape mold, gently drape the slab into the form, letting the sides pop up evenly around the edges—like putting a soft corn tortilla over the top, you want to gently bend the slab into the form and allow the edges to come up. Do not rib the slab into the form. Let the pieces rest together until leather hard, so the curve in the slab will hold its shape. **[G]**

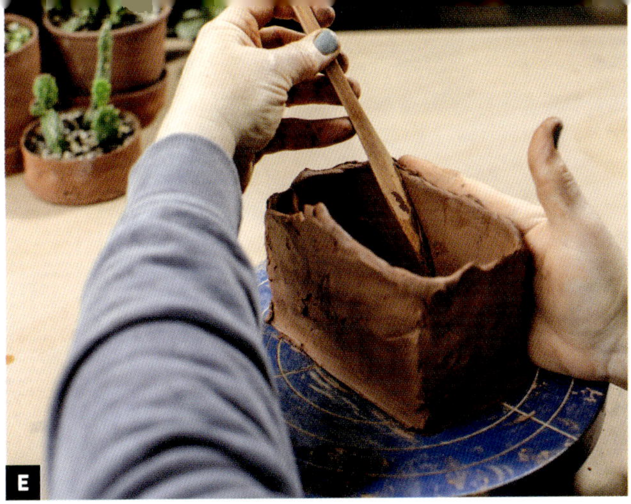
E

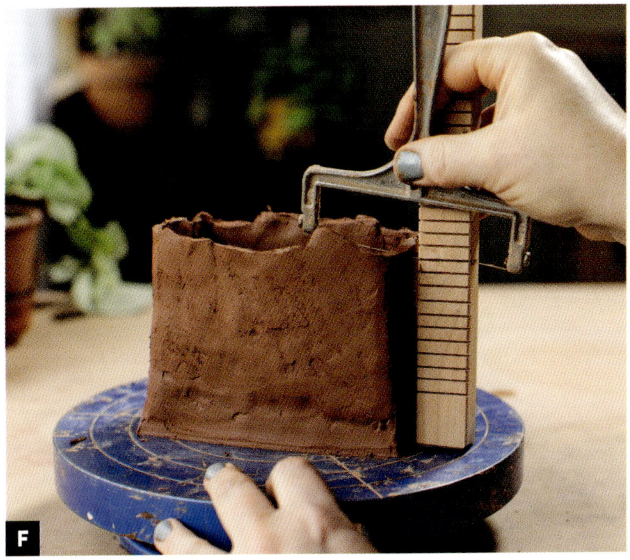
F

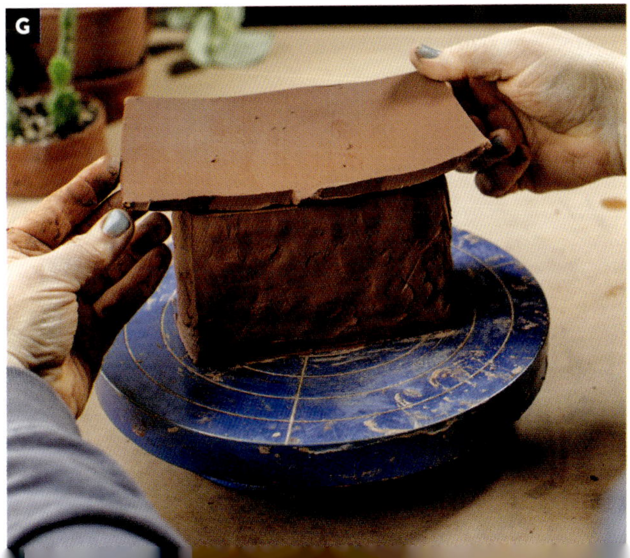
G

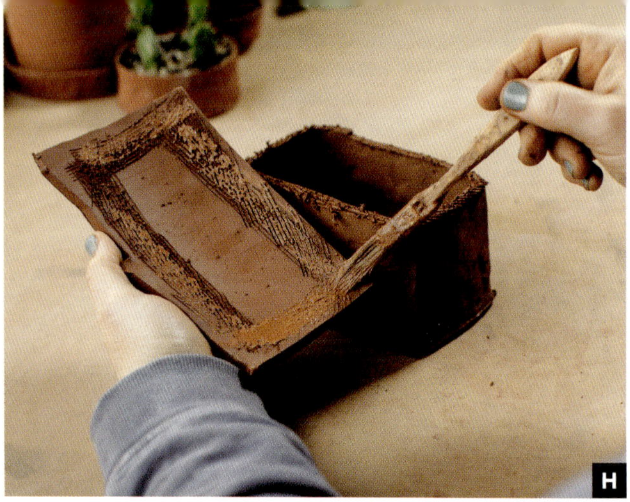

H

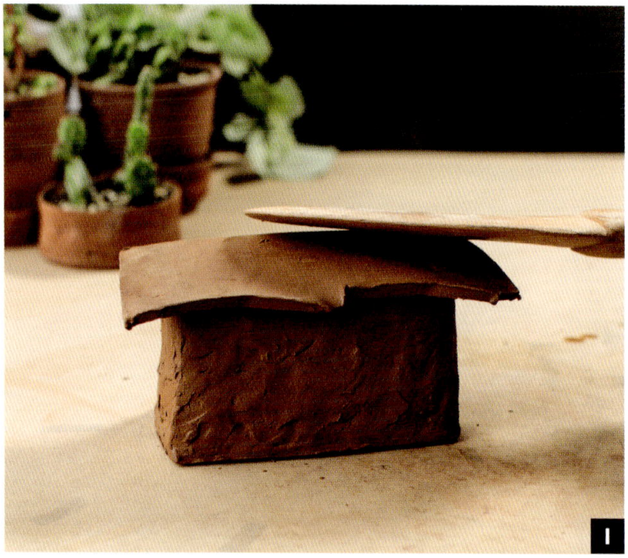

I

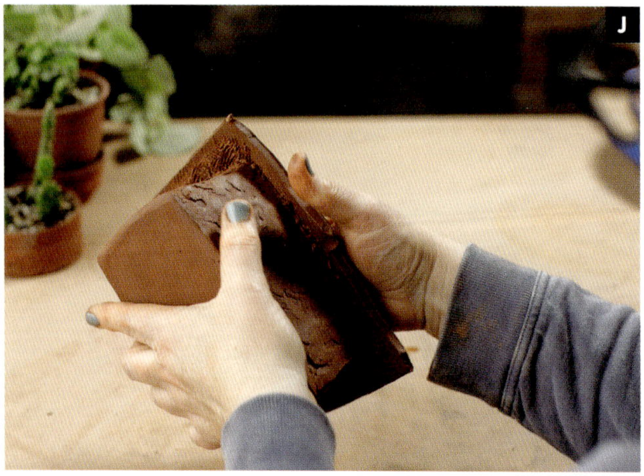

J

Once your slab and object are leather hard, it's time to join the pieces. Flip the slab over and center it on the form; there should be overhang, like the eaves on a house. Using a needle tool, trace around the form onto the slab. You will score on the inside of those marks on the underside of the slab. **[H]**

Score the top edge of the box form, scoring toward the outside edge. This will help the curve of the top slab fit better. Wet one side and attach. Use a paddle or wood spoon to gently compress around the form. **[I]** Now for the lift test—your slab and box should be a medium to firm leather hard at this point. Lift the object up by the excess overhang. Just an inch or two (2.5 cm to 5 cm) off the tabletop will suffice. **[K]**

If it all stays connected, congratulations—you have connection. If, however, the top slab lifts off in spots or altogether (eek!), rescore and attach and do the lift test again. **[J]** This connection point is super important, and you want to make sure it is attached all the way around the form.

Once complete attachment is achieved, use a cheese cutter and the vertical wall as your guide to cut off the excess slab. The edge of the slab becomes part of the vertical wall. **[L]** Using a rib, clean up the connection point and smooth the top of the box, if needed. Let it rest wrapped up in plastic overnight. All the elements should become the same consistency and be ready to work the following day.

For this next step, your box should be a consistent leather hard; this will help keep the form from losing shape or possible warping later. Use a ruler to mark ¾" (1.9 cm) up from the tabletop around the form. Use your ruler and a needle tool to make a line. **[M]** Next, using a scalpel tool, insert on the line and cut horizontally around the form.

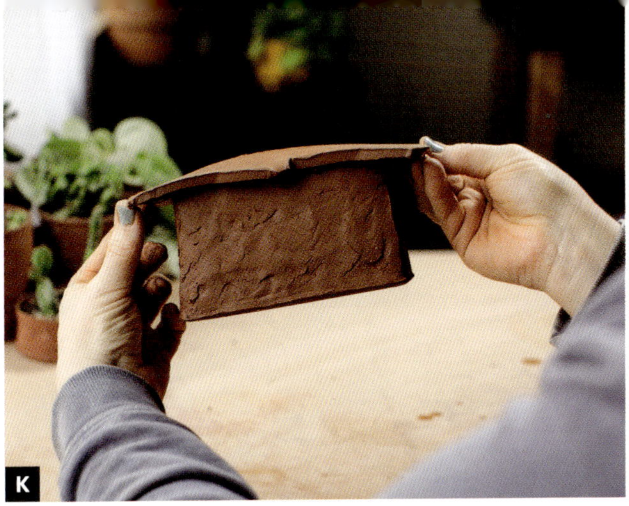
K

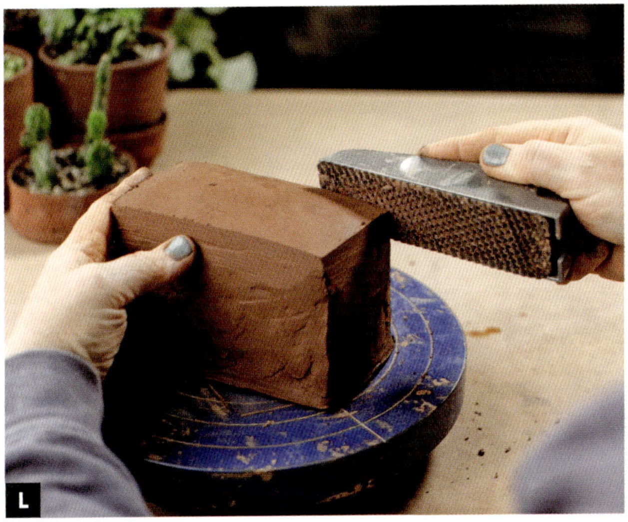
L

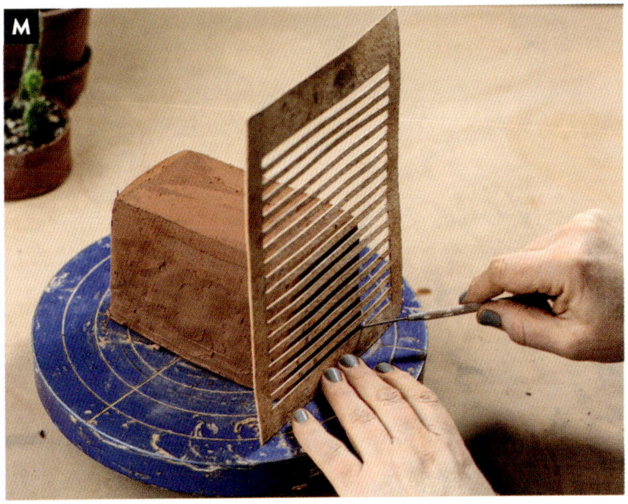
M

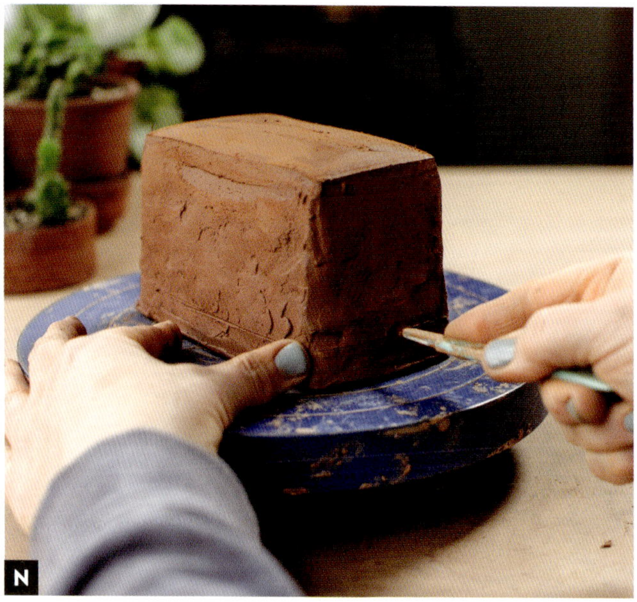

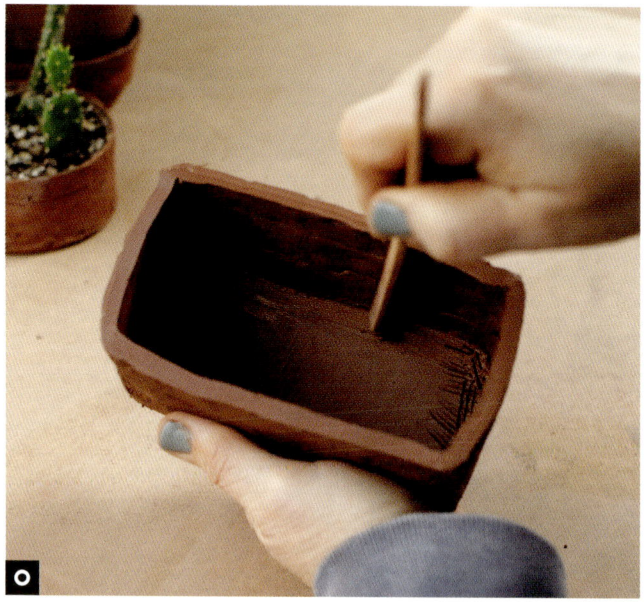

Start cutting someplace mid-wall, in case you need to correct your cut—this is easier to do if you can see it coming versus hitting a corner and being off by ¼" (.63 cm). **[N]** Before you lift the top off, make marks on the lid and the bottom that line up so you have a reference on how the lid should fit together. It will fit only one way (in theory!).

Now that the pieces are apart, cradle the lid in your hand and use the blunt end of a wooden knife or a right-angled rib to clean up the inside score marks and corner. Leave no gaps, and be careful not to distort the shape. **[O]**

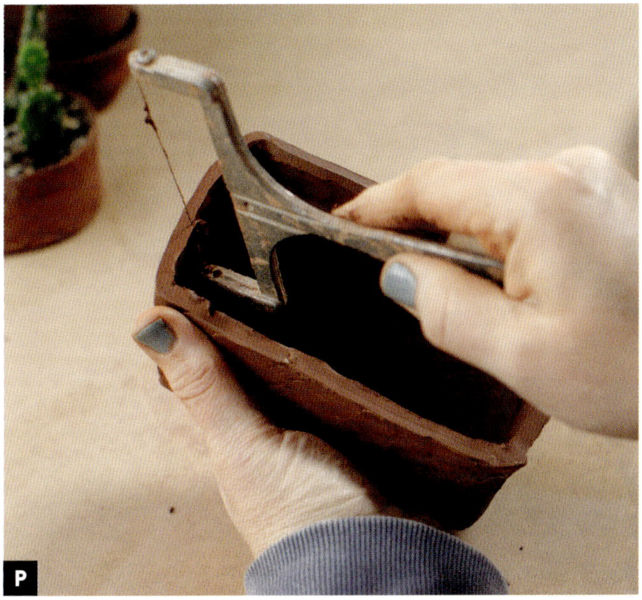

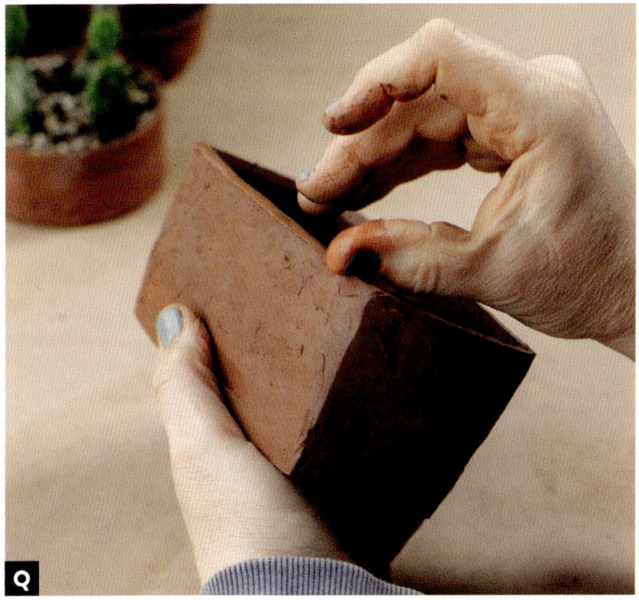

Using a cheese cutter or scalpel, trim the interior wall edge. **[P]** To finish the outside edge of the wall, use the back of your thumbnail and a little water and gently roll the corner up. **[Q]** Set aside.

Now, for the bottom section, again use the back of your thumbnail and a little water and gently roll the outside corner down. This will create a relationship with the lid and a stronger edge less likely to chip.

Make a coil roughly the length of the interior circumference of your footprint. Using a rolling pin or a brayer, make the coil into a long narrow ¼" (.63 cm) slab. Use a ruler to make the slab 1" (2.5 cm) wide and keep the length.

Inserting the Flange

Score the interior wall of the bottom piece.

Score the bottom half (½" [1.3 cm]) of the 1" (2.5 cm) slab—roughly 13" long slab

Wet the long slab and gently start placing it on the interior scored wall, again mid-wall. **[A]**

Pay close attention to the corners, and don't press so hard that you overlap the wall. This wall edge is your lid seat. It's best to taper the flange slab more toward the center of the form, just slightly.

Once it is pressed in place, use a right-angled rib to clean up the inside attachment and the wall seat. **[B] [C]**

Now that your flange is cleaned up, it is probably uneven on the top and too tall. Using a scalpel, cut down the flange to about ½" (1.3 cm) above the wall seat. I do this freehand, but I have had some practice and have a steady hand. Use a ruler and make a guide line if you need to. Use all the tools in your toolbox! Now gently pinch around the edge to soften the hard line just created, gently leaning it toward the center of the form. **[D]**

Here's the moment of truth. Put the lid on the base. Don't mash it on there, just see whether it fits. Find your matching marks, and gently see whether they go together. If they don't, no worries—see where the problems are and use your rib to clean up the lid seat, taper the flange toward the center

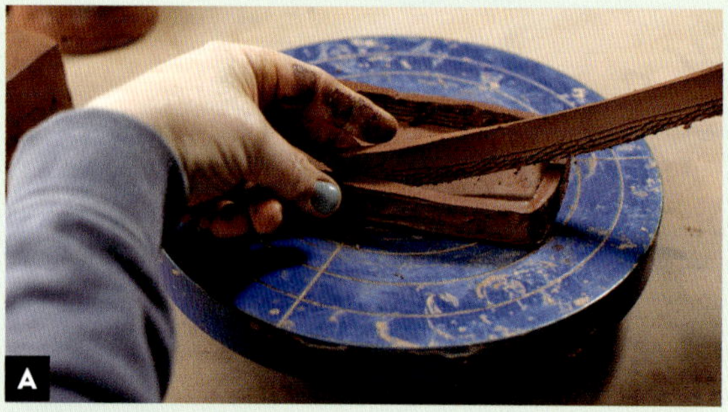

A

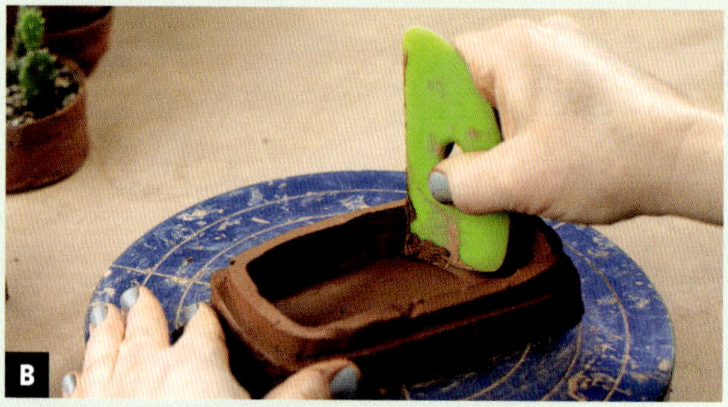

B

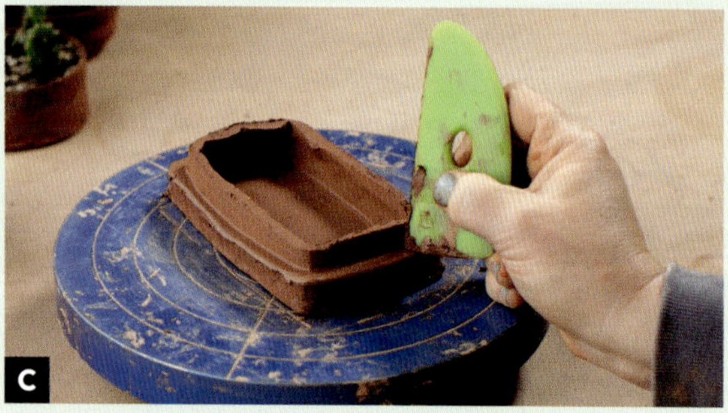

C

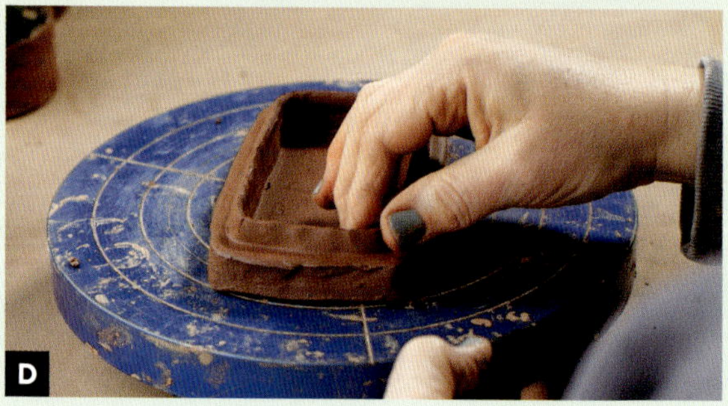

D

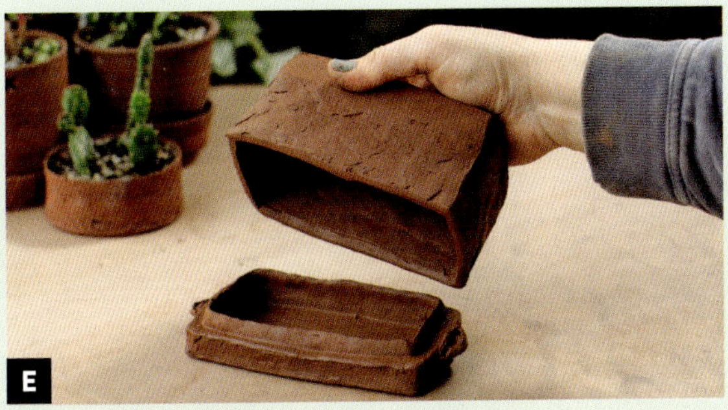

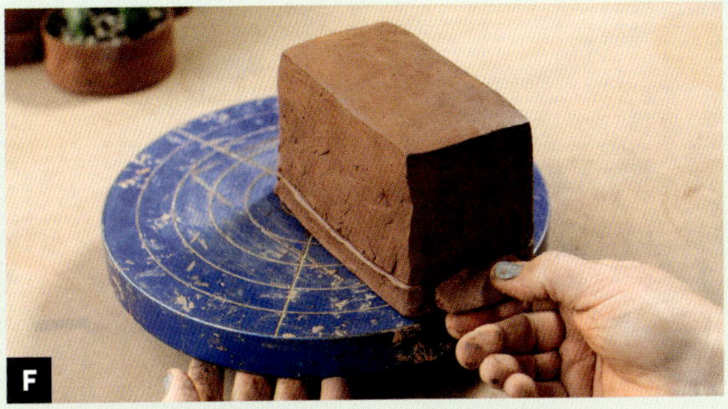

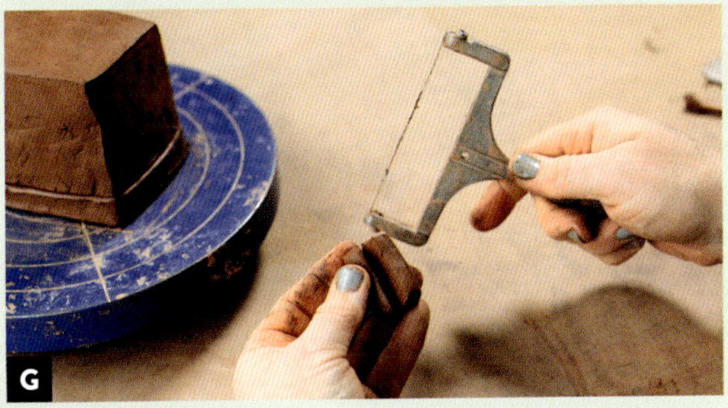

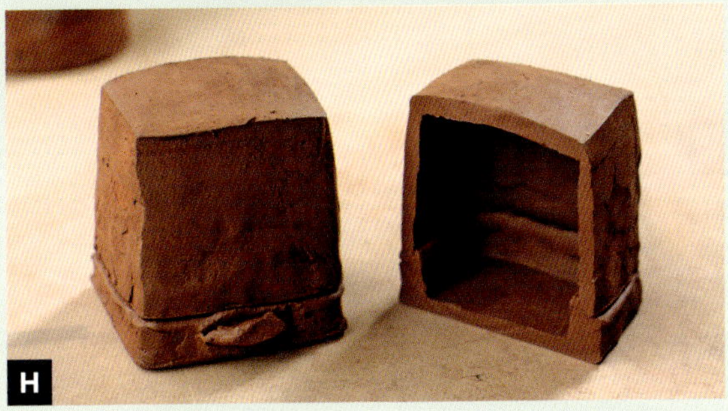

a bit more, or take a little off from the inside of the lid. (A metal rib is good for this.) There are multiple ways to fix the fit. Just go slowly and gently. **[E]**

Once the pieces are together, let it rest. Now is the time to make your key. The example is keyed with glazing, but you can add matching stamps or make and attach a clay tab that lines up. Whatever works for you.

This object doesn't really need handles, but I think it looks a bit naked without them. Roll a 1" (2.5 cm) coil, slip in half. Using your fingers, shape it into a long triangle and attach to the tray portion of the butter box. Refine. **[F] [G]**

There is one last step. After the pot has set up some, I like to make sure the lid comes off and on easily. Work the lid off carefully. Clean up any points that seem sticky, and don't forget about the flange edge. Now it should be more leather hard. Take a small green scrubby or a piece of drywall sandpaper and drag it around the interior of the lid and exterior edge of the flange, taking away the sharp corners. We want to make sure this pot can take a little bit of banging around and survive! Put the box back together and let dry.

NOTE: When it comes to glazing, this style of box should be dried, fired, and then glaze fired with the lid on. This will help with any possible warping, as it will warp as a unit and the lid will still fit. When glazing, make sure your lid seat and flange (bottom) and the inside wall of the lid where it will touch the lid seat and the flange are glaze free. This is really important if you want a lidded box and not a door stop! **[H]**

TAPAS PLATES

They don't serve real tapas here in the United States, not like they do in Spain. On my first trip to Spain, I learned the distinct difference. I was there for close to three weeks with family and friends and ate many amazing meals. The tapas are what I remember most vividly. They arrived when we were done exploring for the day and it was time to sit and enjoy our company. If I remember correctly, tapas are served sometime after 4 p.m. and before the dinner hour, which was maybe 9 p.m. It amazed me to walk into a bar or cafe and order a drink, and when it arrived, it came with food! With one drink, I'd get fried little fishes and with the next drink grilled eggplant with honey drizzled over it, or green beans coated with some unknown delicious spice—all of it amazing. I can't say I would have ordered any of it from a menu, but I loved trying everything that came my way! So this project is not necessarily about making a replica of the little plates, as they were just standard commercial restaurant plates, but to try, in my interpretation, to capture the emotional experience of those moments.

To make work that folks connect with, one needs to find an emotional component that compels exploration. When I look back at those moments in the bar drinking and eating, what I remember is a sense of wonder and the joy I felt in companionship and revelry. Deeper than that feeling, a real sense of being cared for and nurtured in those moments is what still lingers in my thoughts today, some 15 years later. Identifying and connecting those emotions to a tiny little dish helps me dive deep into an investigation of form and color to try to make work that can elicit those emotions from my audience.

Now, you might wonder, how do you make an emotional plate? Well, I think that is mostly an impossible notion! What you want to do is tap into an energy and a spirit of those emotions and bring that to your making with the hope that a small sliver of those thoughts and feelings find their way into your work. That energy, with practice, becomes easier and easier to tap into: think of it as setting an intention, something to strive toward. I sometimes believe that our progress in this area is all but invisible, until suddenly one day, it's present in our work. So keep identifying the energy and feeling you want in your work. I believe that one day it will manifest for you.

There are lots of ways to make small dishes but for this project we are going to mostly rely on our hands and a little bit of slab work and explore one of the more foundational and intimate ways to work with clay: the pinch pot.

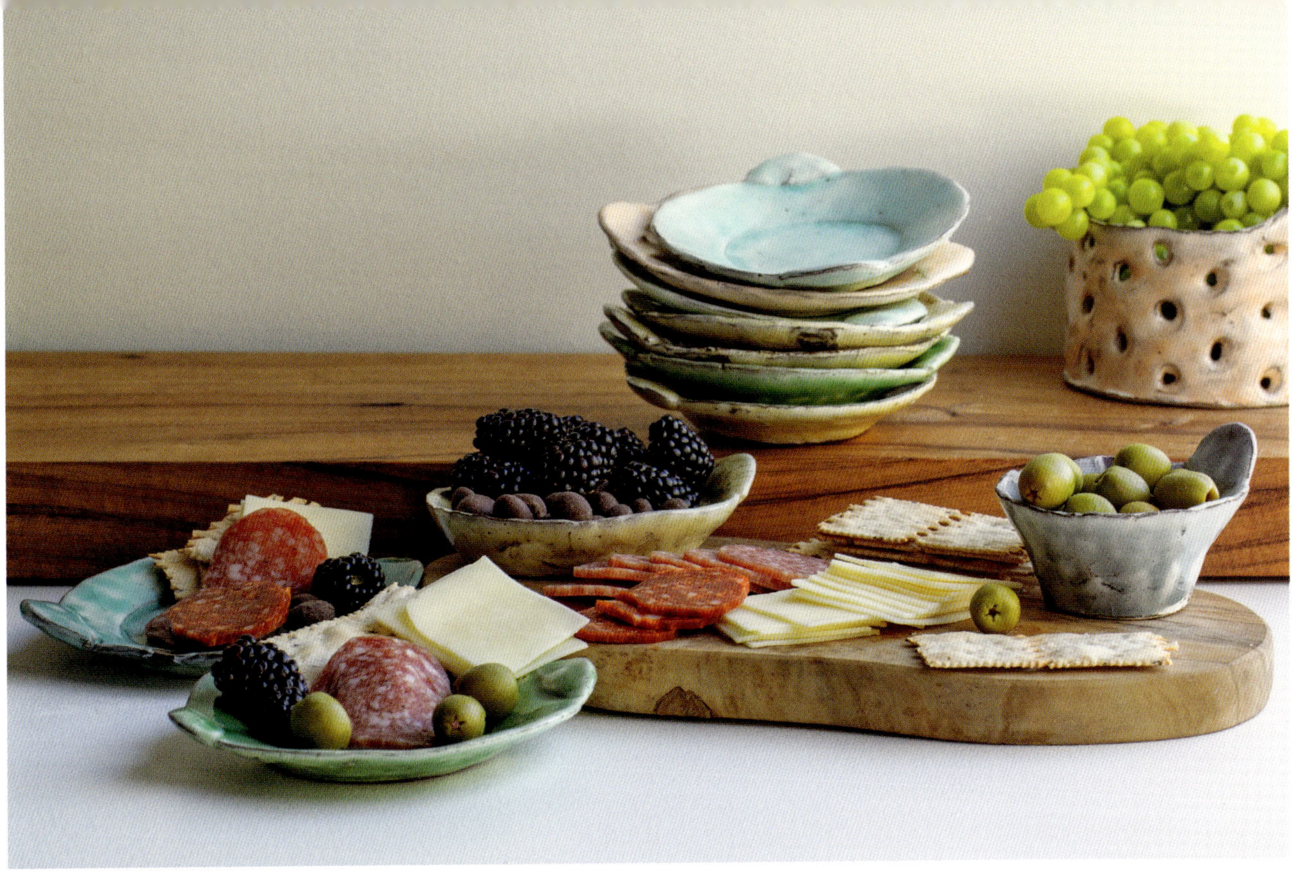

CONE 5 red clay, white slip, celadon style commercial glaze

Something to Think About

Pinch pots are often presented as a very simple project idea. This project may bring up some issues for you. In the early days in my practice, I did not find pinching pots the easiest way to work. If your hands give you trouble, it might even be a painful prospect. This type of project often illuminates a need to work on dexterity and mobility. In my experience, exercises like this often bring a level of frustration and negative self-talk. Be kind to yourself. Go slow and be patient with yourself. Evaluate whether you just need to practice more, with less worry about outcome, or if this process is not for you and your body. If so, move on. Another option is to try a combination of pinch pots with other processes, such as slab and coil building. This is just one of the skills you are adding to your toolbox. It is an important skill to know and have in your back pocket if the need arises. But please remember, in clay, there is always another way a project/problem can be solved.

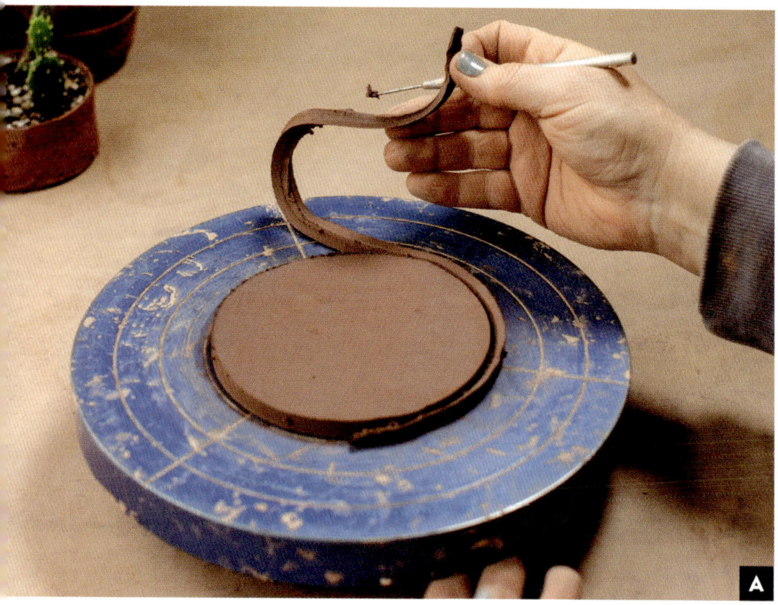

A

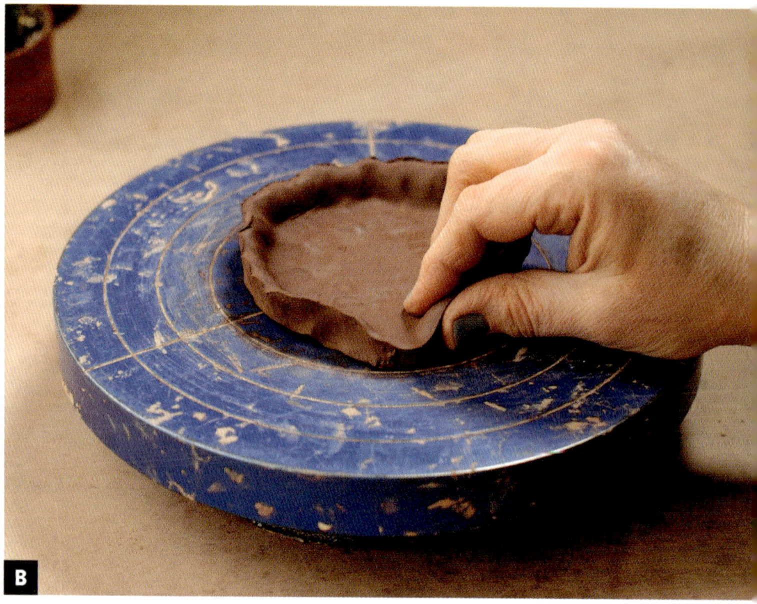

B

TOOLS AND MATERIALS

Basic Tool Kit (page 37)

Brayer

Serrated rib

Sunshine Stick

Measure out a few bits of clay roughly the size of a walnut or small tangerine up to the size of an orange. Play around with scale on this project. You may need more clay to manipulate than you think to get the desired plate size. Roll the clay bits into a little ball. Gently flatten the ball on your work surface and pull it off the tabletop. It is always a good idea to get a little air between the table and the clay. (It can be difficult to a get a piece of clay off the working surface the longer it sits attached.)

Using a rolling pin or a brayer (small roller device), roll the flattened ball into a more recognizably shaped slab. Aim for a circular or oval shape with consistent thickness, just under ½" (1.3 cm) thick. You want the slab to be about 1" to 1½" (2.5 to 3.8 cm) wider than the desired bottom (foot) of the dish. If the shape doesn't resemble a circle or oval, trim it with your needle tool. (You can always place the slab of clay on your banding wheel, spin, and use a needle tool to make a perfect circle.) **[A]**

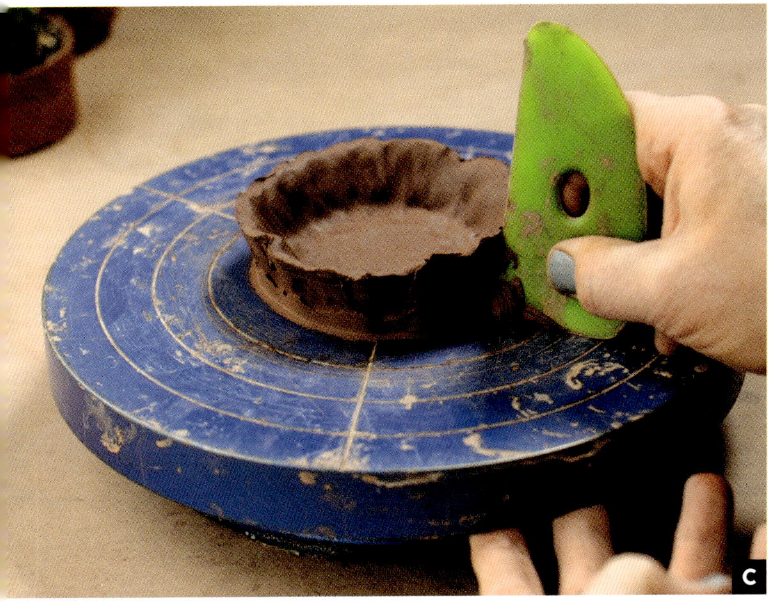

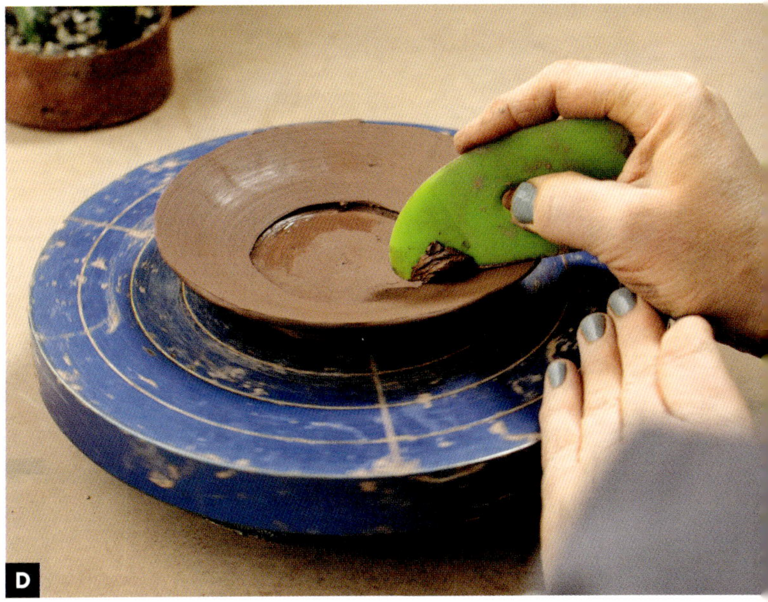

Place the slab in the center of your banding wheel. Using your fingers and thumb, gently work the edge in a more vertical position. Apply more pressure with your fingers or thumb positioned on the outside of the form. Continue working your way around the form, moving the clay up to create a small wall around the piece. **[B]**

Use a rib or your hands to gently shape/pinch the wall to resemble a bowl or small plate lip. Reaffirm (compress) the shape with several passes of your rib. **[C] [D]** The form will have a memory of being more vertical and may bounce back during the drying and firing process. Make sure not to skip the compression process of this step; it will help keep the desired shape.

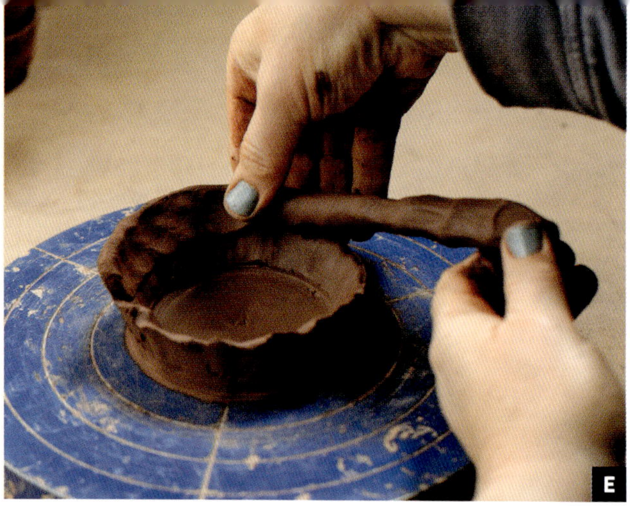

E

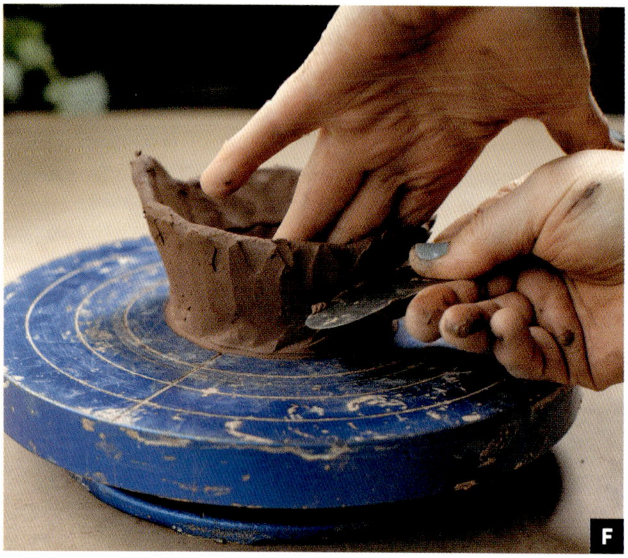

F

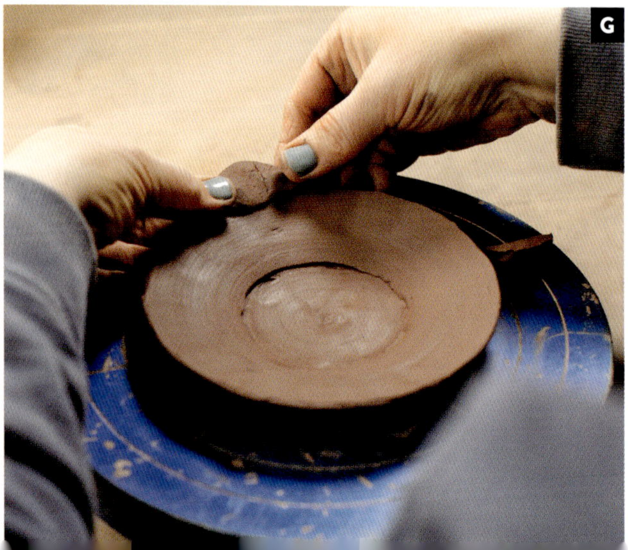

G

If the lip of the plate is not big enough, you may want to add a coil to the top edge. Your object should be soft enough for you to take a bit of clay out of the bag, make a small coil, and attach it to the top edge. Overlap the attachment, rib the wall inside and out for consistency, and then cut off to the desired height and finish the edge (described in the previous step). **[E] [F]**

Now that the shape is where you want it, it is time to finish the top/outside edge. Your pot may have a perfect edge, but often the top edge is more uneven than desired. Use a cut-off tool (Sunshine Stick and cheese cutter) to even up the top, finding your lowest edge point and using that as your guide. Soften the sharp edge with your fingers, pinching the edge between your finger and thumb to compress and define it. There should be a relationship between the lip and the texture of the whole pot.

Add handles. Take a small bit of clay (about the size of a swollen quarter), roll into a ball, and flatten gently. Then cut it in half. Using a scalpel, slice down the center of the cut side, spread open, and sandwich on the edge of the plate. Gently squish and shape into a soft half-moon. **[G]**

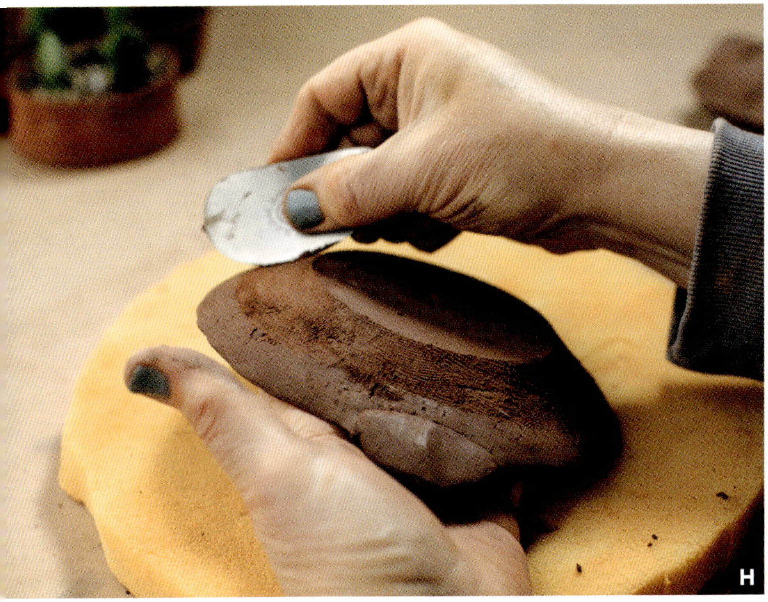

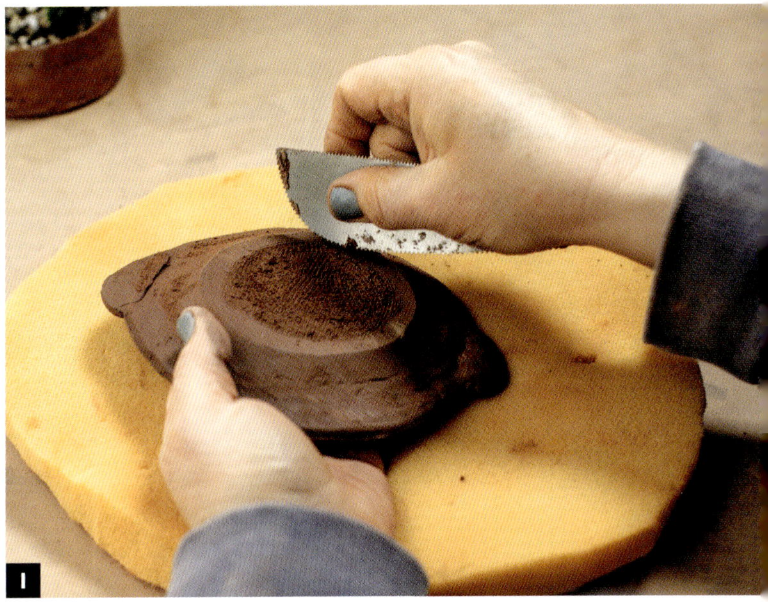

Repeat for the other handle, and place it directly across from the attached handle. Once both are in place and shaped, use your scalpel to cut the edge of the half-moon shape to even out any size discrepancy. Gently pinch the edges to soften and finish them.

Remove the plate from the wheel head—you may need to use a cutoff wire. Let the form get to a leather-hard state.

Create a foot. You may notice that the pot has "lifted" on the bottom outside edge, and become a bit wobbly, which is never a great sign for a plate! To solve this, use a surform or serrated rib to gently take a bit of clay from the center bottom of the plate. Gently give the plate a hint of a foot ring (around the outside edge) and make sure it sits flat. One way to see if the plate is sitting evenly is to gently rub the plate on your working table, and then look at the bottom. Are the scratch marks or burnishing even? Is it scratching only in the center? Time to work the serrated rib or surform across the surface if so. **[H] [I]**

BASKET

One of my favorite objects out there in the world is a basket. Whenever I'm wandering through an antique store or a thrift store in a small town, I am always on the lookout for interesting containers—especially colander-style containers. All shapes and sizes interest me in application and design. Sometimes functional clay objects can be viewed as very limited in their application: bowls, cups, plates, and vases. My hope is that through all the projects in this book you are getting an idea of how versatile clay is. This project is an example of what my teachers told me not to do: cut holes in clay! I have a firm belief that we need to learn the rules of any medium. Knowing your material—in this instance, clay—will help you use it with more clarity and skill. Those skills will grow over time. Then, once you know the rules, you learn to bend them until they snap. For everyone those "rules" will look different as you grow and develop in what interests and excites you.

For me that journey began with travel and visiting architecture. I wondered how to capture the beauty of line and light I saw in cathedral windows. How different they looked from the inside versus the outside. Because clay and functional forms were my thing, I started making boxes with holes cut in them. Over the years, I eventually wandered down the road of colanders, those objects I always loved in the antique stores. What interested me most about this object was how to play with the patterns of the piercings, and how to make that work in a round object that could range from narrow to wide, such as a bowl shape. I still investigate and challenge myself to come up with new patterns and new shapes and love to play with the scale of these forms. I hope you love playing around with this form as much as I do.

This project will help get you comfortable with coil building and piercing. Coil building is my go-to skill; it is my comfort zone, and I find I can work out new ideas and forms very quickly. (Actually, this project could also be built with soft slabs. It might be worth doing a side-by-side comparison to see which works for you. Check the wall tile project on page 78 to get an idea of what soft-slab construction would look like!) I think we all find one or two skills that really can work with our bodies and our approach to creative solutions. Like all new skills, if you have never done this before, it may feel awkward, and you may be a little clumsy at first. Don't get frustrated. Just keep at it and work in this midrange size until you get the hang of it. The more objects you can start and finish, the better you will get. I promise.

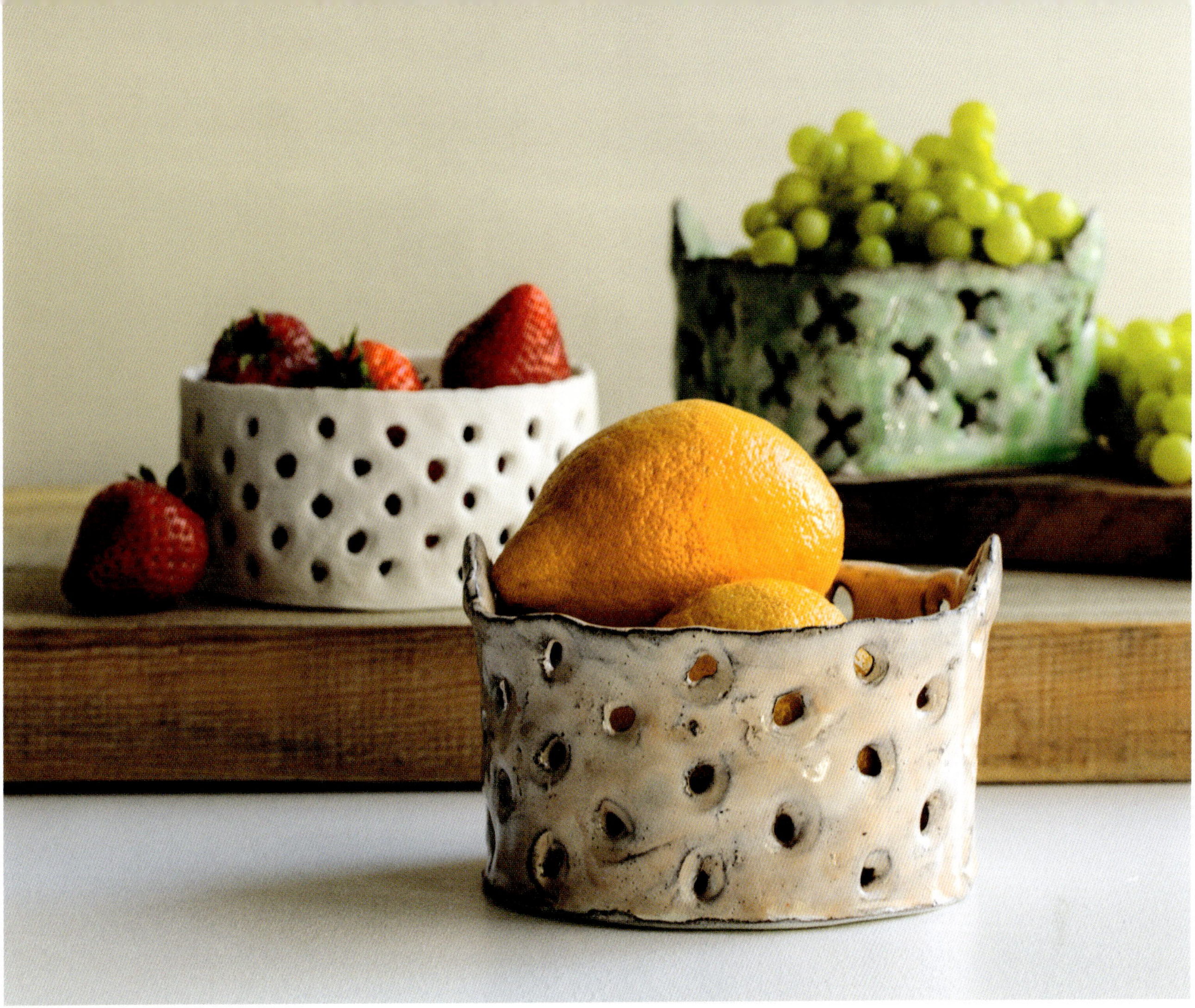

Two different finishes:
1. CONE 5, red clay, white slip, celadon style commercial glaze
2. CONE 5, exposed porcelain clay

TOOLS AND MATERIALS

Basic Tool Kit (page 37)
Templates (pages 164–165)
Sunshine Stick

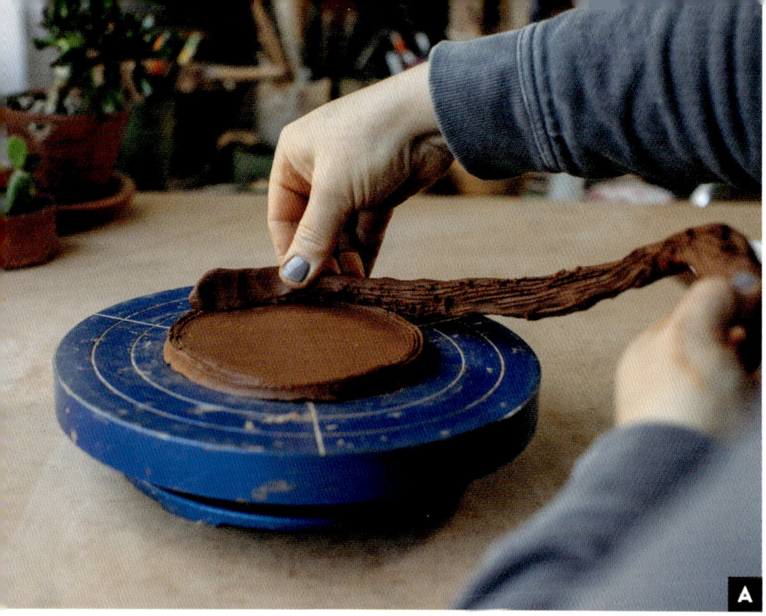
A

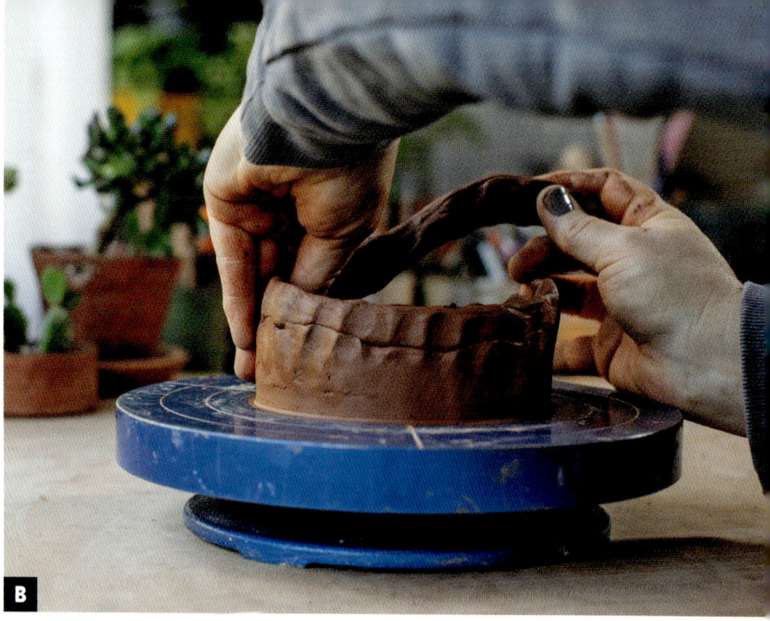
B

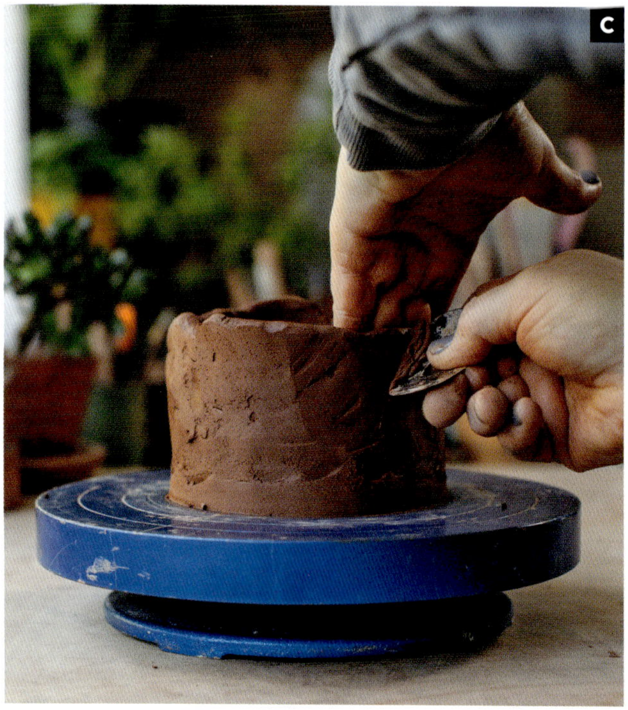
C

Roll out a ¼" (.63)- thick slab for the footprint of your basket. Use the template on page 164 and cut out the shape. As always, you are free to make your own template. My only advice is to avoid any sharp corners to begin with. Remember, we will be creating a piercing pattern that works its way all around the form, and sharp corners can be hard to deal with.

Score around the top outside edge of your footprint and start coil building. See the Foundational Skills section for images and tips if needed (page 45). The thickness of your wall should be about ¼" (.63 cm). If it's much thicker, it will be more difficult to pierce. **[A] [B] [C]**

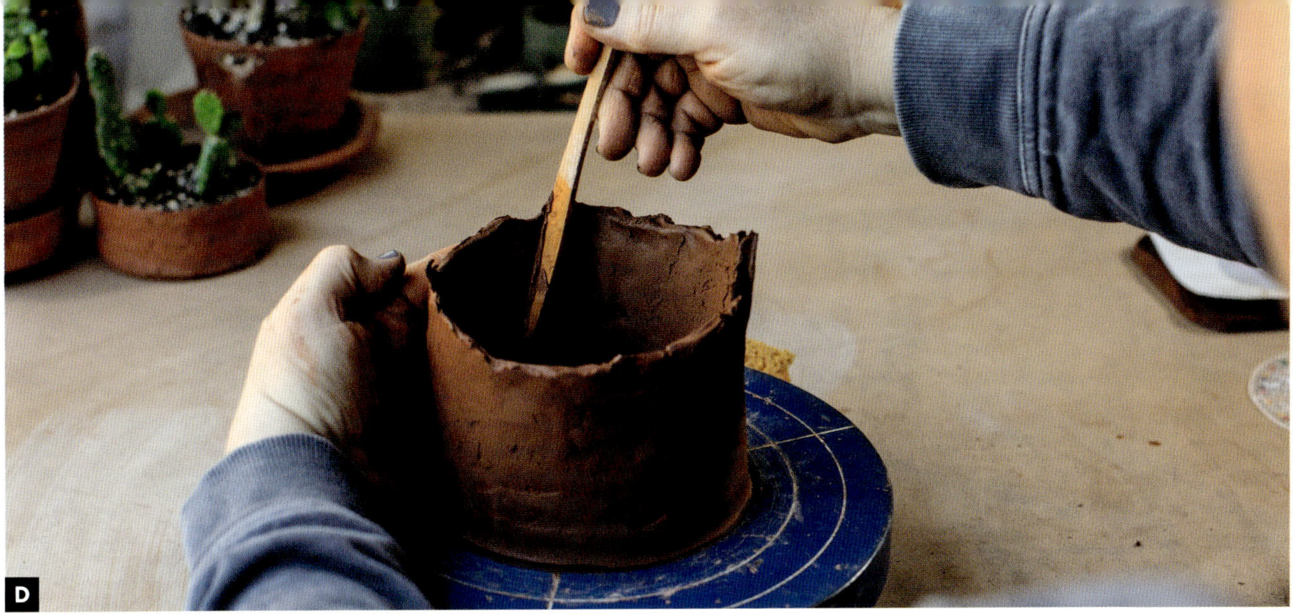

When you reach 4" (10.1 cm) in height, use a cutoff tool to make the wall even to 3.5" (8.9 cm). This should give you a consistent edge and wall thickness. Your entire form should be stable but soft to the touch. Handle it carefully. Using your fingers, softly pinch your way around the top edge to give the lip a soft finished edge. (No sharp edges on functional forms is a good guideline to remember.) In this case, the way you will finish the pierced areas will have a relationship to the lip. (Always look for parts of the pot to relate to each other! This is very important for a "finished" feel to an object. Also, those relationships can help you make choices on a form you when you are unsure how to proceed.)

Now is also your last chance to "shape" your basket. Look at your pot. Is it wonky? Is it too straight up and down? Does it not look like the images? Use a rib or a wooden knife to shape your pot. From the inside area you can use these tools to "swell" the walls and give it a tad more volume. From the outside, try to tame it and collar it in. Look up the section on darting on page 48 if your form needs serious altering.

[D] If you don't like the shape, keep trying, and make it like the image pictured. If it isn't the one here, is it the one in your head? Once you are satisfied, let the pot set up to a medium leather hard state.

TIP *Take that image and make it a reality. Often folks give up too early and live with a form that isn't satisfying for them. At this moment you can always add more coils and reshape the pot to fit your image. Keep at it, even if you destroy the form. You will learn a lot and this is a really quick project to replicate and try again. Part of what you are learning right now is to* make *with your hands and clay what your eyes and brain are interpreting. Like with any new skill, you get better when you practice.*

Roll up the bottom edge. Using your finger and a little water, gently roll the sharp edge where the pot meets the tabletop, making several passes so as to not fold over the edge.

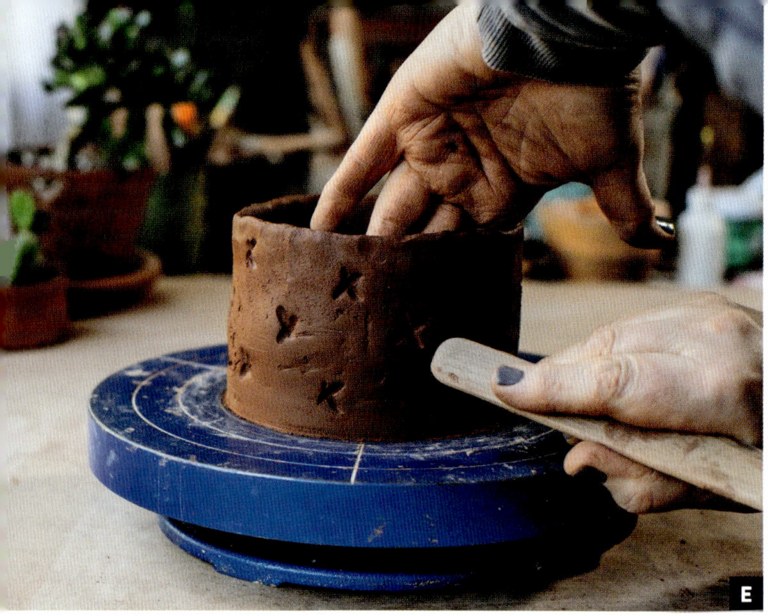

E

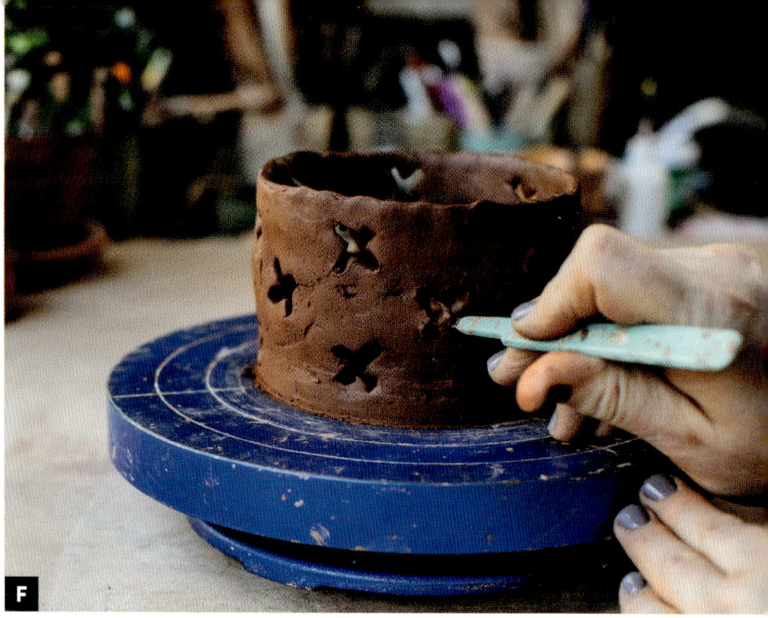

F

Now that your form is finished, it's on to designing the piercing pattern. This pattern will wrap around the entire form. The bottom will also have a pierced element so the basket can function as a colander. The best tools for this part are a bendy clear ruler and a needle tool. Gently, but visibly, make a grid on the pot.

Using the wide end of your needle tool or the blunt end of your wood knife, move vertically to make a mark at every other intersection. Do the same on the next row, but start at the intersection one up, so you have an alternating pattern. **[E]** Make these marks, even if you're a pro at piercing. I have learned the hard way (too many times to mention) to mark out my pattern. Thinking you will remember the pattern (because how could you forget) but then getting caught up in piercing and making a small pattern mistake can completely ruin your design and pot. Also, making these marks will give you an idea on how the pattern will look and whether you want to change the layout of the design. All you have to do is take a rib and scrape away your marks and lay out a different grid. Don't forget the bottom!

TIP *Make sure you account for the wall and floor thickness when gridding and piercing.*

With the grid in place, marks made, and design approved, make your cuts. Using a scalpel, cut out small circles or *X*'s, like in the example, at the marks. **[F]** Cut a couple and then gently pinch the circle between your fingers. Do not mash it . . . remember, no sharp edges. You want to close in the hole slightly and soften the cut marks. This is the finished edge of the cutouts. **[G]** Depending on the thickness of your clay and the size of your cutout, the hole might be nonexistent. Adjust your cutout size accordingly. This might also affect your pattern, so do a few samples before you cut out all your marks. Remember, it is easy to

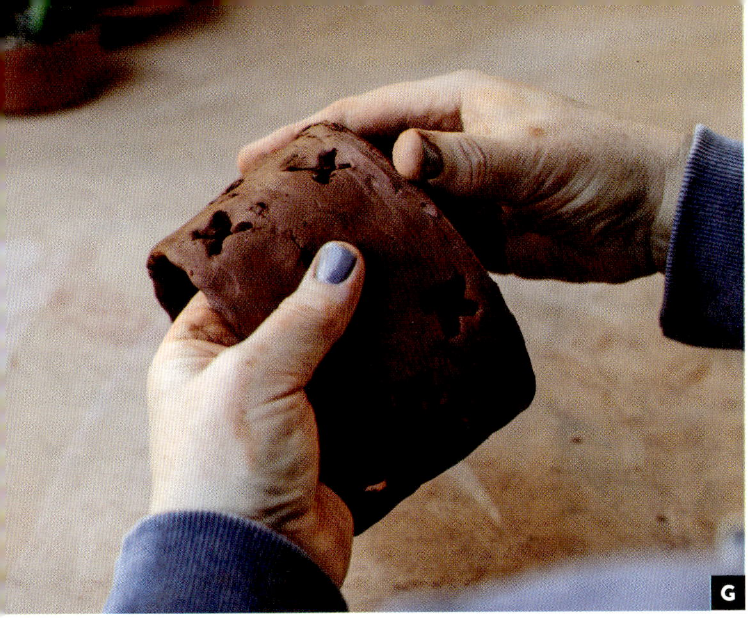

take away clay but adding it is more challenging, so err on the smaller side and then move on to larger holes if needed. Once all your cutouts are done, pinch them in. You may need to recut some holes or adjust the final look with your scalpel. Remember, you are compressing these piercings with your fingers from both sides. So make sure you are doing that for the bottom as well. (No squishing against the work surface!)

TIP *Compressing these cutouts will help reduce possible cracking. But with any cutout, there is a risk of cracking. So don't sweat it too much in the beginning and just practice and see where the piercing exploration takes you. Avoid sharp corner cutouts and cutouts spaced close together in the beginning.*

Give your piece the once over, and check in on the lip and make sure you haven't scuffed it up while piercing. Your piece may still be soft to the touch, so handle and clean it up gently. When it looks good, set it on the shelf to dry slowly (draped under plastic is a good idea).

COFFEE POUR-OVER

There is no arguing with coffee connoisseurs on how best to prepare their coffee. We, as makers, have an opportunity to contribute to the slow morning ritual that coffee lovers enjoy. A lot of modern life is about speeding up and efficiency, and you have chosen a hobby that is all about slowing down and paying attention to details and the rhythms of yourself and the materials. What is exciting and satisfying about functional work is how it leads us as makers down a path of investigation, and how the result of that investigation is an object that becomes an important part of someone's day. It adds to their ritual, and it adds beauty to their experience that changes how they experience the world around them.

The notion that beauty can impact our daily life is a bit of a pillar in my personal philosophy. The truth of it has only grown through my life and exploration of making art. Sometimes in making we can get wrapped up in our own exploration and ego. Sitting at your studio table can be a somewhat solitary existence. Although we are making work first for ourselves, ultimately, we make work to communicate and connect with others. That is how investigating a form such as a coffee pour-over can be important, even if you are not a coffee drinker. You learn not only what is technically important about the process of brewing coffee, which adds to your problem-solving skills, but also how to contribute to a singular moment of another human as an artist. What can you contribute to the beauty of the moment?

This project will involve working with soft and hard slab construction to build a functional coffee pour-over, using templates to piece together a somewhat complex form. There will also be the exploration of handle attachment.

TOOLS AND MATERIALS

Basic Tool Kit (page 37)

Templates (pages 165–166)

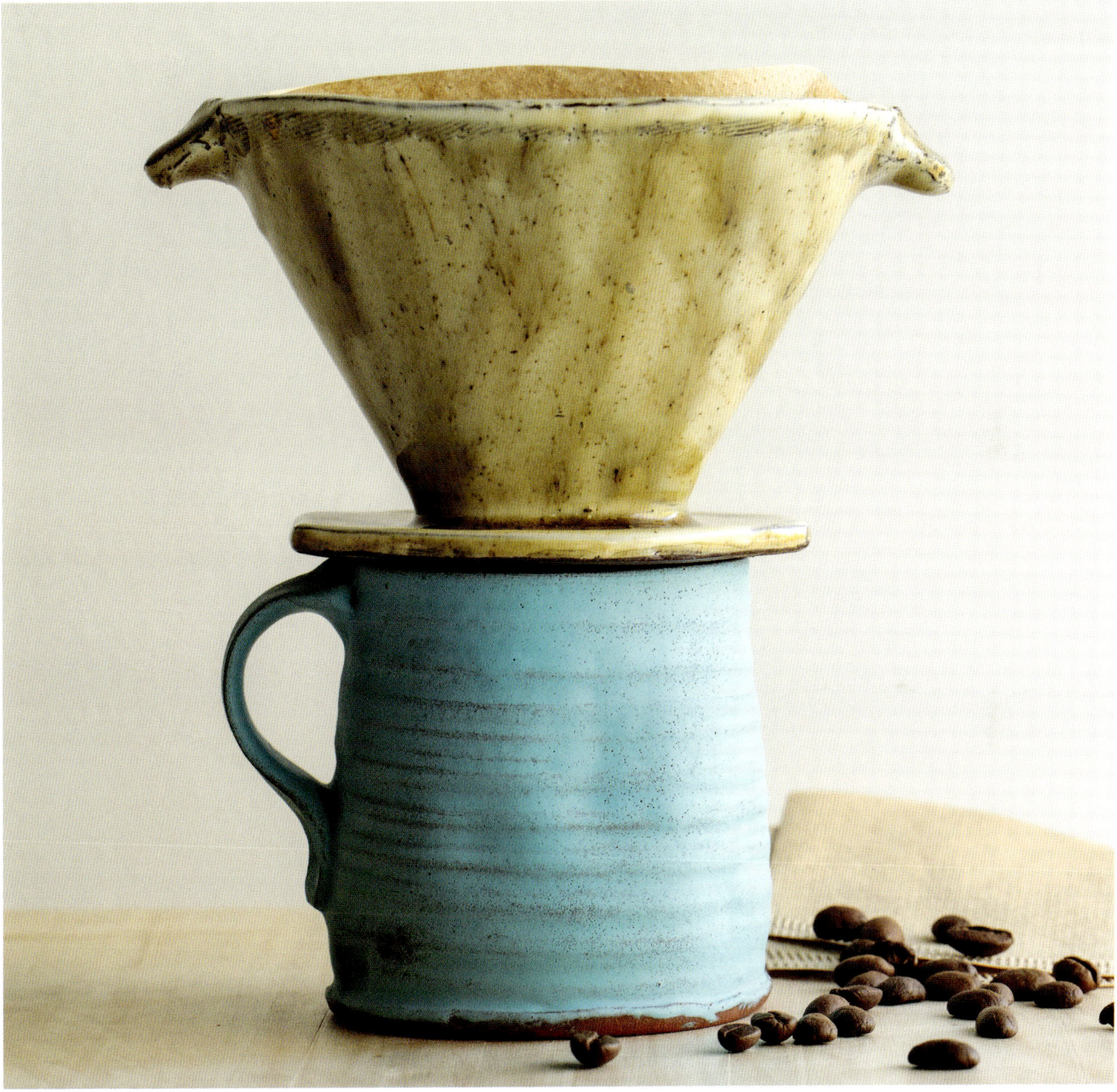

1. Pour-Over. **CONE** 5 red clay, white slip and celadon style commercial glaze
2. Mug, wheel thrown by author. **CONE** 3 red clay, commercial glaze, sandblasted

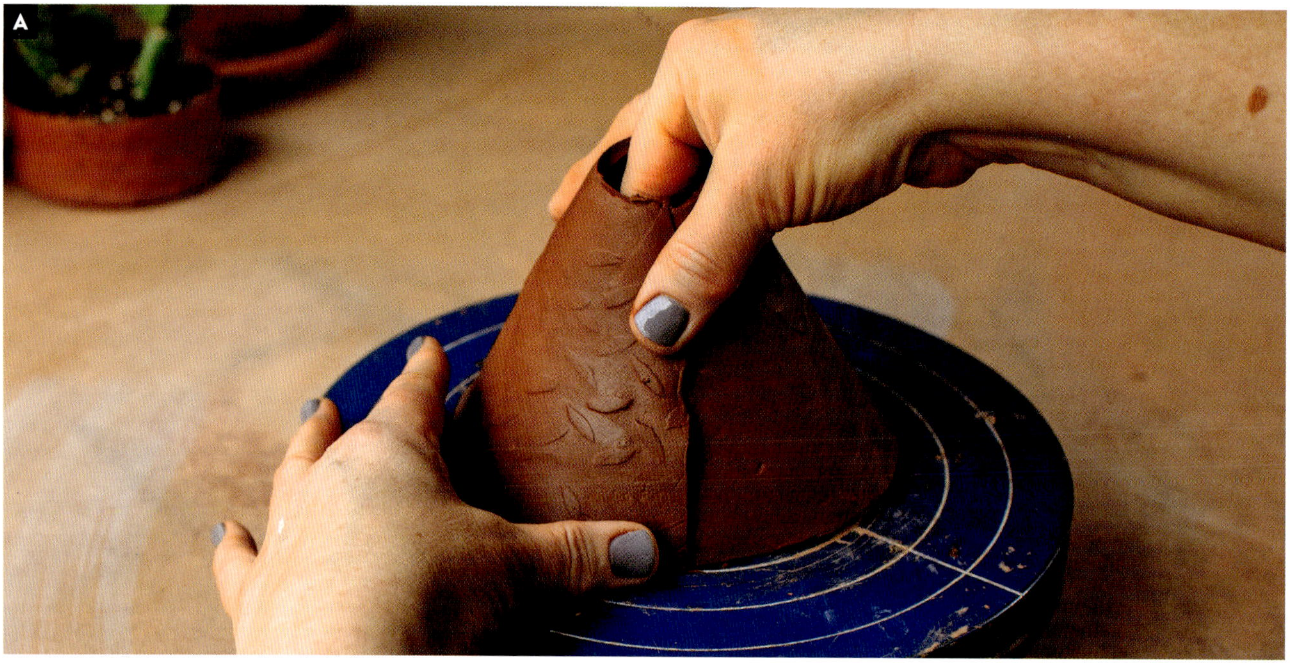

Roll out a ¼" (.63 cm)-thick slab, aiming for about 10" to 12" (25.4 to 30.5 cm) squared. Lay the templates from page 165 out on the slab and cut them out with a needle tool. Allow the slabs to stiffen up to a soft leather-hard state. This will make assembly a tad easier than working with super soft slabs.

OPTIONAL While waiting for the slab to firm up, make a small dish for the pour-over to rest on. Cut out the circle from your slab roughly 3" (7.6 cm) across, and a 1½" (⅜ cm)-wide strip, roughly 8" (20.3 cm) long. Bevel the outside of the circle and the bottom edge of the strip. Score each side and transpose one of the scored surfaces. Place it on a bat or piece of paper to limit the need to peel the piece off your working surface when finished. Attach the beveled edges together, keeping the wall as vertical as possible.

When the wall edges come together, bevel the edges, score, and attach. Clean up the outside and inside attachments with a right-angled rib. If the top edge needs evening, use a cutoff tool and then finish the edge. For this example, I used the cheese cutter to take off the inside and outside edge of the top lip. Set aside and leave to firm up.

Assemble the large cone. Work wide-side down. Bevel and score the vertical edge of the slab, wet one side, and attach. Gently clean up the attachment using a metal rib or wooden knife to make the seam disappear inside and out. Let the cone set up, and rest the cone with the large side down on the tabletop/bat. Your edges may be uneven, but that is okay for now. That will be addressed after the form has been allowed to set up and rest for a bit. This "resting" allows for the seam to adhere. **[A]**

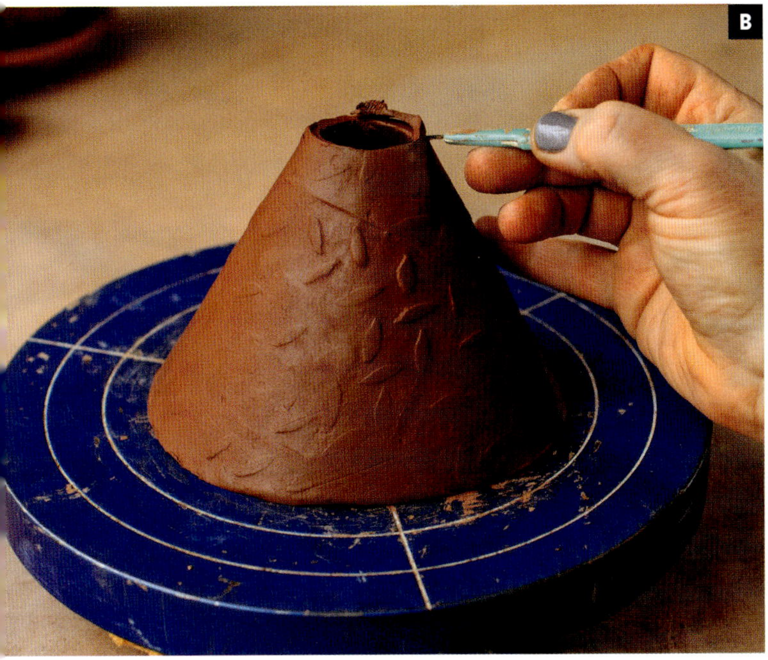

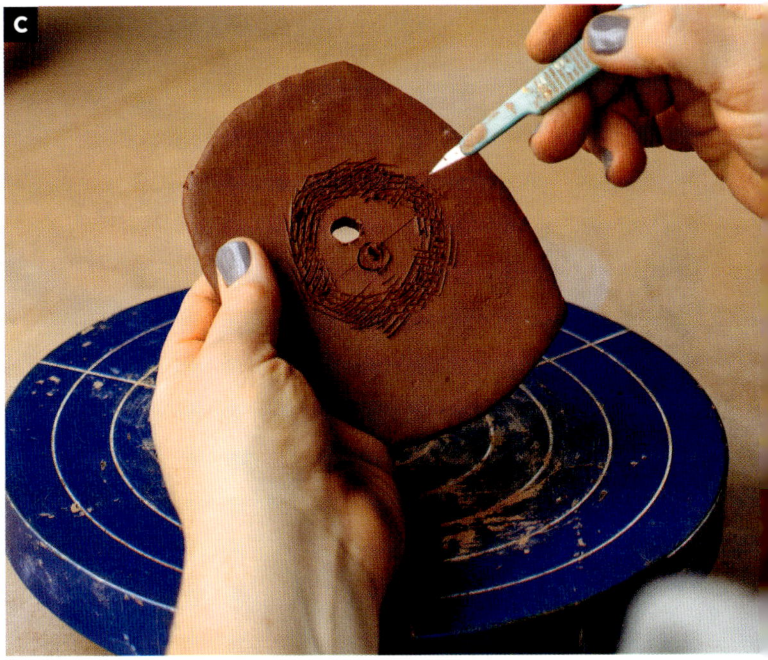

Using a rib, compress both sides of the disc shape; it should be the most set up of all your pieces. Using a brayer or rib, compress the edge of the disc shape. Then, using a green scrubby/soft red rib/drywall sandpaper, work round the edge and take away any sharp spots. This is the part of the pour-over that will get the most abuse, so it's important to make sure it is strong. Maintain a flat disc shape and avoid bending or excessive thinness on the edge.

Use a surform or scalpel to level off the narrow section of the large cone. Proceed gently and with caution near the attachment point. Work around the form in a circular motion and level it off as flat as possible. You want the opening to remain about 1" to 1½" (2.5 to 3.8 cm) across. **[B]**

Using a scalpel or drill bit, cut out holes in the bottom of the disc. They can be small or large, but use the inside of the cone as your reference point for how much space you have to pierce. (This may take some experimenting with and research to know what will work for the brewing of coffee.) Clean up the cutout section and address/finish the top edge of the cone. **[C]** Allow it to rest right side up on the disc, especially if the disc isn't leather hard yet. Before you move to the final steps, there should be no bend whatsoever in that disc.

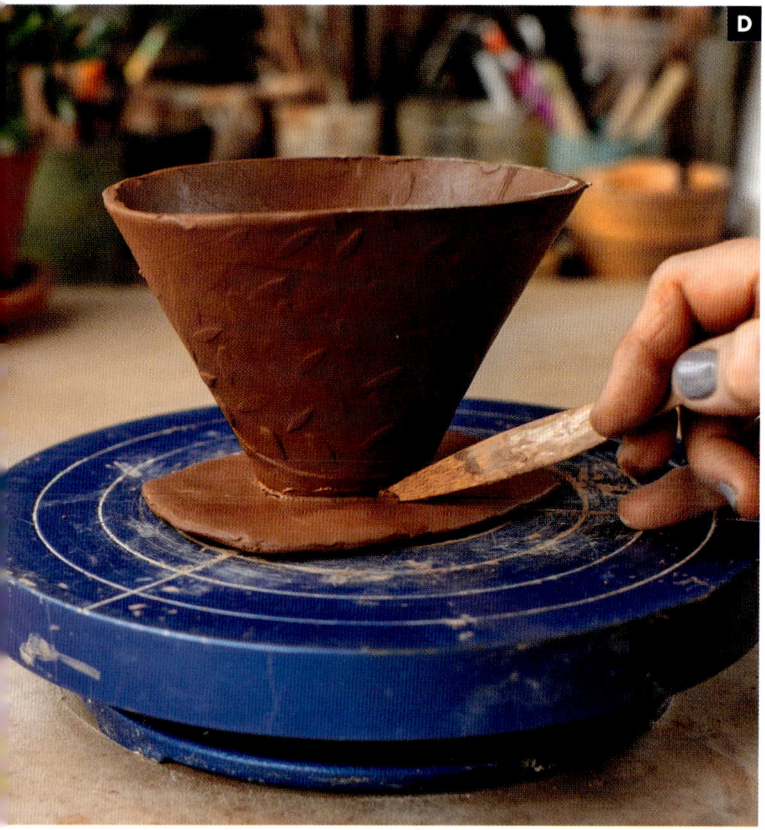

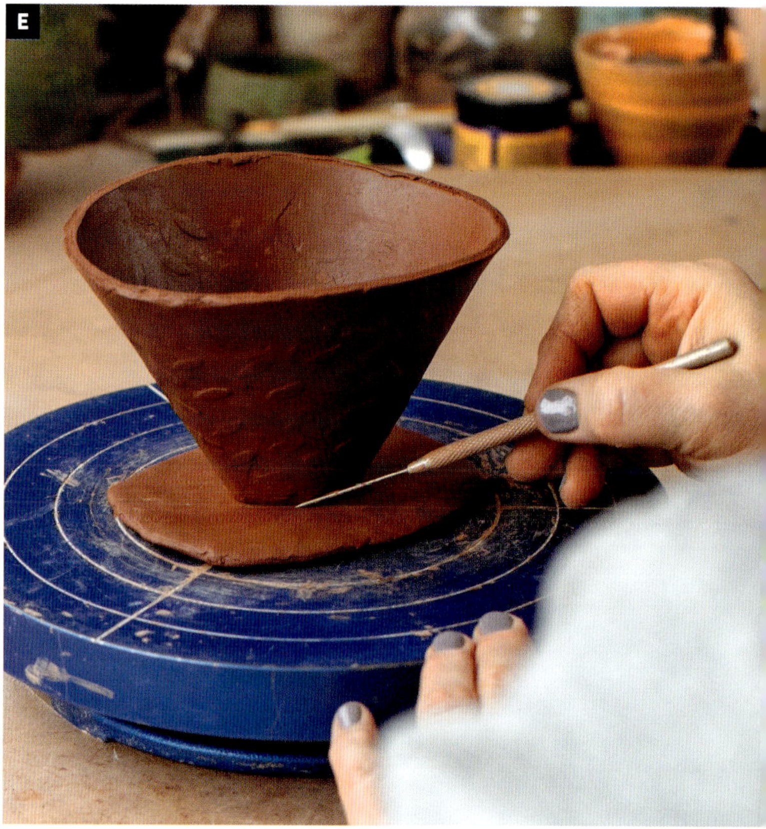

Turn the cone right side up (narrow end on the worksurface), and make sure it isn't leaning in any direction. The cone should be stable and centered.

Work firmly but gently; you don't want to distort the shape of the cone. **[D]** This small coil will increase the surface area of the attachment and add a bit of strength at this narrow connection point.

Grab the disc and center the cone, narrow side down. Using a needle tool, trace around the outside and inside of the cone onto the disc. **[E]** This will give you an idea of where to score. Score both the bottom of the cone and the disc (inside the circle). Be generous with your scoring—this attachment point is important. Wet one side and attach. Use a rib and wooden knife to clean up the attachment. If there are gaps or unevenness in the attachment, make a very tiny coil, backfill the outside attachment, and compress with your fingers and then with a tool.

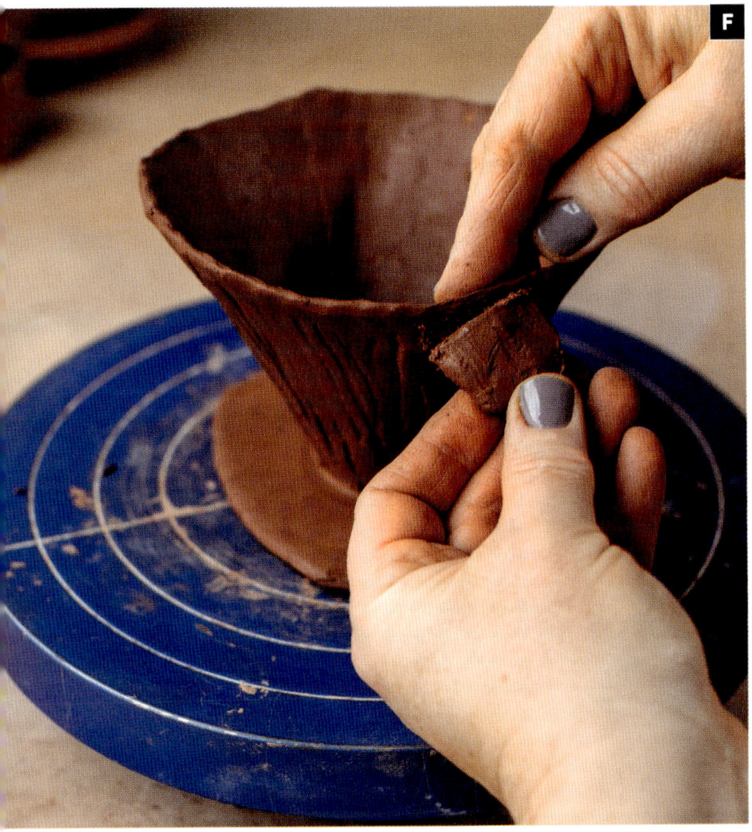

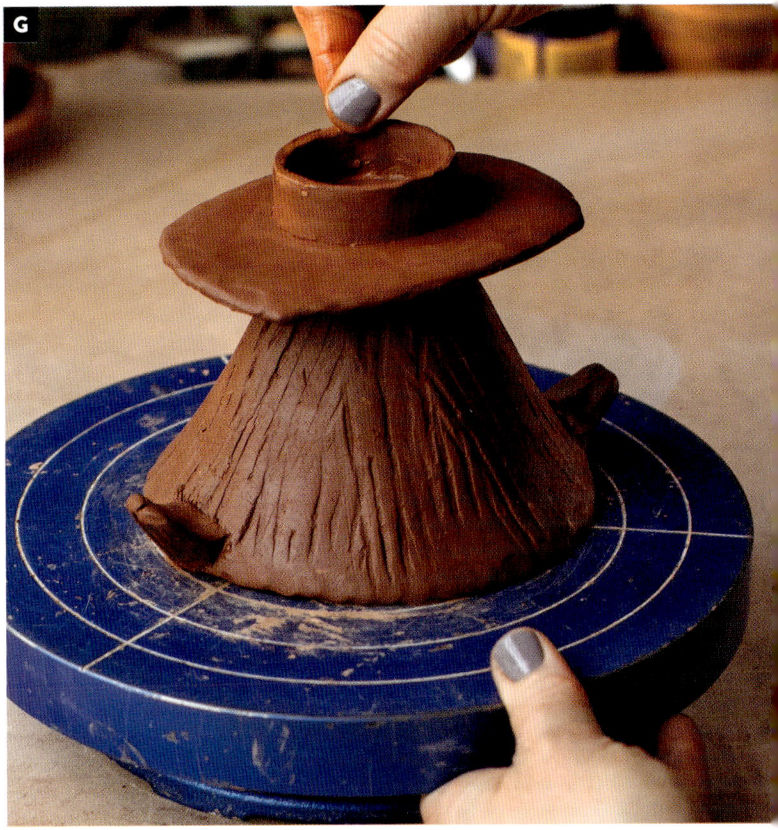

Now it's time to make and attach the handle. This can be a more traditional-style handle, like on a mug, or a nub off the top. It depends on what you would like. The piece needs something to hold on to that is removed from the heat of the steeping area. I made a couple of small nubbin handles across from each other. **[F]**

Once the piece has set up, meaning all the attachments are firm and the handles are set, you are ready to attach the last bit. Gently flip the cone over and set it on a soft work surface, such as a piece of foam, to protect the lip of the cone. Using a ½" (1.3 cm) strip of clay, make a circle roughly 2.5" (6.3 cm) across (it needs to fit inside your resting dish and a mug), bevel, and attach the ends. Center on the disc, score, and attach. Clean up the seams. **[G]** Allow to dry upside down.

MATCH STRIKER

Saving the best for last? This may be my favorite project in the book! Besides being adorable and practical, I had the most fun working out the design. I had a picture in my head: the perfect match striker. I sat down to make my vision and it totally didn't work. This is something I am always trying to get my students to understand: our first idea is mostly likely not our best idea and most definitely not our last idea. What comes out in the making are the realities of the object, what will work and what won't, and new ideas.

In the development of this little match striker, I started playing with several ideas after my imagining didn't pan out. When one prototypes a new object, it is important to lay out the needed components. The elements of a match striker are: someplace to strike a match (unglazed clay surface), someplace to store fresh matches, and someplace to deposit the hot used matchstick. I always recommend sketching out some possible ideas with a pen and paper, but sometimes that doesn't feel right or translate into a 3D form, and it is necessary to sketch with clay. Seeing things in three dimensions is sometimes how our brains need to process these kinds of objects.

When sketching with clay, I try and work quickly and make several very different iterations of a form. Often I'll set a goal—say five iterations in an hour. This makes sure I'm not focusing on craftsmanship but more on the design and the overall feel of the object. Craftsmanship will come later, when I decide on a direction to investigate. Sometimes how an object comes together initially can be very clumsy, but after I have the idea and form developed, I will reverse engineer a better/cleaner way for the object to be built. What was surprising on the development of this object was how different each match striker was in overall feeling and appearance. I knew immediately which one spoke to me and felt like "the one."

A quick side note on the other "failed" match strikers. I didn't toss these into the recycle bin but cleaned them up and thought I'd use them for some glaze testers and to possibly share with you the prototyping process. After they came through the process, I realized there was another gem in there that interested me and will be an avenue that is ripe for exploration. Don't be quick to toss aside all your experiments—sometimes there is a diamond in the rough that doesn't spark your interest immediately, but you will warm to over time and contemplation. Let's get making!

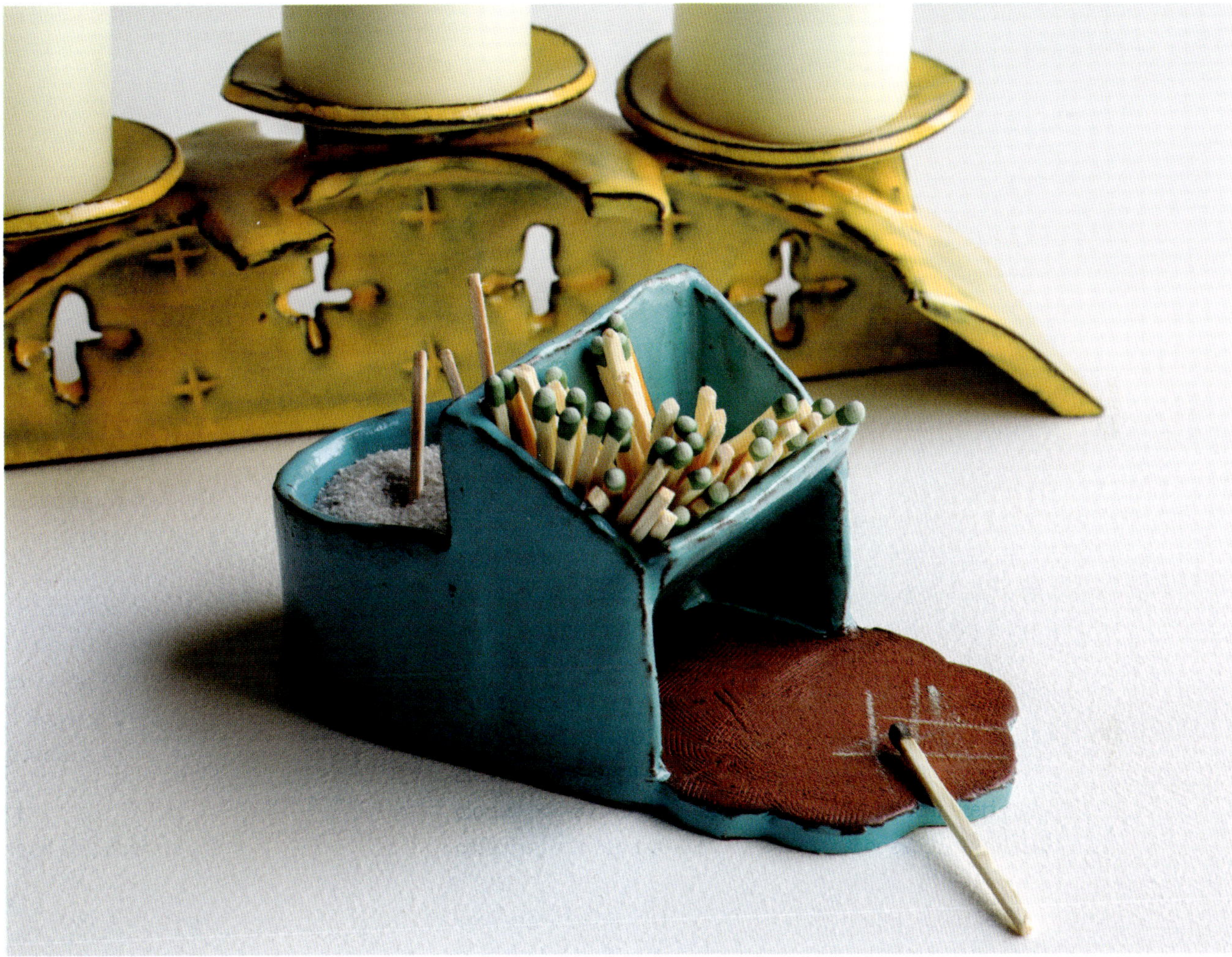

CONE 3, exposed raw clay and commercial glaze

TOOLS AND MATERIALS

Basic Tool Kit (page 37)

Serrated rib

Template (page 167)

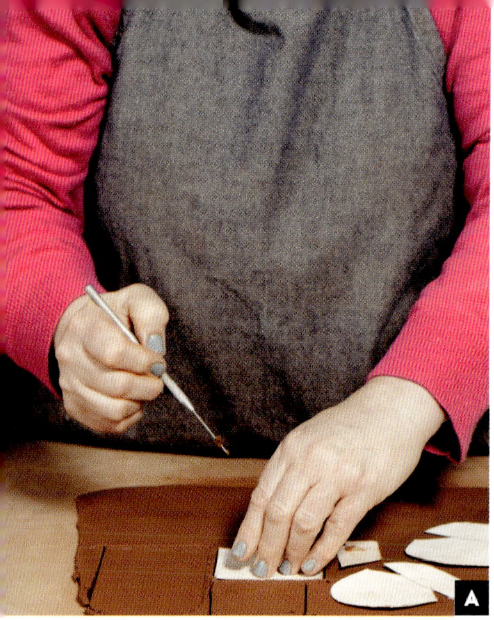

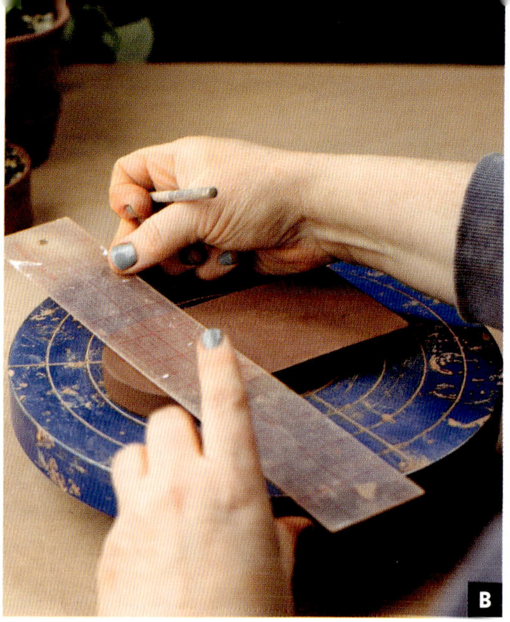

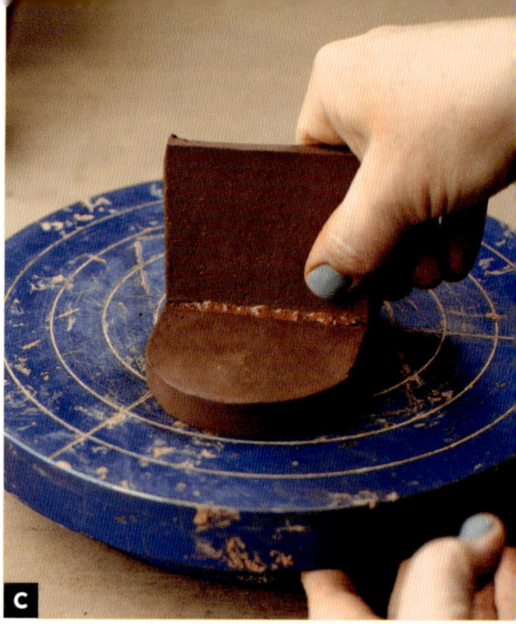

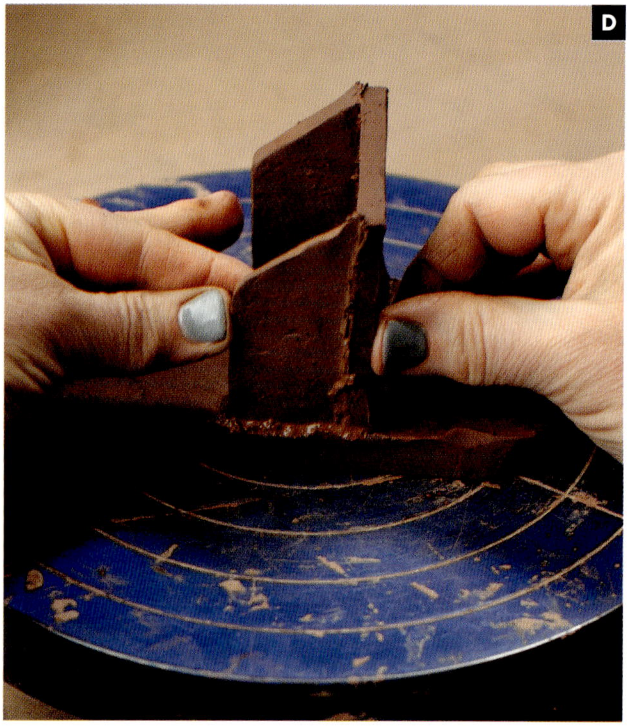

Roll out a ¼" (.63 cm)-thick slab. (If you want to roll two slabs, the bottom footprint can be thicker, but for the walls I recommend the ¼" [.63 cm] slab.) Cut out the template pieces from page 167, five in total, and let them firm up to leather hard. **[A]**

You are now ready to assemble the pieces. On your working surface, place the footprint, the largest piece. Measure 2.5" (6.3 cm) from the curved edge, making a straight line with your needle tool. Score along this line. **[B]** Take the largest square template piece and score the bottom edge. (You can hold it up to the footprint to double-check whether it fits.) Attach the pieces. **[C]**

Find the two matching side pieces (they have the sloped cut). Score the long edge and the bottom, score the wall and the footprint, wet one side of the attachment, and assemble. Clean up and make sure the pieces are vertical and even with the footprint. **[D]**

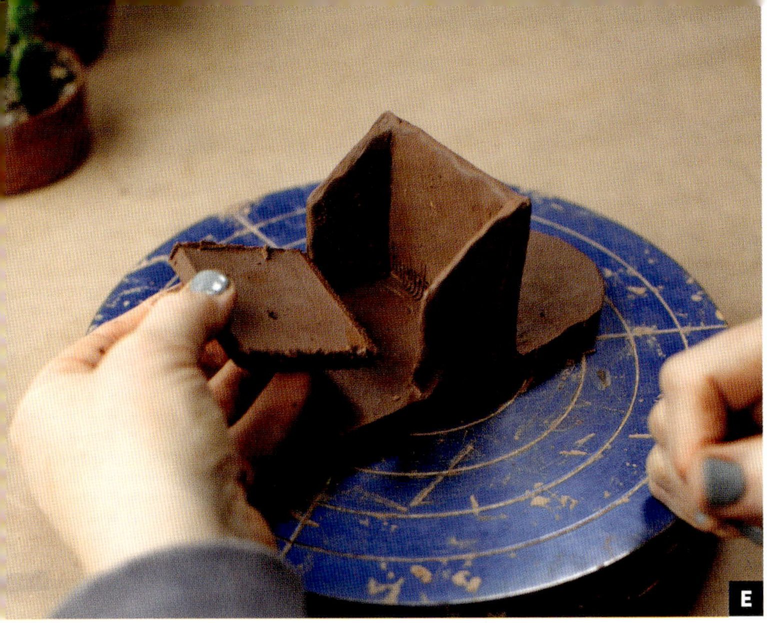

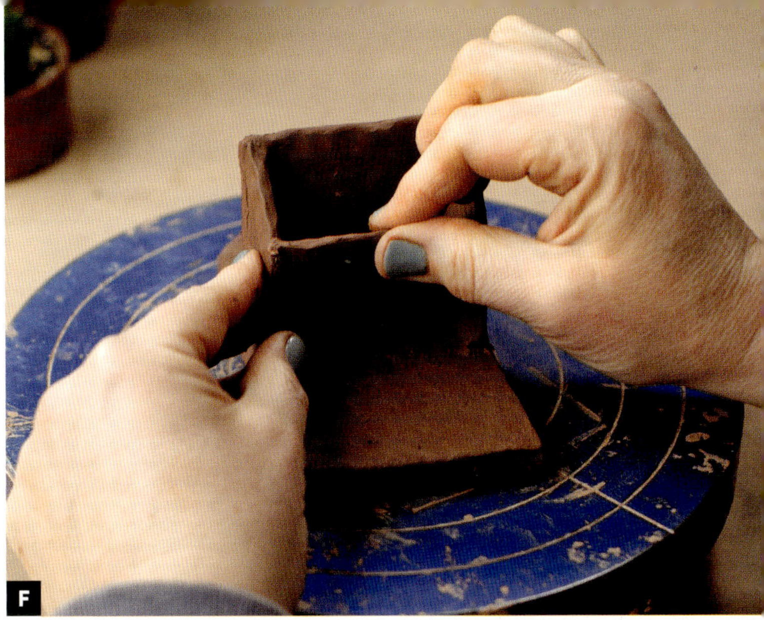

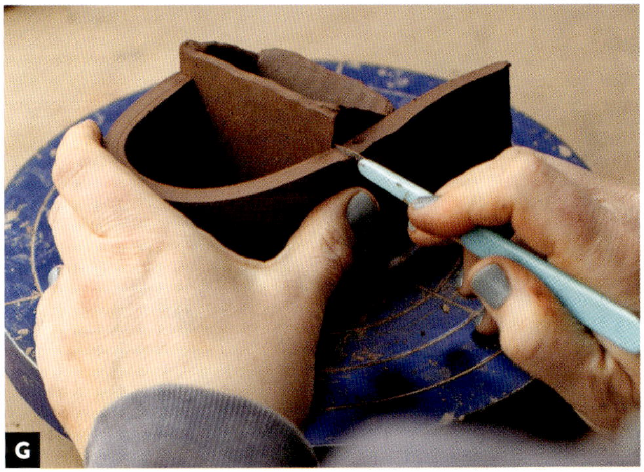

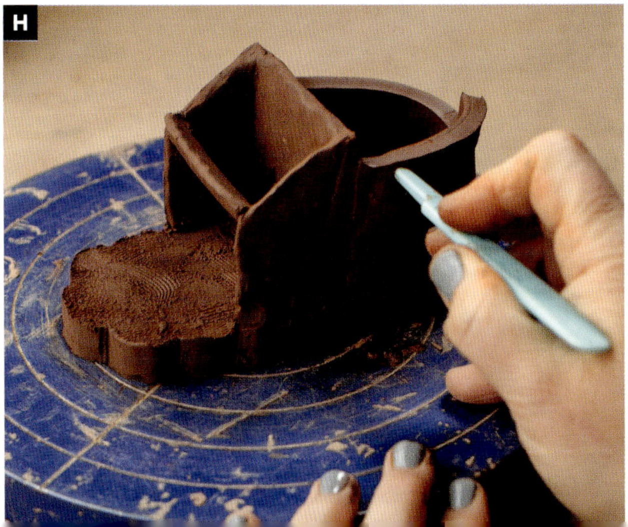

Using the last template piece, cut it down to fit in between the two side pieces. **[E]** Assemble on the diagonal, bevel the bottom edge to rest against the wall, and line up the slab to reach just past the corners of the sloped pieces. Use your needle tool to trace where you need to score. Score and attach and clean up the seams. **[F]**

Roll out a fresh slab ¼" (.63 cm) thick, 3" (7.6 cm) wide and roughly 6" to 8" (15.2 to 20.3 cm) long. Bevel the curved edge of the footprint. Bevel the bottom edge of the slab to match. Score both sides and up the front outside edge of the wall. Cut slab to fit, score the edges, and attach to the footprint and wall. Clean up the interior and exterior seams, using a rib and wooden knife. **[G]**

Using a scalpel, find the center of the dish and make a ½" (1.3) cut straight down. Cut from there to the top of the slab attachment at an angle, and repeat for the other side. This will create a roughly symmetrical sloped wall. Use your knife or surform to even this if it is way off. (This takes a bit of practice.) **[H]**

Take a serrated rib and texture the match strike area. This area will remain unglazed and needs to be rough enough to light a strike-anywhere match. After you have applied the texture, finish the edge. I made a quick paper cutout of a semantical scalloped shape that fit the strike plate and used a scalpel to cut the edge, rolling the edges to soften the cut.

OPTIONAL *Use your fingers to gently pinch all the edges of the pot to soften those lines. (This may be difficult if your pieces are getting closer to a bone-dry state. You want there to be a little bit of give to the wall edge.) Finishing an edge is the last personal touch, so play around and see what works for you.* **[I]**

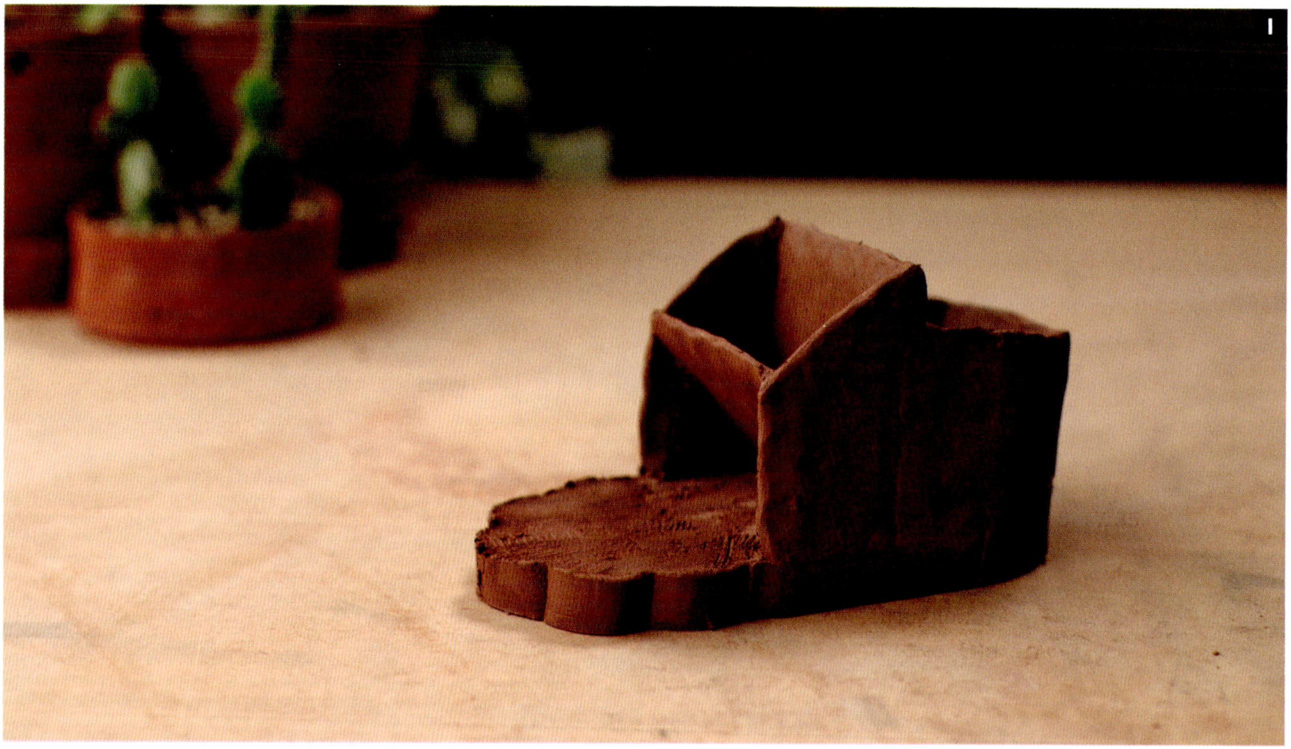

I

GALLERY

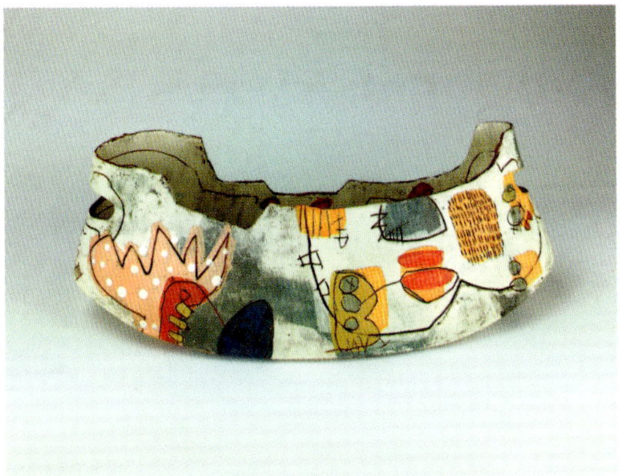

Rebecca Zweibel, *Boat.*
Photo Courtesy of the Artist

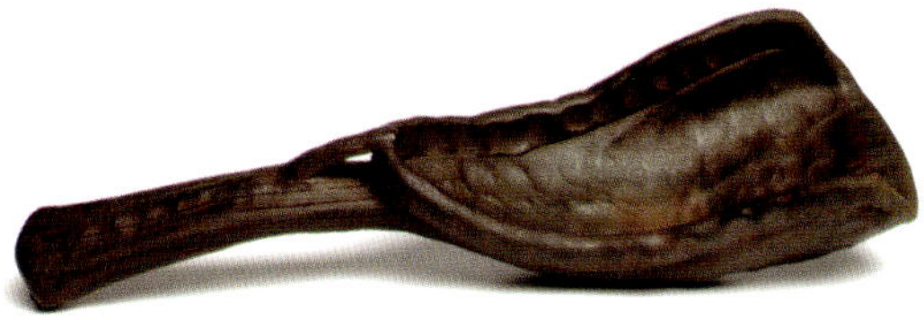

Liz Vukelich, *Scoop*, slab built.
Photo Courtesy of the Artist

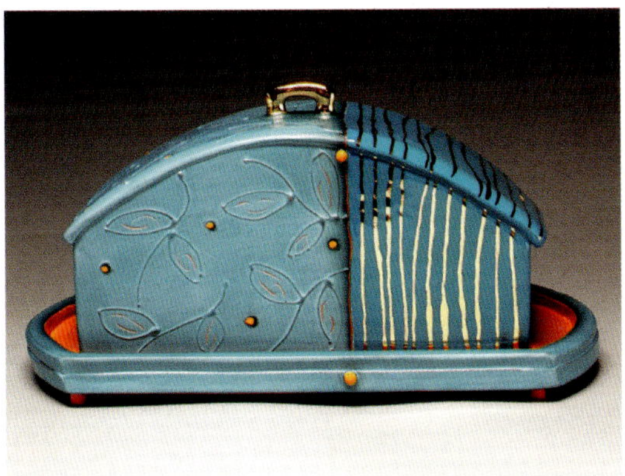

Liz Zlot Summerfield, *Butter Dish*, slab built.
Photo Courtesy of the Artist

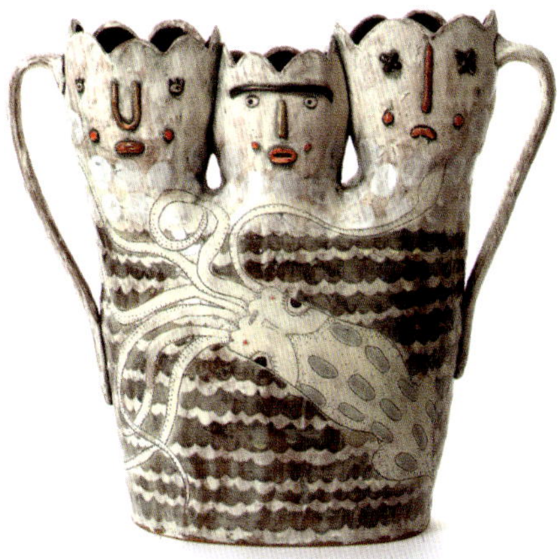

Lynne Hobaica, *Three Headed Vase*, coil built.
Photo Courtesy of the Artist

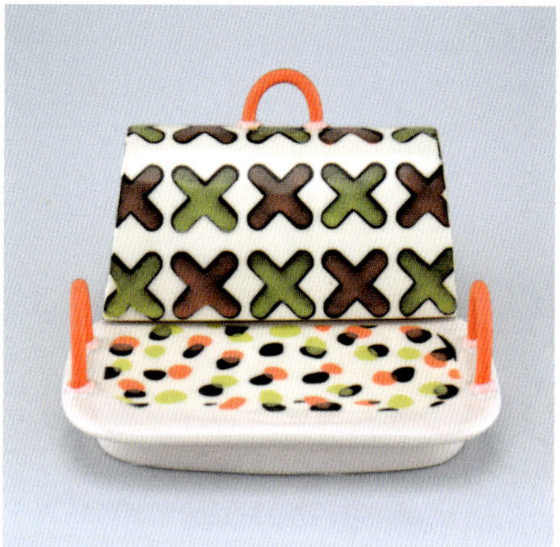

Adrienne Eliades, *Butter Box*, slab built.
Photo Courtesy of the Artist

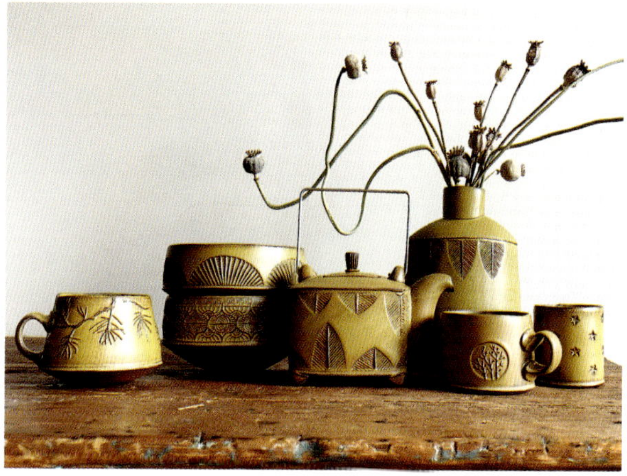

Sarah Pike, *Pike Pots on a Table*, slab built and stamped.
Photo Courtesy of the Artist

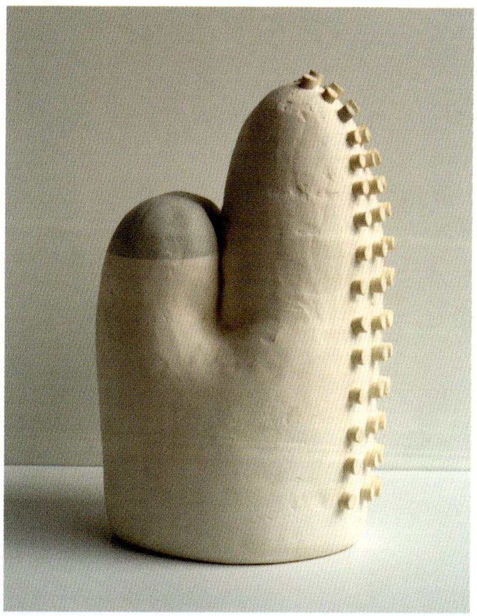

Alyce Carrier, *Mitten*, coil built.
Photo Courtesy of the Artist

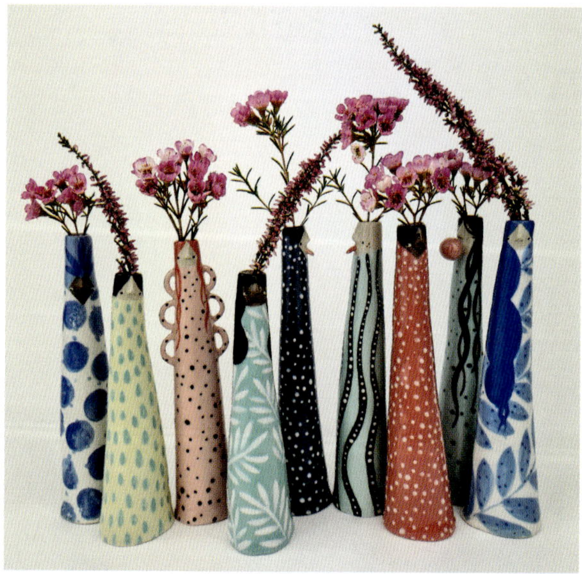

Sandra Apperloo, *Vases*, slab built.
Photo Courtesy of the Artist

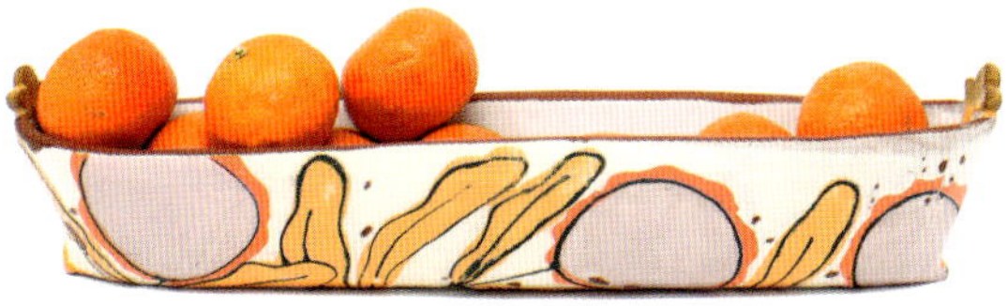

Catie Miller, *Boat Tray*, slab and pinch.
Photo Courtesy of the Artist

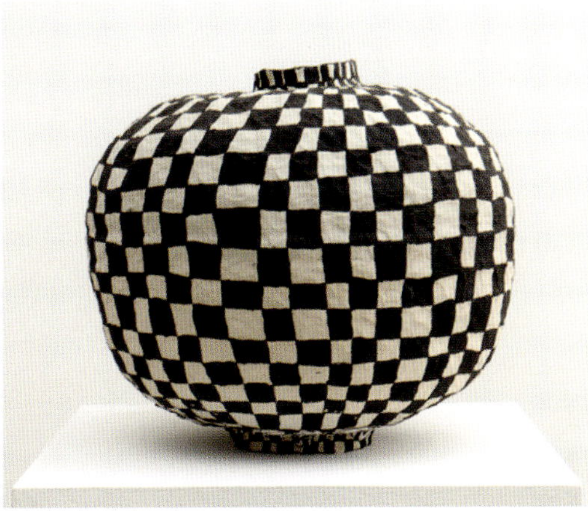

Brittany Mojo, *Vessel*, coil built.
Photo Courtesy of the Artist and The Pit, Los Angeles. Photograph by Jeff McLane.

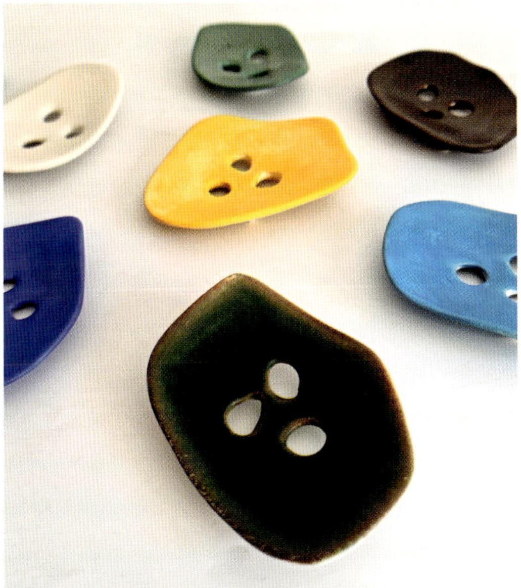

Maria Baleva, *Soap Dishes*, slab built.
Photo Courtesy of the Artist

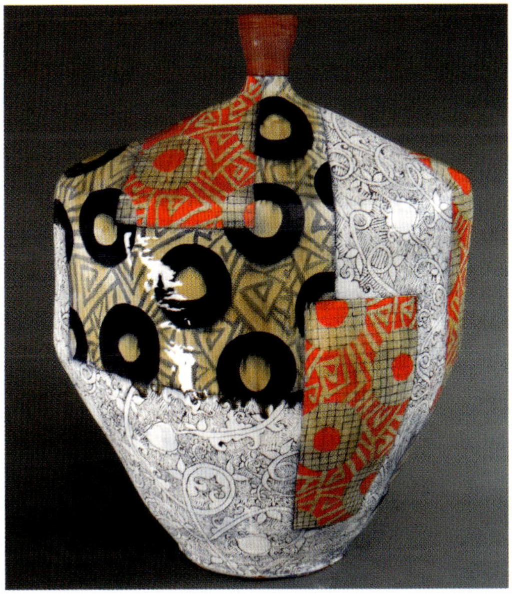

Adero Willard, *Embodiments*.
Photo Courtesy of the Artist

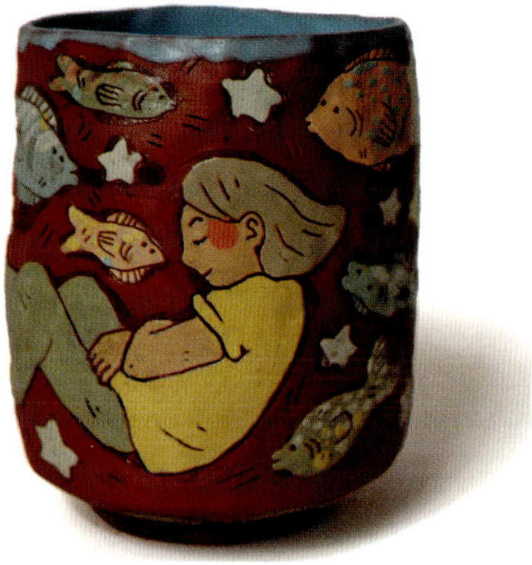

Laura Casas, *Pet Fish Dream*, coil built.
Photo Courtesy of the Artist

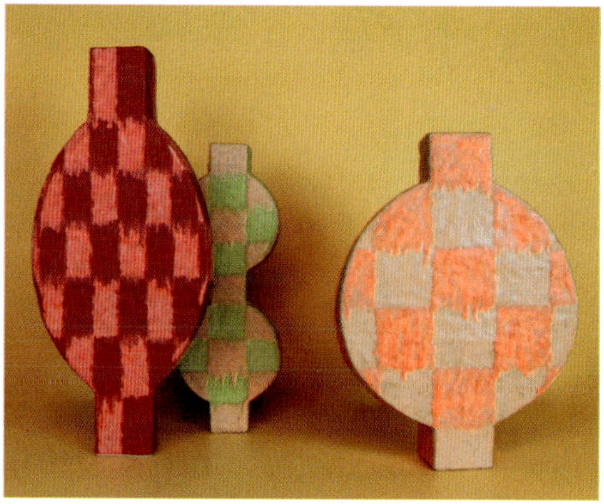

Kelsie Rudolph, *Vessels*, pinch and slab.
Photo Courtesy of the Artist

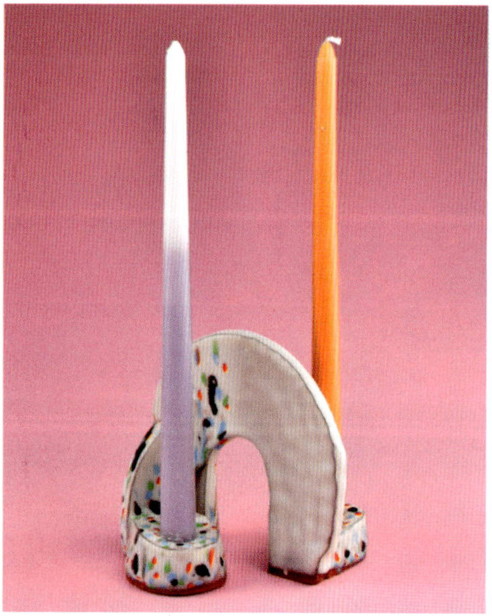

Brian Jones, *Candleholder*, slab built.
Photo Courtesy of the Artist

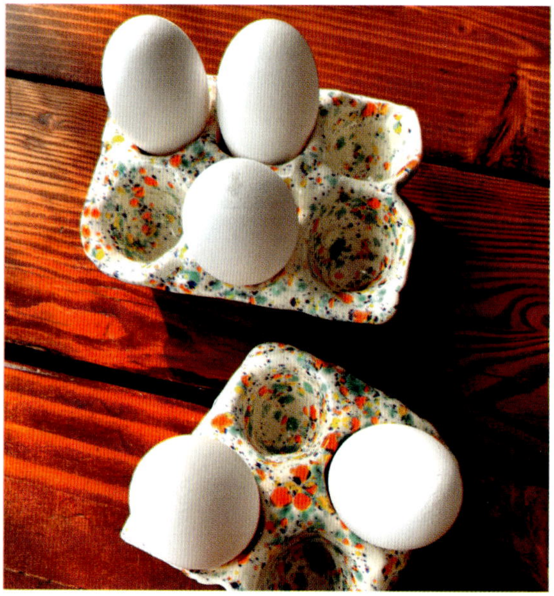

Jasika Nicole, *Egg Carton*, slab and pinched.
Photo Courtesy of the Artist

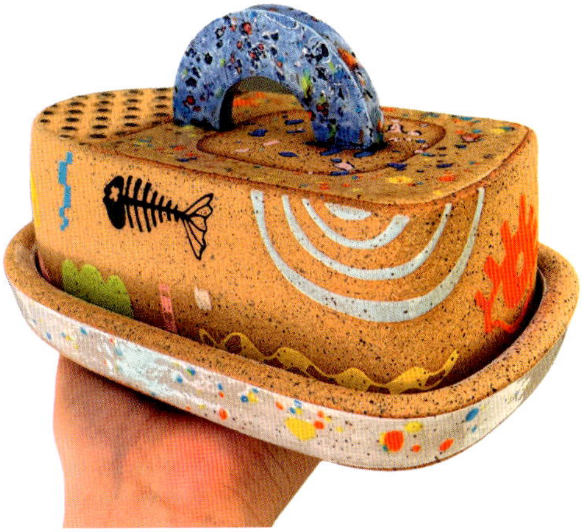

Didem Mert, *Bling Collage Butter Get Some*, slab and coil built.
Photo Courtesy of the Artist

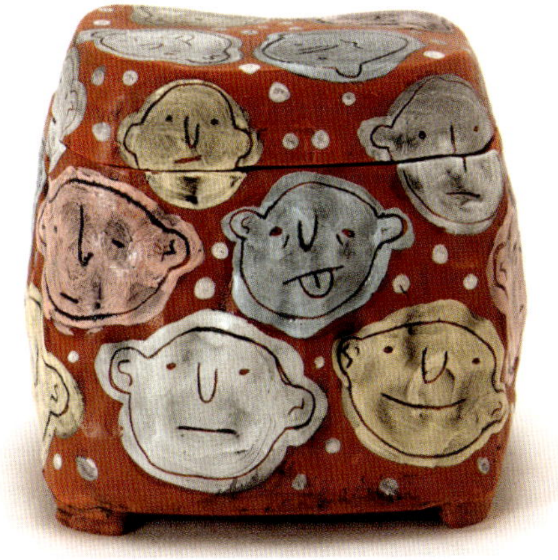

Laura Casas, *Face Box*, coil built.
Photo Courtesy of the Artist

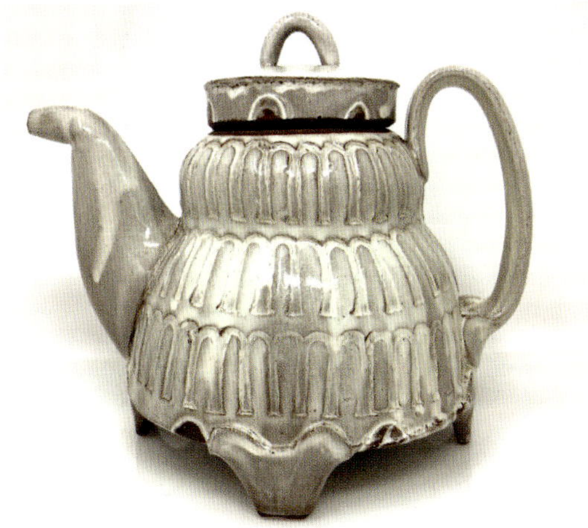

Jennifer Allen, *Teapot*, slab built.
Photo Courtesy of the Artist

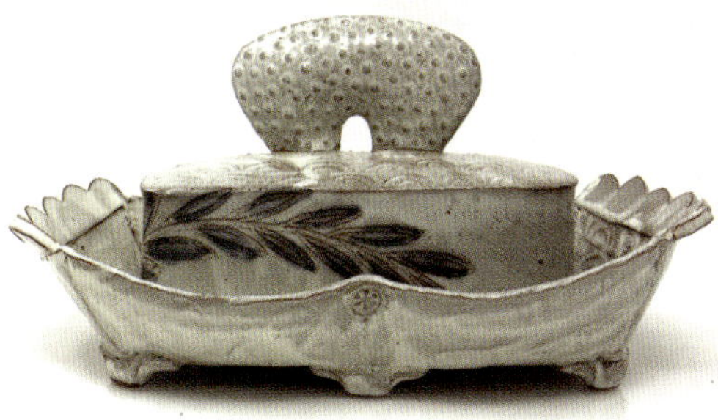

Jennifer Allen, *Butter Dish*, slab built.
Photo Courtesy of the Artist

TEMPLATES

CANDELABRA

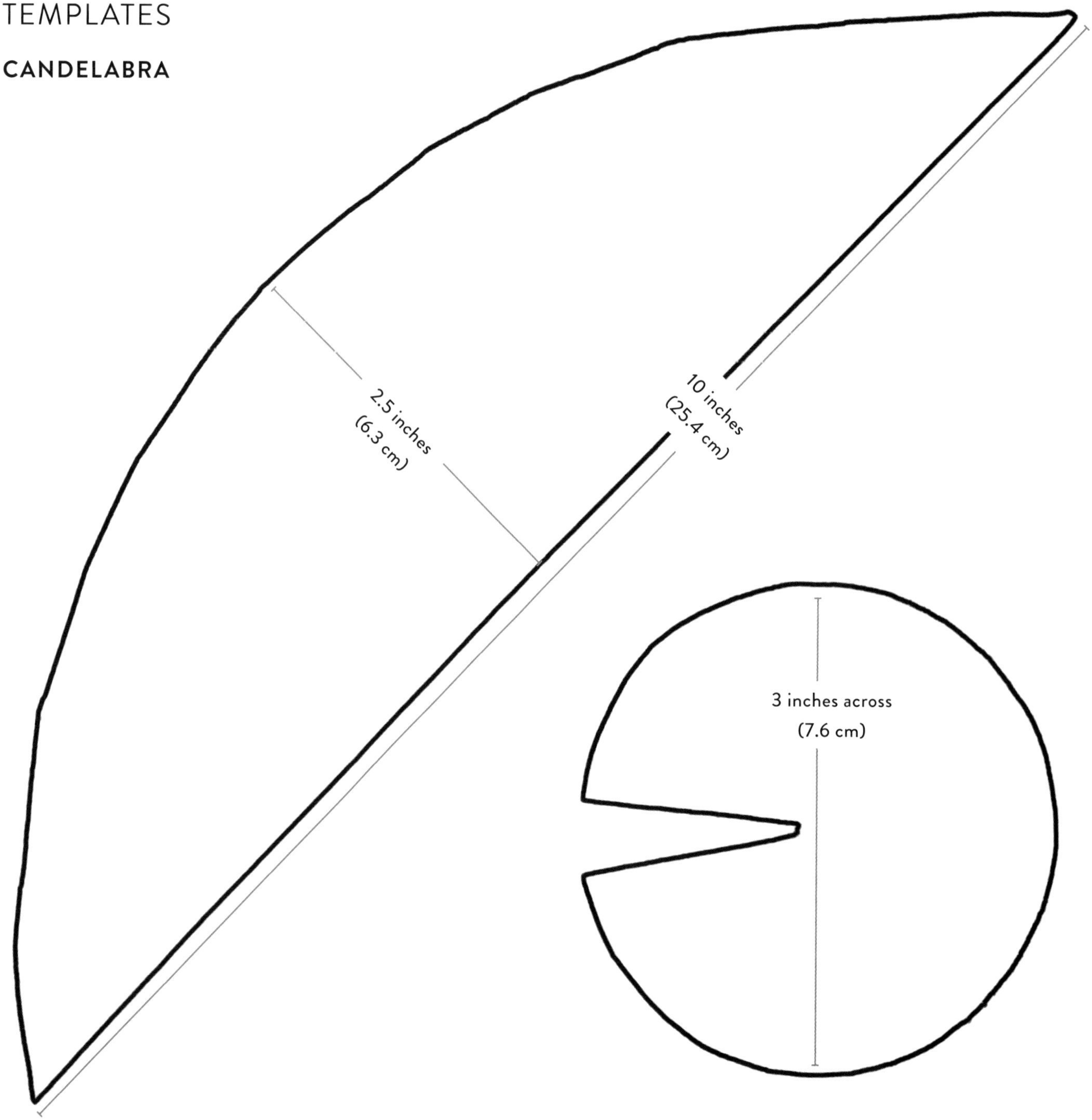

TEMPLATES

SCOOPS

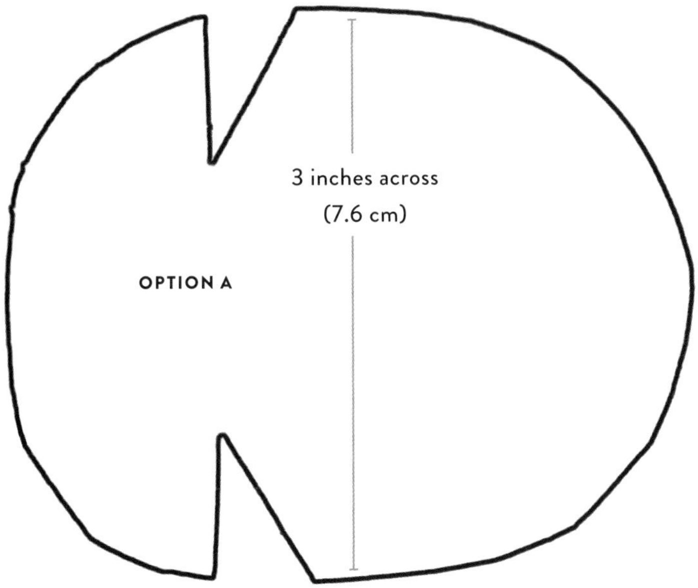

3.5 inches (8.9 cm) long and 3 inches (7.6 cm) wide

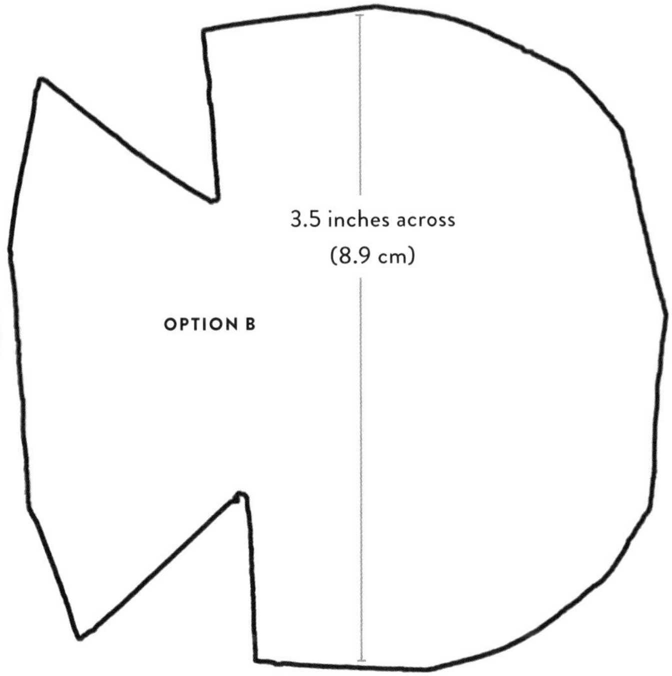

3.5 inches (8.9 cm) long and 3.5 inches (8.9 cm) wide

CITRUS REAMER

ENLARGE BY 50%

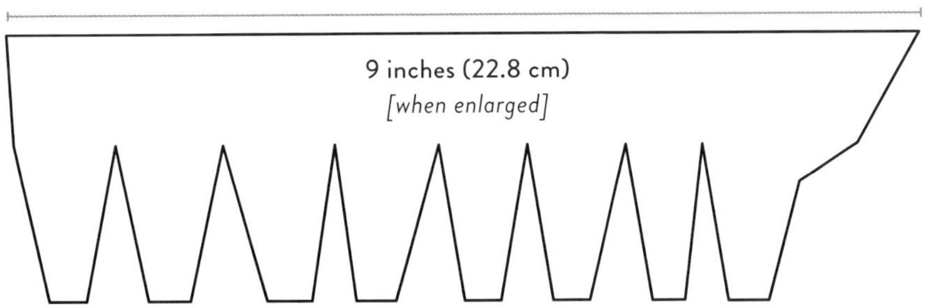

TEMPLATES

BASKET BASE

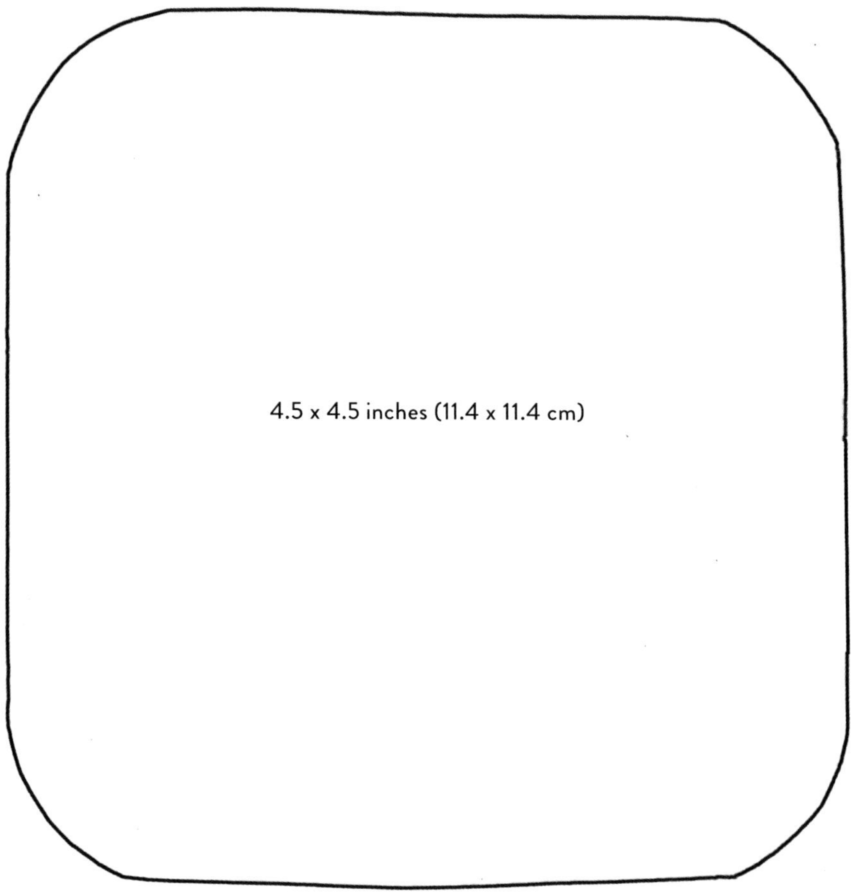

TEMPLATES

EXTERIOR: BASKET ROUND
INTERIOR: COFFEE POUR-OVER BASE

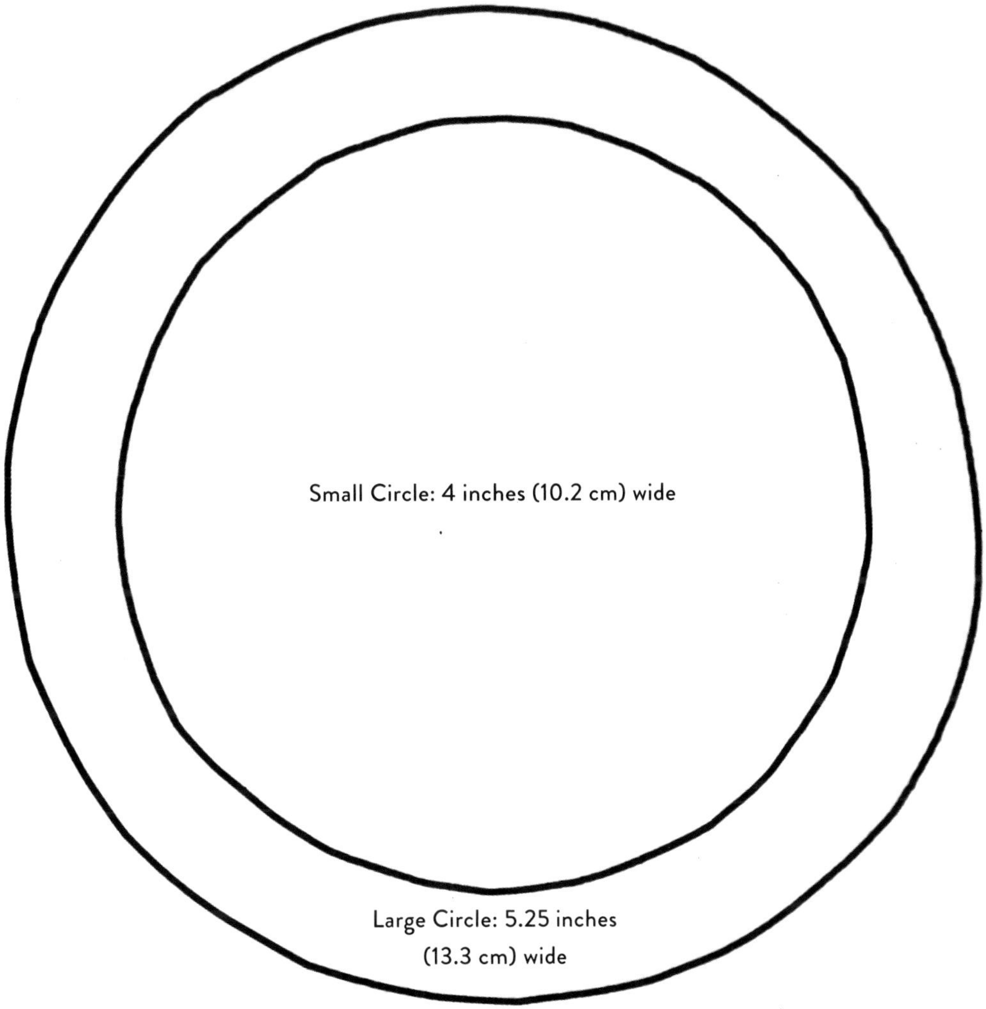

TEMPLATES

COFFEE POUR-OVER

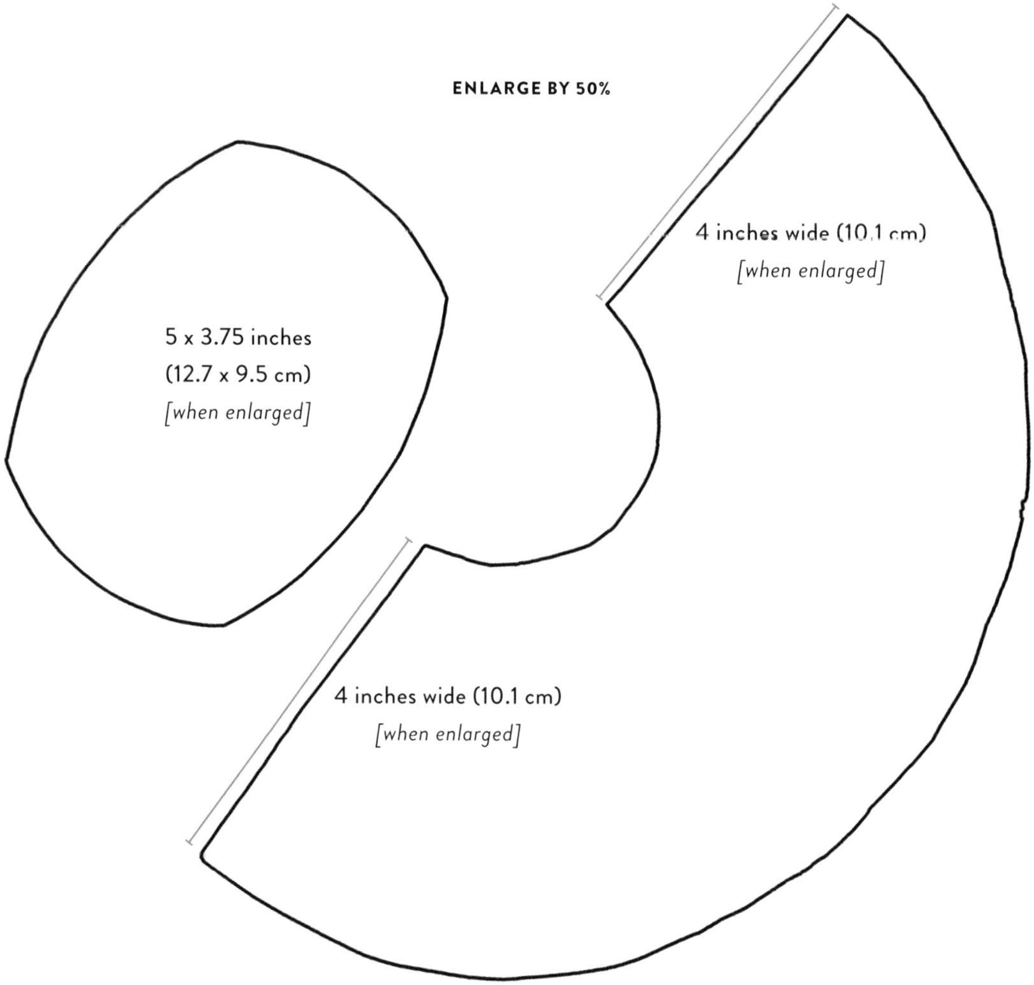

TEMPLATES

MATCH STRIKER

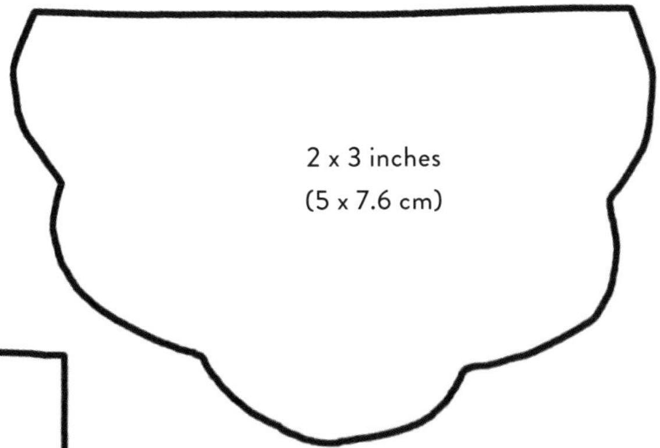

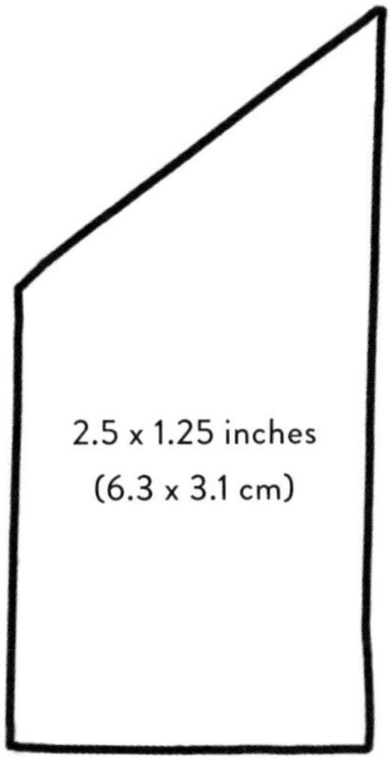

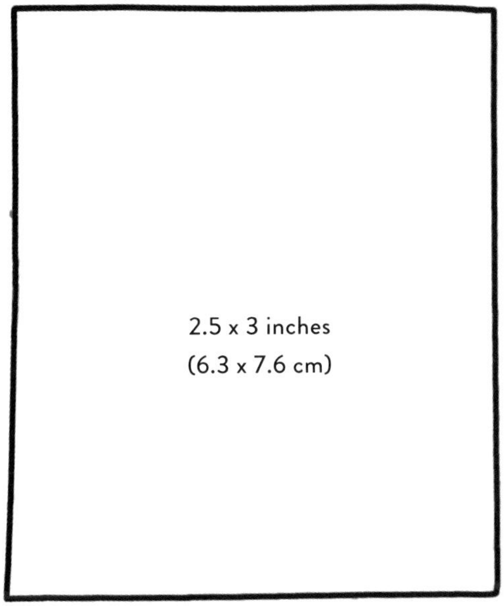

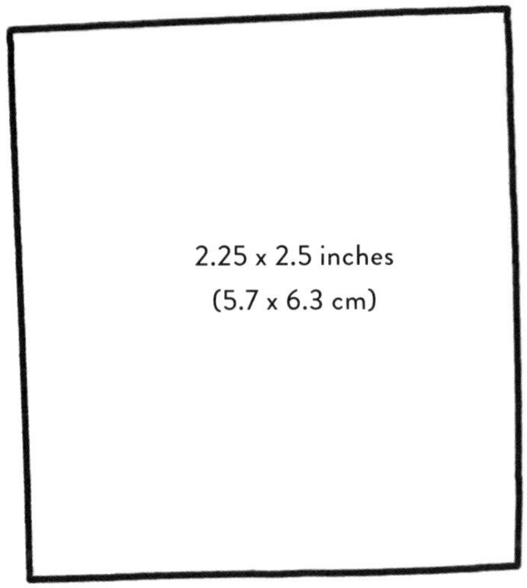

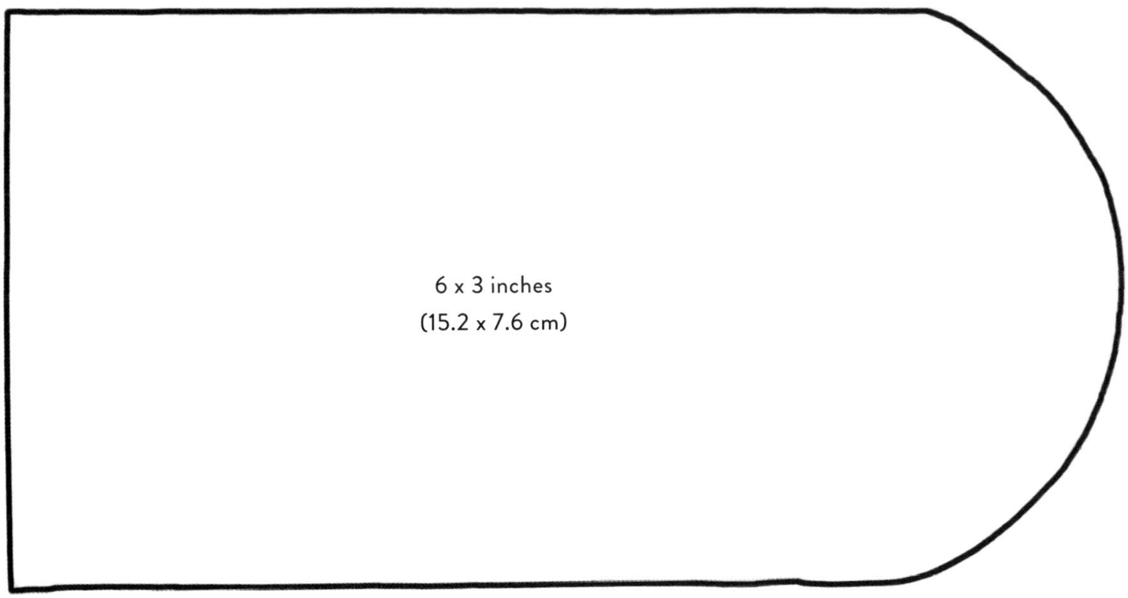

RESOURCES

PUBLICATIONS AND ARTIST RESOURCES

American Craft Magazine
www.craftcouncil.org/magazine

Ceramics: Art and Perception
www.mansfieldceramics.com/product-category/magazine

Field Guide for Ceramic Artisans
www.ceramicsfieldguide.org

Ceramic Arts Daily
https://ceramicartsnetwork.org/daily/

Ceramics Monthly
https://ceramicartsnetwork.org/ceramics-monthly/

Ceramic Review
www.ceramicreview.com

Clay Times
www.claytimes.com

Critical Craft Forum
www.criticalcraftforum.com

Craft in America
www.craftinamerica.org

The Journal of Australian Ceramics
www.australianceramics.com/journal

New Ceramics
www.new-ceramics.com

Pottery Making Illustrated
https://ceramicartsnetwork.org/pottery-making-illustrated/

Professional Artist
www.professionalartistmag.com

Studio Potter Journal
https://studiopotter.org/journal

Favorite Tools

Mudtools
https://mudtools.com/

Dirty Girls Pottery Tools
https://dirtygirlspotterytools.com/

Shimpo Banding Wheel
www1.ceramics.nidec-shimpo.com/banding-wheels

MKM Pottery Tools
Decorating Disc
ps://mkmpotterytools.com/

CircleMatic Template System
Sandi Pierantozzi
www.circlematic.com

Sunshine Cobb Ceramics - Tools
www.sunshinecobb.com

Ceramics Equipment and Materials Suppliers

Aardvark Clay
Santa Ana, CA
www.aardvarkclay.com

American Art and Clay Company
Indianapolis, IN
www.amaco.com

Archie Bray Clay Business
Helena, MT
https://archiebrayclay.com/

Axner Pottery and Ceramic Supplies
Oviedo, FL
www.axner.com

Bailey Ceramic Supply
Kingston, NY
www.baileypottery.com

Big Ceramic Store
Sparks, NV
https://bigceramicstore.com/

The Ceramic Shop
Philadelphia PA
www.theceramicshop.com

Clay Art Supply
Tacoma, WA
https://clayartcenter.net/

Clay King
Spartanburg, SC
www.clay-king.com

Clay Planet
Santa Clara, CA
https://shop.clay-planet.com/

Continental Clay Company
Denver, CO, and Minneapolis, MN
www.continentalclay.com

Crane Yard Clay
Kansas City, MO
https://kcclay.com/

Georgie's Ceramic and Clay Co.
Portland, OR
https://georgies.com/

Highwater Clays
Asheville, NC
https://highwaterclays.com/

Laguna Clay
City of Industry, CA
www.lagunaclay.com

Mid-South Ceramic Supply Co.
Nashville, TN
www.midsouthceramics.com

New Mexico Clay
Albuquerque, NM
https://nmclay.com/

Seattle Pottery Supply
Seattle, WA
https://seattlepotterysupply.com/

Sheffield Pottery
Sheffield, MA
www.sheffield-pottery.com

Skutt Kilns
Portland, OR
https://skutt.com/

Standard Ceramic Supply Company
Pittsburgh, PA
https://standardceramic.com/

Venco
Western Australia
www.venco.com.au

Recommended Reading

Amazing Glaze: Techniques, Recipes, Finishing, and Firing, Gabriel Kline

Amazing Glaze: Recipes and Combinations, Gabriel Kline

Electric Kiln Ceramics: A Guide to Clays, Glazes, and Electric Kilns, Richard Zakin and Frederick Bartolovic

Glaze: The Ultimate Ceramic Artist's Guide to Glaze and Color, Brian Taylor and Kate Doody

Graphic Clay: Ceramic Surfaces & Printed Image Transfer Techniques, Jason Bige Burnett

Mastering Cone 6 Glazes: Improving Durability, Fit and Aesthetics, John Hesselberth and Ron Roy

Mastering Hand Building: Techniques, Tips, and Tricks for Slabs, Coils, and More, Sunshine Cobb

Mastering Kilns & Firing: Raku, Pit and Barrel, Wood Firing, and More, Lindsay Oesterritter

Creative Pottery: Innovative Techniques & Experimental Designs in Thrown & Handbuilt Ceramics, Deb Schwartzkopf

Online Databases, Artist Collectives, and Member Organizations

Access Ceramics
https://accessceramics.org/

Art Axis
https://artaxis.org

Ceramic Arts Network
https://ceramicartsnetwork.org/

Digital Fire
www.digitalfire.com/index.php

Glazy
https://glazy.org/

Kamm Teapot Foundation
https://kammteapotfoundation.org/

National Council on Education for the Ceramic Arts
https://nceca.net/

The Rosenfield Collection
www.rosenfieldcollection.com

Recommended Podcasts

The Potters Cast – Paul Blais

Tales of a Red Clay Rambler – Ben Carter

The Mud Peddlers: Ceramic Art Behind the Scenes – Lindsey M. Dillon and Donte Earth Nation

The Maker's Playbook – Rebecca Ickes Carra

ACKNOWLEDGMENTS

This project was born out of the Covid-19 lockdown: what happened during 2020 changed so much of my outlook and studio practice. In my isolation, I started sharing videos of me rambling on about things in the studio, or some of the thoughts I was having, or issues we as a collective were encountering. I started hosting online project-based workshops, as all my jobs for the year had been canceled. This helped me cope, and folks reached out and shared how much it helped them find some solidarity in their feelings with what has happening in the world and in our lives. There was a profound need to connect in the isolation of lockdown, to find structure and purpose during an unsettling time. Everyone lost access to their community studios almost overnight. I made a quick video of what one might take home to have a small "kitchen table" studio during what we thought would be a two-week lockdown. That time is what inspired me to make this project book. This little book is about keeping you company at the kitchen (studio) table and taking a real look at what you need to have a making practice and how that can support you in your journey as a human. Thank you for allowing me the privilege to be part of that exploration.

Thank you to all of my students, supporters, and readers: your continual support makes me a better person, artist, and teacher. You make my life and practice possible. Thank you for reaching out with kindness and generosity. I never expected it and I am so grateful. I will forever be in awe of you!

To my sister, Feather, you are my rock. I am so glad we were born into the same family, but I believe we would have found each other even if we weren't tossed together at birth. Thank you for appreciating my craziness and being my biggest cheerleader and sounding board.

To my youngest brother, Sunrise, thank you for getting me that VR headset. I would have never tried it on my own, but it literally saved me. Giving me beautiful places to virtually visit and work on my fitness, when the real world was filled with darkness and shadow. Thank you for showing me a little crack to let the light back in!

To my Helena Pod, who knew we would ever be a pod! I would have come out the other side of 2020 a very different person if not for our Friday night family dinners. You help keep me sane during regular life and especially during the insane times. Our time together was an unexpected gift of the lockdown. While I could write a paragraph on each of you, Giselle Hicks, Steve Roberts, Mel Griffin, and David Peters, THANK YOU for your generosity, love, and support. You all are amazing friends and tremendous cooks! Also, a shoutout to the doggos of the group, whose friendship and contributions cannot be forgotten: snuggles to Pearly, Wiley, and Rey.

To the Lindse/ays in my life. What would I do without you both? Truthfully, I have no idea. Thank you for always being up for a morning chat. I love that we can talk about the dumbest thing to the most serious of matters. You are my best-est of friends. I swear the next book is going to be "The Care and Feeding of Lindsa/eys." You both provide endless material and support, laughter through the tears. Lindsay O. and Lindsey C.—love you both!

Miss Carey Shaw, thank you for always being just a phone call away! I miss our morning breakfast dates and bike rides around Sacramento. If not for you, I would never have rediscovered my love of bike riding, even though we are the worst workout partners in history! We do value our sleep! You call and connect in such truth and emotion it keeps me grounded and aware of myself. Thank you for always being willing to go there! Love you, woman!

To my roommate during the lockdown, Sadie Clarendon, I am so glad you were here. I feel like we took care of each other . . . making coffee and talking about all life's problems and the glaringly obvious solutions! I miss Remy intimidating you with her love. You were and are a lifesaver. And thank you, I think, for introducing me to TikTok, and to the dance and makeup tutorials that saved us! Love you.

To my editor Thom O'Hearn, without you this project never would have happened. Thank you for believing in me.

To Athena Longsdale, photographer on this project, thank you for listening and working with me to make the pictures in this book spectacular. Thank you especially for the beautiful headshots you managed to get on a day I felt less than beautiful or spectacular! You truly helped me capture the vision I had for this book.

To the amazing artists in the galleries in this book, thank you for sharing your genius with me and the world at large. I invited each of you because you inspire me and I am glad to be on this makers' journey alongside each of you. Even if we never meet in person, I am grateful you are out there making beautiful, amazing work.

Even though they can't read, I am thankful and want to acknowledge my sweet kittens, Remy, Hall, and Oscar (and my foster babies, Stella and Brandon, who have gone on to find forever homes but were integral to keeping me in front of my computer writing). They surround/ed me with joy, snuggles, and mischievousness. They keep me company and make me happy to come home and share my space with them. Yep, I'm officially a cat lady!

This book is dedicated to my grandmother, Jeanne Liebau. From cooking to watercolors to sculpting to storytelling, she had a lifelong dedication to adding creative practices to her life. She modeled the importance of nurturing one's spirit with creativity. You are my inspiration. You would have gotten a kick out of me writing a couple books. I miss you every day!

ABOUT THE AUTHOR

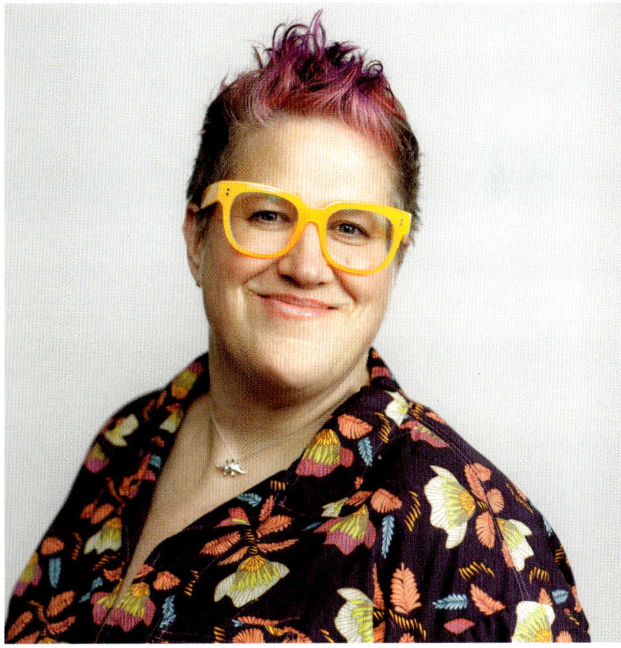

Sunshine Cobb is a potter who lives with her three cats in Helena, Montana. As a full-time studio artist who specializes in handmade functional pottery, she frequently travels the country as an invited lecturing and demonstrating artist. Her work has drawn both critical praise for its whimsical, rustic style and national and international commercial success. She is considered an important contemporary functional potter, hailed in both academic and commercial circles, and is consistently featured in art exhibitions throughout the country.

Utilizing traditional techniques, her work embodies the importance of handmade pottery in an era of disposability, while representing a new model of a functional potter in the modern era. Her unique style is inspired by everything from roaming junkyards and thrift shops to her love of plants and working with textiles. She insists that her work remain functional, an object that finds its way into our busy days, creating a connection between the maker and its user.

With a strong following and online media presence, she represents an innovator in online business models in the ever-changing ceramics field and a leading advocate for functional art in modern living. She devotes time and effort into growing and improving a ceramics community locally and nationally.

She was educated at California State University of Sacramento with a BA in Studio Arts and an MFA in Ceramics from Utah State University.

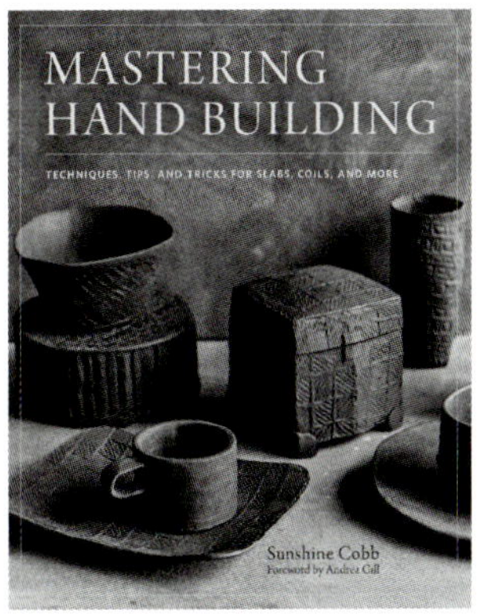

ALSO AVAILABLE FROM SUNSHINE COBB:

Mastering Hand Building
978-0-7603-5273-1

INDEX